The Book of Forms

Other Books by Lewis Turco

Poetry

A Book of Fears, 1998

Bordello: A Portfolio of Poemprints, with George O'Connell, 1996

Emily Dickinson: Woman of Letters, 1993

The Shifting Web: New and Selected Poems, 1989

The Fog: A Chamber Opera in One Act, with Walter Hekster, 1987

The Compleat Melancholick, 1985

American Still Lifes, 1981

Pocoangelini: A Fantography & Other Poems, 1971

The Inhabitant, 1970

Awaken, Bells Falling: Poems 1959–1967, 1968

First Poems, 1960

Nonfiction

The Book of Literary Terms, 1999

Shaking the Family Tree: A Remembrance, 1998

The Public Poet, 1991

Dialogue, 1989

The New Book of Forms, 1986

Visions and Revisions of American Poetry, 1986

Poetry: An Introduction Through Writing, 1973

The Book of Forms: A Handbook of Poetics, 1968

Lewis Turco

THE BOOK
OF FORMS

A Handbook of Poetics

THIRD EDITION

University Press of New England

Hanover and London

University Press of New England, Hanover, NH 03755
© 2000 by University Press of New England
All rights reserved
Printed in the United States of America   5 4
CIP data appear at the end of the book

ACKNOWLEDGMENTS

The Book of Forms, Third Edition is based upon these previous publications: *The Book of Forms* (New York: E. P. Dutton), © 1968 by Lewis Turco; copyright renewed 1996; *Creative Writing in Poetry* (Albany: State University of New York), © 1970 by the State University of New York, all rights reserved 1998 by Lewis Turco; *Poetry: An Introduction Through Writing* (Reston: Reston Publishing Co.), © 1973 by Reston Publishing Co., all rights, including reversions of rights, reserved 1985, 1986 by Lewis Turco; and *The Public Poet, Five Lectures on the Art and Craft of Poetry* (Ashland: Ashland Poetry Press), © 1991 by Lewis Turco.

"Re" by Vito Hannibal Acconci is from *Young American Poets,* edited by Paul Carroll (Chicago: Follett Publishing Company), © 1968. Reprinted by permission of the author.

"Canst Thou Draw?" by Manoah Bodman is from *The New Book of Forms* by Lewis Turco (Hanover: University Press of New England), © 1986, and from *The Life and Poetry of Manoah Bodman, Bard of the Berkshires,* edited by Lewis Turco (Lanham: University Press of America) © 1999. Reprinted by permission of Lewis Turco.

"Hymn to the Creator" by Caedmon, v. (version by) Wesli Court, is from *The Davidson Miscellany* 14:2 (Fall), © 1978. Reprinted by permission of the author.

"The Obsession" by Wesli Court is from *Patterns of Poetry,* ed. Miller Williams (Baton Rouge: Louisiana State University Press), © 1986, and from *The New Book of Forms* by Lewis Turco (Hanover: University Press of New England), © 1986. Reprinted by permission of the author.

Continued on page 308

This book is dedicated to all those of my students
who received their Poetic Licenses,
even the class that called me "Uncle Lew."

Contents

PART III. TRADITIONAL VERSE FORMS

Preface to the Third Edition

Like the original *The Book of Forms: A Handbook of Poetics,* which was published in 1968, and *The New Book of Forms,* published in 1986—both of which became standards in the fields of poetics and prosodics—*The Book of Forms, Third Edition* is intended as a text and reference work for students and teachers of poetry in general and of verse composition in particular. Although the emphasis is on the forms of poetry, this volume contains all the information essential to a study of verse and verse techniques from the Middle Ages to the present.

However, *The Book of Forms* now has a companion volume, *The Book of Literary Terms: The Genres of Fiction, Drama, Nonfiction, Literary Criticism, and Scholarship,* which uses the same codification and systematization for all of the literary genres other than poetry: fiction, drama, nonfiction, criticism, and literary scholarship. *The Book of Literary Terms* provides a comprehensive guide to and definitions of all significant terms, forms, and styles in these genres. All subgenres and their historical examples are defined and described, all significant terms explicated, and all important styles illustrated and explicated.

This third edition of *The Book of Forms* begins with a discussion of the two modes of writing—prose and verse, and the "levels" of poetry—the typographical, the sonic, the sensory, and the ideational levels. These sections clarify terms such as *rhythm, cadence* and *meter,* and provide clear explanations of the processes and methods of versification. Figurative language is defined and discussed, as are considerations such as diction, style, syntax, and overtone.

Parts II and III are The Book of Forms proper. Part II is a

"Form–Finder Index" in which all the forms contained in the volume are listed and divided, first into *specific forms,* and then into *general forms.* Under "specific forms" there are further subdivisions, beginning with *one-line forms* and working through to *two-hundred-ten-line forms.*

Should one wish to know the form of a poem one is studying, rather than leaf through all the forms in the book, one may first determine (1) the *rhyme scheme* of the poem or stanza in question and (2) its *meter.* Then one may (3) *count the lines in the form* and turn to the Form-Finder. There, under the appropriate heading, will be found a short list of stanza and whole poem patterns, from which one can determine the exact name of the poem form in question.

Similarly, should a student of verse composition wish to use a form of a specific length, he or she can consult the Form-Finder to discover an interesting structure. Many students find there is no quicker way to improve their writing than through formal experimentation and attempts to solve specific technical problems.

Part III, following the Form-Finder, is the most comprehensive compilation of the verse forms traditionally used in British and American prosody ever gathered between covers. Over seven hundred forms are listed alphabetically, many of which have been added for this third edition of *The Book of Forms.*

Our heritage of forms is rich. We are heirs not only of British metrical systems, but also of systems derived from continental Europe, the Middle East, and Asia. Our history of verse forms goes back to the Celts, the Anglo-Saxons, and the Normans, and we have derived much from the systems of the Semites, the Greeks, the Italians, and the French. The verse forms set forth here have all been utilized by poets of the English-speaking world. During every period of English letters, craftsfolk, loresmen, and bards have explored the possibilities of the formal structures of verse and extended the range of those structures.

This new version of *The Book of Forms* adds many examples of poems written in each form by poets from all periods. Each form is described succinctly in prose. Where necessary, a unique schematic diagramming system (for years imitated by others in books and on the internet) lays the pattern of the form out on the page so that its structure is clear. Generally, there follows at least one poem exemplifying the form, always in a modern English version. The entry ends with complete cross-references so that readers can discover relationships and similarities among many of the forms.

All unattributed poems in this volume are by Lewis Turco.

Oswego, New York
May 1999

Part I   The Elements of Poetry

Introduction

The terms *poetry* and *poesy* are often used interchangeably, but the former means that body of literature which is identified as being poems, and the latter means the act of composing poetry. There are three traditional major genres of poetry and any number of minor ones. The *major genres* of poetry are *dramatic poetry*, which is poetry written in *dialogue*; lyric poetry or *songs*; and *narrative poetry*, story poems. These genres are considered in order following the Form-Finder Index.

There have been many poets and critics throughout the ages, in particular during the *Romantic period*, who have maintained that lyric poetry is the only "*pure poetry*," for this genre has no narrative, argumentative, or didactic purpose. The ancient narrative forms, such as *epics*, *romances*, and *ballads*, however, were originally considered to be poems, and they correspond to our modern *novel*, *novella*, and *short story*. For discussions of these genres, see the companion volume, *The Book of Literary Terms*.

Because in most of the European world all poems, whether songs, stories, or plays, were originally written in the mode called *verse*, popular confusion has resulted since the introduction, during the Renaissance, of the mode called *prose* as a vehicle for narrative and drama. However, in the earliest Middle Eastern literature, which became the basis for much European literature, the oldest lyrics and narratives were written in *prose mode*, not *verse mode*, as in the oldest long narrative poem on record, the Chaldean *Epic of Gilgamesh*. In the Hebrew Old Testament, songs were also written in the prose mode, as for instance *The Song of Songs* and the *Psalms*; there is even evidence that the earliest known drama may have been *The Book of Job* in its original version. Moreover, among the Norse there are both prose and verse *eddas*—anthologies of ancient Icelandic poetry.

Thus, in the Western *Judeo-Christian tradition* there is ample precedent for writing any of the *genres—song, narrative poetry*, and *dramatic poetry*, in either of the *modes—prose* or *verse*; therefore, genres do not depend on the modes in which they are written. "Verse," a mode, is not equivalent to "poetry," a genre. To ask the question "What is the difference between prose and poetry?" is to compare anchors with bullets. One must ask, "What is the difference between poetry and fiction?" or "What is the difference between prose and verse?"

Modes of Writing

The *Oxford English Dictionary* defines *prose* as "The ordinary form of written or spoken language, **without** metrical *structure*" [emphasis added], and it defines *verse* as "a succession of words arranged according to natural or recognized rules of prosody and forming a complete **metrical** line [emphasis added]." To put it even more simply, *prose* is **unmetered language** and *verse* is **metered language**. To "meter" is to count. Generally, what the poet counts is syllables.

The Levels of Poetry

If *fiction* is "the art of written narrative," and *drama* is "the art of theatrical narrative," both of these using *language as a vehicle* to tell a story, and the various *nonfiction* genres are "the art of rhetorical exposition," using *language as a vehicle* to make didactic or argumentative points, then what is *poetry*, since it can do, and originally did, all of these things? Since poetry is the product of the poet who is interested in the vehicle itself, in *language* as the medium for expression, then poetry is "the *art* of language." Like the other genres (see *The Book of Literary Terms*), poetry also has four elements, but in this case they are *levels* of language usage, those of *typography*, *sound*, *tropes* ("figures of speech"), and *theme*. And there is *fusion* as well—how do all these levels come together to make a poem?

Prosody

In order to write poetry, one must have some kind of language system, or *prosody*—a theory of poetry *composition* or *an organizing principle*—within the bounds of which one can build the *structure* of the poem. *Form*, then, whether it be "*internal*" and "*organic*," or "*external*" and "*formal*," is of major importance. The poet may use any aspect of language on which to base a prosody, but most English language prosodies have to do with counting syllables.

Meter ("numbers") means "measure," and when one measures a *line* by counting syllables in that line, one is writing *verse*, not prose. If one is counting simply the number of syllables in a line and measuring out a certain number of them *per* line, then one is using *syllabic prosody*, and one is writing *syllabic verse*. If one is counting in each line only those syllables that, for some reason, are more **hea-**vi-ly **em-**pha-sized (*stressed*) than others, then one is using *accentual prosody*, and one is writing *accentual verse*.

If one is counting not only **all** the syllables in the line, but all the *stressed syllables* as well, and arranging them in an *alternating pattern* of some kind—in series of "*verse feet*"—then one is using *accentual-syllabic prosody*. If one is not counting syllables at all, but is arranging lines in *grammatical parallels* or *phrasal units*, then one is not writing verse but *prose*, which many people erroneously refer to as *free verse*, q.v.

The Typographical Level

A prosody based upon the *typographical level*—what poems look like on the page—is called *carmen figuratum*, or *spatial prosody*. An ordinary poem—that is, a poem written in prose or verse, but in *shaped stanzas*—is variously called *hieroglyphic verse, pattern verse,* or the *calligramme*, but a *concrete poem* is an *ideograph*, a figure that represents something else, but without naming it, like a character in the Chinese language, whose impact is almost wholly visual; for instance, in English the ideograph & (an *ampersand*) may be pronounced "and," "besides," or "also," as in, "We went to the party & found many others there, including Bob and Fred; & Jane—& Bill and Nancy off in a corner somewhere." "Town Square" is a *concrete* or *picture poem*.

Town Square

```
town town town town town town town
town                            town
town            town            town
town            square          town
town            sq ua re        town
town           s q u   a r e    town
town           s q u a r e      town
town           s q u   a r e    town
town            sq ua re        town
town            square          town
town            town            town
town                            town
town town town town town town town
```

Spatial verse may utilize *positive* or *negative shaping*; the former utilizes the words to make the shape, and the latter utilizes the words to surround the shape. "Easter Wings" is a famous *calligramme* that uses positive shaping:

> *Easter Wings*
> Lord, who created man in wealth and store,
>   Though foolishly he lost the same,
>   Decaying more and more,
>   Till he became
>   Most poor:
>   With thee
>   O let me rise
>   As larks, harmoniously,
>   And sing this day thy victories:
> Then shall the fall further the flight in me.
>
> My tender age in sorrow did begin:
>   And still with sicknesses and shame
>   Thou did so punish sin,
>   That I became
>   Most thin.
>   With thee
>   Let me combine
>   And feel this day thy victory,
>   For, if I imp my wing on thine,   [impose]
>   Affliction shall advance the flight in me.
>   —George Herbert

Proportion in figure has to do with the shape of the *stanza* (*stave*) or *strophe* of poems that are not written in *spatial prosody*. Essentially, "stanza" and "strophe" mean the same thing: shorter *divisions of a poem*; however, a distinction may be made if one thinks of *strophes* as short divisions of a poem having no specific length, and *stanzas* as having specific lengths. A poem of one strophe or stanza is *monostrophic*; of two, *distrophic* (if it rhymes, a *twime*); or three, *tristrophic* (*thrime*), and so on. Often lines of the same length in a stanza will be *indented* the same number of spaces or will begin at the *margin*; similarly, the poet may indent or not indent lines according to the *rhyme scheme*. Another convention capitalizes the *initial letters* of the lines of a poem, and sometimes these initials will form an *acrostic* (described later). Longer divisions of poems are *cantos, fits,* and *movements*. A *coda* (*cauda, tail*) is a concluding *demistrophe* (partial stanza) that appears in certain forms such as the French *sestina* and the *ballade*, often as an *envoi* (*envoy*). Poems that are not broken into stanzaic or strophic divisions are called *astrophic*.

The Sonic Level

Prose Poetry

Some nonmetrical systems for writing poetry are based upon *constructional schemes*—sets of correlated things such as grammatically parallel sentence *structures*—and these systems ought properly to be considered as *prose prosodies* when verse systems are not in use for structuring poems. Parallel sentence structures are *constructional schemes*, and the prosody that uses them is called *grammatical parallelism*.

Proportion by treatment has to do with choosing the meters, forms, length of lines, stanzas and strophes to suit the *architectonics* (the overall structure) of the whole poem in order to treat the subject of the poem in an appropriate and effective manner.

Prose poems written in parallel structures will set up *prose rhythms* that have some of the effect of verse, but they will not be *free verse* because verse is metered language and prose is not. Amy Lowell (1874–1925) called prose poetry that utilized many sonic devices *polyphonic prose* rather than "free" verse.

Constructional schemes, like all *schemes,* are strategies for constructing *sentences*. They have to do with the ways in which *words*, *phrases*, *clauses*, and larger units are grammatically balanced in sentences. *Synonymia* is a *paraphrase* in parallel structures ("I love you; you are my beloved"); *synthesis* is *consequence* in parallel structures ("I love you; therefore, I am yours"); *antithesis* is the *opposition* of ideas (*antinomy*) expressed in parallel structures ("I love you, and I loathe you"); *auxesis* is the building up, in parallel structures, of a *catalog* or *series* that ultimately closes at the *zenith* (high point) of the set (the *climax:* "I love your eyes, hair, breasts; I love the way you walk and speak; I love you"). *Epithonema* is *climactic summation* at the conclusion of a sequence.

Meiosis is the building up, in parallel structures, of a *catalog* or *series* that ultimately closes at the *nadir* (*low point*) of the set (the *anticlimax*), as in, "We struggled through dense forests; we forded raging torrents; we battled the terrors of storm and starvation to reach the road; we took the bus home."

Kenneth Fearing conducted some sophisticated experiments in lyric prose. His "Dirge" exhibits all sorts of parallel structures, including meiosis or anticlimax. Just when a particular catalog or parallel series begins to threaten dullness, Fearing changed his structures and his rhythms—"Dirge" is, in many ways, a jazz poem. Poe's "The Bells" has been called the first jazz poem, and it is interesting to note that there is a bell effect in Fearing's poem as well, but there is a question whether the tolling at the end of the poem is climactic or anticlimactic.

If one were to draw a series of lines to indicate the movements of the first series of parallels, they would be a series of rising half-circles, always beginning and ending at the same spot:

Dirge

1-2-3 was the number he played but today the number came 3-2-1; bought his Carbide at 30 and it went to 29; had the favorite at Bowie but the track was slow—

But the next series would be a flat half-line followed by a series of slightly rising half-lines, for the first half of the parallel structure is an apostrophe directed to the dead man; the second "half" of the single sentence forming the strophe is a series of sarcastic rhetorical questions:

O, executive type, would you like to drive a floating power, knee-action, silk-upholstered six? Wed a Hollywood star? Shoot the course in 58? Draw to the ace, king, jack?

The next strophe continues the apostrophe in a pair of parallel threats:

O, fellow with a will who won't take no, watch out for three ciga-
rettes on the same, single match; O, democratic voter born in
August under Mars, beware of liquidated rails—

Then Fearing again switches to third-person narration in a series of synthetic parallels, the first half proclaiming his individual-
ity, the series of negative consequences illustrating the dead man's
futile life:

Denouement to denouement, he took a personal pride in the certain, certain way he lived his own, private life, but nevertheless,
they shut off his gas; nevertheless, the bank foreclosed; nevertheless, the landlord called; nevertheless, the radio broke,

but this last strophe turns out to be itself the first half of another
synthetic parallel which splits into a catalog of final actions:

And twelve o'clock arrived just once too often, just the same he
wore one grey tweed suit, bought one straw hat, drank one
straight Scotch, walked one short step, took one long look, drew
one deep breath, just one too many,

Then there is a third set of recapitulative consequences—all
strophes since the second constitute a single sentence:

And wow he died as wow he lived, going whop to the office and
blooie home to sleep and biff got married and bam had children
and oof got fired, zowie did he live and zowie did he die,

and the climax, the funeral itself, with another series of sarcastic
rhetorical questions:

With who the hell are you at the corner of his casket, and where the
hell we going on the right hand silver knob, and who the hell
cares walking second from the end with an American Beauty
wreath from why the hell not, . . .

We note that this is still a single sentence, sarcasm building upon sarcasm, the impersonality of this urban Everyman well established by now. The next strophe would be a sentence fragment if it were independent, and in a manner of speaking, it is, the two narrative viewpoints—second and third person—implied; that is to say, it may be read, "He is very much missed . . ." or "You are very much missed." The ambiguity implies a third possibility: We will all be very much missed by faceless and unfeeling institutions when we die:

Very much missed by the circulation staff of the *New York Evening Post;* deeply, deeply mourned by the B.M.T., . . .

At last the sarcasm modulates into what is a set of irrelevant and random objects, and finally the tolling of the nameless bell for a nameless citizen:

Wham, Mr. Roosevelt; pow, Sears Roebuck; awk, big dipper; bop, summer rain; bong, Mr., bong, Mr., bong, Mr., bong.
—Kenneth Fearing

Meiosis is often a technique of *satire* or *self-derogation,* an anticlimactic method of *irony* or *sarcasm—heavy irony—*that diminishes the importance of something, as in, "He's a big fellow indeed—big-headed and big-bellied."

Chiasmus is *cross-parallelism* in parallel structures: "I vied with the wind, she fought the air, and as she lost, I was victorious." *Syneciosis* cross-couples *antonyms,* words antithetical in meaning or opposite, in such a way as to make them agree: "We are ourselves **victim** and **victor**. You were and are ourselves." The words in boldface are the antonyms. *Parison* is construction using parallel clauses of equal weight, as in the first stanza of Chidiock Tichborne's "Elegy: On the Evening of His Execution," which is also an example of *catalog* or *recapitulative verse* because of the repeated parallels:

Elegy: On the Evening of His Execution

My prime of youth is but a frost of cares,
My feast of joy is but a dish of pain,
My crop of corn is but a field of tares,
And all my good is but vain hope of gain;
The day is past, and yet I saw no sun,
And now I live, and now my life is done.

My tale was heard and yet it was not told,
My fruit is fallen, and yet my leaves are green,
My youth is spent and yet I am not old,
I saw the world and yet I was not seen;
My thread is cut and yet it is not spun,
And now I live, and now my life is done.

I sought my death and found it in my womb,
I looked for life and saw it was a shade,
I trod the earth and knew it was my tomb,
And now I die, and now I was but made;
My glass is full, and now my glass is run,
And now I live, and now my life is done.
                                        —Chidiock Tichborne

Walt Whitman's "I Hear America Singing" is a *prose poem* that
is one *sentence* long, comprised entirely of grammatically parallel
lists. In it there are several lists or *catalogs*: of types of people—la-
borers of one kind or another—of jobs, of *prepositional phrases* and
other modifiers. One can see the parallel structures by running
one's eye down the left-hand *margin* of the poem, where the *article*
"the" appears in a column. Besides these constructional schemes,
one finds a *repetitional scheme* also: the repetition of the verb "singing" throughout the poem:

I Hear America Singing

I hear America singing, the varied carols I hear,
    Those of mechanics, each one singing his as it should be blithe
        and strong,

The carpenter singing his as he measures his plank or beam,

The mason singing his as he makes ready for work, or leaves off
work,

The boatman singing what belongs to him in his boat, the deck-
hand singing on the steamboat deck,

The shoemaker singing as he sits on his bench, the hatter singing
as he stands,

The wood-cutter's song, the plowboy's on his way in the morning, or at noon intermission or at sundown,

The delicious singing of the mother, or of the young wife at
work, or of the girl sewing or washing,

Each singing what belongs to him or her and to none else,

The day what belongs to the day—at night the party of young
fellows, robust, friendly,

Singing with open mouths their strong melodious songs.

                                                    —Walt Whitman

In his poem "Chicago" Carl Sandburg combined one technique from the craft of short fiction, the *circle-back ending*, with a
repetitional scheme, the *refrain*, and the parallel structure of the catalog. The first *strophe* (section) of the poem reads,

Hog Butcher for the World,
Tool Maker, Stacker of Wheat,
Player with railroads and the Nation's Freight Handler;
Stormy, husky, brawling,
City of the Big Shoulders:

and the last reads,

Laughing the stormy, husky, brawling laughter of Youth, half-naked,
sweating, proud to be Hog Butcher, Tool Maker, Stacker of
Wheat, Player with Railroads and Freight Handler to the Nation.

Clearly, the first strophe is little more than the prose of the last
strophe *line-phrased* or, to use a current term, "*lineated*"; that is,
the *dependent clause* is lineated according to the phrases of which

the clause is comprised. To put it another way, the last strophe is the first strophe unlineated. One can illustrate by taking the Whitman poem just cited and breaking it up into line phrases so that it will more closely resemble verse—what many people erroneously call "*free verse*" (*vers libre*). That phrase is clearly a *contradiction in terms*, for "verse," in which some sort of syllables are being counted, cannot be free. Lineating a prose passage does not convert it to verse, nor does it convert one genre—*fiction*, *drama*, or *nonfiction* (as in this case)—to the genre of poetry.

Isoverbal Prosody

The ancient Hebrews sometimes imposed other strictures upon their grammatic parallels. For instance, a perfect parallel is one that not only divides the sentence into balanced clauses, it also requires that the same number of words, or even syllables, appear in each half of the parallel. The following line is a *perfect parallel*, for there are six words in each half, as the numbers above the words indicate:

EXAMPLE 1.

1   2   3   4   5   6   1   2   3   4   5   6
In the sky there is darkness; / birds settle out of the air.

The poetry writing system based upon *word-count* is called *isoverbal prosody*. If there were an isoverbal poem written with lines all of which contained the same number of words, it would be called *normative isoverbal prosody*. This is a couplet written in normative isoverbal prosody:

EXAMPLE 2.

In the sky there is darkness;
Birds settle out of the air.

If one were to write *stanzas* that contained differing numbers of words in the first stanza, but kept the same number of words in each corresponding *line* in succeeding stanzas, then one would be writing in *quantitative isoverbal prosody*.

The lines just shown were cited as a perfect parallel because there are six words in each half of the sentence, but one might have observed that it is perfect also because there are seven syllables in each of the two *clauses,* so that this *isocolonic line* is doubly perfect—the upper numbers indicate words, the lower ones indicate syllables:

EXAMPLE 3.

1	2	3	4	5	6		1	2	3	4	5	6

In the sky there is darkness; / birds settle out of the air.

1	2	3	4	5	6 7		1	2 3	4	5	6	7

Parenthetical Prosody

Parenthetics is also a prose system or prosody. In his poem "l(a" Cummings used two techniques primarily: parenthetics and grammatical dispersion. Cummings would sometimes write a poem in a traditional form, such as a sonnet, and then he would disguise the original form by "dispersing" the lines according to some pattern different from its original structure, perhaps breaking it up into lines that are really phrases or a few words, or by cutting lines at caesuras, or by running together two or more lines. In this case Cummings typographically dispersed a single word, "loneliness," and a short independent clause, "a leaf falls," breaking them up into clusters of one, two, or three letters; then he inserted the clause parenthetically into the word, thus turning the construct into a spatial or "picture" poem that falls down the page as a leaf falls to the ground:

l(a

l(a

le

af
fa

ll

s)
one
l

iness
—E. E. Cummings

This is not an arbitrary construct, for the typographical level is important in this impressionist poem, which makes its impression largely through the way the poem looks on the page. Cummings' use of dispersion here isolates on the page individual letters such as the letter *el*, used in place of the numeral 1 that, on old typewriters such as writers operated in the precomputer era, was left off the keyboard. By means of dispersion, Cummings even brought out the fact that the word "one" is part of "loneliness." (As one of the rock groups of the 1970s sang, "One is the loneliest number that you'll ever do.") Techniques like this are what might be called *sight puns*, plays on words that only the eye can catch. It would be almost impossible to read this poem aloud and have the audience catch this play, for it must be seen to be understood.

However, reading "l(a" aloud would make clear the fact that Cummings was also interested in the sonic level of the poem. It is full of soft sounds and sibilances: The els make a moaning, windy noise, and the esses and effs sound like leaves rustling in that wind.

In his poem "She," Russell Salamon began by taking *parentheses* themselves as his center:

().

He then took a sentence, "my hands cup her cup," broke it after the subject, and inserted the set of parens into the break:

my hands ( ) cup her cup.

This is a metaphor: my hands are a set of parentheses. Next, a second sentence, "all parentheses in which I am warm drizzle-rain inside her," thus:

All parentheses in which I am
[my hands ( ) cup her cup]
warm drizzle-rain inside her.

And a third, "sizzling on snowscapes of her skin, her face, her arms, her thighs, forests full of soundless flowers waited once unseen, translucid; she carries rain constellations to fill flute basins where," with some changed punctuation and a bit of typographical dispersion, appears this way:

sizzling on snowscapes of her skin.
Her face, her arms, her thighs,
all parentheses in which I am
[my hands ( ) cup her cup]
warm drizzle-rain inside her.
Forests full of soundless flowers
waited once unseen, translucid.
She carries rain constellations
to fill flute basins where

And finally, "My finger touch dis[s]olves into a shiverlong echo of rains; we wash our morning faces off":

My finger touch dissolves
into a shiverlong echo of rains/
sizzling on snowscapes of her skin.
(Her face, her arms, her thighs,
all parentheses in which I am
[my hands ( ) cup her cup]
warm drizzle-rain inside her.
Forests full of soundless flowers

waited once unseen, translucid.
She carries rain constellations
to fill f lute basins where
/we wash our morning faces off

The split between f and lute in the penultimate line appears as it was originally printed in *Parent[hetical Pop]pies*; it may or may not be a typographical error.

Others have written parenthetics since, and made other parenthetical experiments, as for instance Vito Hannibal Acconci in his poem titled "Re." Here, Acconci worked primarily with sets of parentheses themselves—there were to be three in each line:

(   ) (   ) (   )

Only one set in each line was to be filled with words:

(here) (   ) (   )

As the poem progressed, there would also be a progression in the set of parentheses to be filled; that is, it would be the second set in line two, the third set in line three, and then the order would be reversed—the second in line four, the first in line five, and so on back and forth to the end:

```
(here) (       ) (       )
(   ) (there) (                 )
(   ) (                 ) (here and there—I say here)
(                 ) (I do not say now) (         )
(I do not say it now) (         ) (                 )
(           ) (then and there—I say there) (     )
(                 ) (       ) (say there)
(       ) (I do not say then) (           )
(I do not say, then, this) (           ) (   )
(                 ) (then I say) (       )
(         ) (           ) (here and there)
(         ) (first here) (                 )
(I said here second) (                 ) (           )
```

```
(            ) (I do not talk first) (   )
(          ) (          ) (there then)
(        ) (here goes) (           )
(I do not say what goes) (        ) (        )
(              ) (I do not go on saying) (  )
(            ) (              ) (there is)
(     ) (that is not to say) (            )
(I do not say that) (          ) (          )
(          ) (here below) (               )
(      ) (               ) (I do not talk down)
(          ) (under my words) (            )
(under discussion) (            ) (          )
(        ) (all there) (             )
(    ) (    ) (I do not say all)
(          ) (all I say) (    )
```

People who see this poem for the first time are baffled by it. But the poem says visually, as well as in so many words, that "only about one-third of what one has to say can be communicated to others." This poem, however, is a paradox, because it expresses this theme completely, which contradicts the theme! The last two lines are, in fact, explicit: "I do not say all / all I say." Acconci invented a *form* that does exactly what he wanted it to do.

Syllabic Prosody

If one *lineates* the *sentence* in Example 2, shown earlier, it will constitute a true *verse couplet*:

```
 1   2    3     4   5   6   7
In the sky there is darkness;
   1     2 3   4    5   6   7
Birds settle out of the air
```

If all the other lines in the poem contained seven syllables, it would have been written in *normative syllabic prosody*.

Accentual Prosody

The major *form* of English *accentual prosody* (*strong stress verse*) is
Anglo-Saxon prosody, in which the oldest European epic written in
a *vernacular tongue* (as distinguished from the *classical tongues* of
Greek and Latin), *Beowulf,* was written, not to mention such later
poems as William Langland's *The Vision of Piers Plowman* and *Sir
Gawain and the Green Knight.* Anglo-Saxon prosody has continued
to be written fitfully over the centuries, even in contemporary
times, and there are other, more modern strong-stress forms, such
as Gerard Manley Hopkins' *variable accentual* "*sprung rhythm*"
system and William Carlos Williams' *triversen* stanza.

The basis for accentual verse is the counting of *stressed* (*accented*)
syllables in a line of verse, paying no attention to the number of
unstressed syllables. For the rules of scansion in English see pp.
37–38.

Following is a modern version of a famous poem, written in
Anglo-Saxon prosody, "The Wanderer." This anonymous Old
English *lament* appears here, as it does in the original version, in
Anglo-Saxon prosody. Alexander (see Bibliography) notes that
"These bleak soliloquies . . . together with their linking passage,
are set within a more Christian framework by a prologue and an
epilogue, both of five lines." This "framework" turns the poem
into a *harangue* by a *prototype* of Coleridge's "The Ancient Mari-
ner"—a mad old man who buttonholes the reader with a whining
story. Get rid of the *prologue* and the *epilogue,* which were surely
the additions of a medieval monk, and the poem becomes a pow-
erful, compelling, and structurally solid work of great beauty. The
first four *stichs* (*lines*) have been *scanned* to show the stress pattern
of *Anglo-Saxon prosody,* and markers indicate the *alliterations/asso-
nances* and the *medial caesura* (pause) in each stich.

The features of this particular form of strong-stress accentual
verse are these: Each line (called a *stich*) of verse contains four
stresses (it is therefore *normative accentual verse*); two or three of
these syllables are *overstressed* by means of *alliteration.* This term

means that the first syllable of a word is accented, first, by means of *pronunciation* (that is, the way in which we ordinarily pronounce the word—with the accent on the first syllable), and, second, by means of the *repetition* of *consonant sounds* (that is, in two or more words the stressed first syllable begins with a sound of the alphabet other than the *vowels*).

Besides the four strong stresses in the stich and the alliterations, each stich is broken in half by a pause called a *caesura*. This pause may be built into the poem by *phrasing* (there is usually a slight pause between the phrases of a sentence, often indicated by a *comma* [,] or a *semicolon* [;] or a *dash* [—], or by manipulating *measures* (*meters*) or *sounds*, as in *hiatus*, which is a caesura between identical or like sounds so that the audience may distinguish between syllables: "I will / lift / time out of / fetter." Each half of the stich is called a *hemistich*.

In English lines of four beats or longer, *a natural caesura*—only a brief hesitation—occurs very often after the second or third **stressed** syllable (´ = a stressed syllable, • = a caesura):

´   ´ •   ´   ´

Alone I am driven • each day by dawn

Qualitative caesura is caused by the *manipulation of measures*—that is, by changing up the rhythm of the stich (˘ = an unstressed syllable):

´ ˘ ´ ˘ • ˘ ´   ´

Fasten darkness • in deep moods

The first half has two "*falling rhythms*"— ´ ˘ ´ ˘ (we would call them trochees if we were doing accentual-syllabic prosody), and we can see that the second half of the stich reverses this rhythm ˘ ´ (we call this an iamb later on). There is a pause at the point of rhythmic change in the stich.

Punctuational caesura is caused by punctuation occurring somewhere in the center of the line because of phrasing:

To wake and wander, • to cry my cares.

Compensatory caesura occurs when the caesura compensates for a missing unstressed syllable in the line:

   ´ ᵕ ´ [ᵕ] ´ ᵕ ᵕ | ´
Winter-drear[y], over the wave.

In this stich falling rhythms are set up in the beginning of each hemistich; the mind's ear wants to hear ´ᵕ ´ᵕ ´ᵕ ´ᵕ, but the fourth syllable is missing, so we hear a pause at that point to compensate for that unstressed syllable,

´ ᵕ´[ᵕ] • ´ᵕ ´ᵕ
xx x[x] • xx xx

The Wanderer

    ´   ´   •   ´   ´
Alone I am **d**riven • each **d**ay by **d**awn
   ´   ´   ´   ´
To **w**ake and **w**ander, • to **c**ry my **c**ares.
 ´   ´   ´   ´
Now there are **n**one • among the quick
    ´   ´   ´   ´
To whom I **d**are • to **b**are my heart,

Tell my thought. Too truly I ken	[know]
That in a man it is no vice	
To keep his counsel chest-locked,	
Hold close his mind-hoard.	[thoughts]
No weary wit may scorn weird,	[fate]
Nor wrecked will work hope;	
Wherefore, belike, fame-chasers	
Fasten darkness in deep moods;	
Therefore, I must curb my mind—	

Cut off from kindred, cast from country,
Care-overborne—bind it in fetters,
For long ago the ground's grip   [burial]
Took my weal-lord. Wretched, I went,   [patron]
Winter-drear, over the wave.
I sought the hall of a gold-giver   [patron again]
Where, far or near, I might find
Him whose meadhall would host the castaway,
Grant comfort to one cursed,
Hail me heartily.

    He who struggles
Knows how cruel a companion is care
To him who has few shield-friends.   [fellow warriors]
The path presses him, no purse of gold;
Not Midgard's glory, but heart's cavern   [Earth's]
He recalls hall-men, treasure-sharing;
In youth-yore his loaf-lord   [patron]
Sat him to feast. This joy is fallen.
He who is forced to forgo the word
Of his liege-lord learns this lore:
How sleep and sorrow, twined together,
Bind in a bight the bitter outcast.
Dwelling in dream, he and his lord
Clasp and kiss, lay on knee
Hand and head, as betimes
In days dwindled, upon the gift-stool.

Then he wakens, the forsaken man,
And spies before him bleak spume;
Seamews swimming, stroking feathers;
Swirling hail; hoarsnow falling.
His heart's wounds hurt anew
For his loved lord. Grief blossoms.
The wraiths of kinsmen gather in thought;
He cries out gladly, scans eagerly
The throngs of his hearth—they scud away.
Long-boatmen's ghosts bring not many
Old lays there. Care freshens

In him who sends forward too oft
His warm heart over weary tides.

In Midgard I wit not why   [know not]
My mind is not mired
When it roves the lives of earls,

How in a stroke they forswore their halls,
Those mood-proud theigns. Thus does Midgard,
Each day and all, age and fall.

No man is wise who has not won
His winters-lore. The wise man bides,
Not hot-hearted, nor speech-hasty,
Nor weak in war, nor wanting in reckoning,
Nor too goods-grasping, too glad, too mild,
Nor boast-breasted, before he kens.

The sage forbears folly-boasting
Till fierce wit fully wots   [knows]
Which wind will take his spleen.

A wise man grasps how grim
This world shall be when its wealth wastes,
Even as now, in numberless places,
Earth's walls fall, wind-riven,
Rimed with hoar-ruined houses.
The wine-halls moulder; their wrights lie
In wolfbane, their bandsmen slain
Under the tower. The sword took some
In its course; a bird carried
One over Ocean; one the werewolf
Dealt to death; one stretched
His drear-eyed earl in an earthen trench.
The Man-Maker has marred this hearth   [God]
So men's laughter has sunk to stillness:

That wight who looked on these walls wisely,   [chap, fellow]

Who sounded deeply this dark life,
Would hark back to the blood spilled,
Weigh it well. His word would be,
"Where is the steed that served these men?
Where is the horde and the hoard-sharer?
Where is the fastness, the feast, the fanfare?"

Bright Cup! Burnished knight!
Eager earl! Your age tarnished
In night's helm, torn out of time!

There stands, instead of staunch theigns,
A louring wall wrought with worm-wrines;   [worm-furrows]
The earls eat dust beneath the ash-spear—
Thirsty biter! Their weird is proud.

Storms stutter on the stone hill,
The ground battered by bitter hail,
Weather-wrath. Bleakness breaks
And night-shade spreads, sends from the North
The hobnail sleet to harry man.

In Midgard all is crossed and melled;   [meddled]
Weird's-will wrenches the world.   [fate]
Wealth is our loan, friends our lending;
Mankind is lent, kinsmen lent:
Earth's frame shall stand forsaken.
                        —Anonymous Anglo-Saxon

Although the term "pod" in Latin means "foot," and there are no *verse feet* involved in strong stress prosody, nevertheless *"pod"* traditionally means "strong accent." The standard *prefixes* (mono = 1, di = 2, tri = 3, tetra = 4, penta = 5, hexa = 6, hepta = 7, octa = 8, nona = 9, deca = 10, hendeca = 11) attached to *"podic"* will indicate the number of stresses in the stich. In the refrain of "Wulf and Eadwacer" there are two stresses, on "**we**" and the second syllable of "un**done**," so the meter of the refrain is *dipodic*. One would assume that, because there are four stresses in the full stichs of that poem and of "The Wanderer," the meter would be *tetrapodic*, but not so: because of the *medial caesura* that splits the stich, the meter is *dipodic*. If there were no caesura in the stich, then it would be *tetrapodic*.

Podics

Podics is a "*folk meter*," and it is often found in anonymously written *nursery rhymes*, *ballads*, and *madsongs*. However, many literary poets such as John Skelton in the early Renaissance, the eighteenth-century Scots poet Robert Burns, and such twentieth-century poets as John Crowe Ransom, Vachel Lindsay, Ralph Hodgson, and Theodore Roethke have used it successfully.

Podics uses *rhyme*, but it does not regularly alternate stressed and unstressed syllables. Podics is a holdover, in folk poetry, of the old Anglo-Saxon prosody. After Geoffrey Chaucer, his contemporary John Gower, and other fourteenth-century poets combined the Norman French syllabic system with the native English strong stress prosody, thus inventing accentual-syllabic prosody, the common folk, including the balladeers of the Scottish-English border, continued to hear the ancient alliterative stich and echoic devices, so they continued to write using the old prosody, but they added true rhyme and stanza forms, which they adopted from the Normans. Many *nursery rhymes* and *lullabies* are nothing more than two rhyming stichs (a *distich*) of Anglo-Saxon prosody:

The cock's on the midden • a-blowing his horn;

The bull's in the barn • a-threshing of corn;

The maids in the meadow • are making of hay;

The ducks in the river • are swimming away.

Notice the *alliterations* in some of the stichs, and the added rhymes (the *rhyme scheme* is *aa, bb*): these distichs look like ordinary *couplets* of accentual-syllabic prosody, and they even sound something like them, but add *breves* over the unstressed syllables, and no regular pattern of *verse feet* appears:

> The cock's on the midden • blowing his horn;
> The bull's in the barn • threshing the corn;
> The maids in the meadow • are making of hay;
> The ducks in the river • are swimming away.

If this were accentual-syllabic verse, we would be looking for a *running foot* (common rhythm)—that is, a regularly recurring pattern of a single kind of verse foot. The first foot in the first line is an iamb ($\smile$ $\prime$); the second is an anapest ($\smile$ $\smile$ $\prime$); the third is another iamb, and the fourth another anapest. In line two there is an iamb, an anapest, a trochee ($\prime$ $\smile$) and an iamb. Line four shows an iamb and three anapests in a row—this is the only line in which a particular verse foot predominates. But what stays absolutely steady is the strong stressing: There are four strong stresses in each line; this poem, therefore, is written in podic meters.

Sometimes these stichs are line-phrased; that is, they are broken at the caesura to become dipodic lines:

> The cock's on the midden •
> Blowing his horn;
> The bull's in the barn •
> Threshing the corn;
>
> The maids in the meadow •
> Are making of hay;
> The ducks in the river •
> Are swimming away.

The rhyme scheme now becomes *abcb defe*. Notice another feature of podic verse—*falling endings*: **mid**den, **mea**dow, **ri**ver.

Many nursery rhymes and ballads have this *form*:

´　　　´ •　　　´　　　´
Jack and Jill • went up the hill
　´　　　´　　´
To fetch a pail of water;
´　•　´　　•　　　´　　　　´
Jack fell down • and broke his crown,
　´　•　　　´　　　´
And Jill came tumbling after.

Up Jack got and home did trot
As fast as he could caper,
To Old Dame Dob, who patched his nob
With vinegar and brown paper.

When Jill came in, how she did grin,
To see Jack's paper plaster;
Dame Dob, vexed, did whip her next
For causing Jack's disaster.

—Anonymous

This is nothing more than rhyming *song measure*—a Norse *edda measure quatrain* whose first and third lines are stichs of Anglo-Saxon prosody, and whose second and fourth lines are tripodic; that is, they are quatrains rhyming *abcb* consisting of two couplets made of a full stich followed by a tripodic line. There are *falling rhymes* and *falling endings*, the only thing new added being the *internal rhymes* in the full stichs: the hemistichs rhyme. Secondary stresses do not figure in the system, **only** the strong stresses.

This podic quatrain stanza is called *ballad stanza*, and many ballads are written in it (but not all of them, for the definition of a *ballad* is simply "a relatively short lyric narrative," and it may be written in any stanza *form*). *Ballad stanza* written in accentual-syllabic prosody rather than in podic prosody is called *common measure* or *common meter*, and it is the form of many *hymns* and other songs—*lyrics*.

Although there are no verse feet to be found in podic prosody, nevertheless J. R. R. Tolkien (see Bibliography) isolated six *basic hemistichs* in Anglo-Saxon prosody, and these basic half-lines have been retained in many podic poems: (1) The *double-fall* (´ ˘ ´ ˘) as in "**Mis**tress **Ma**ry | **Quite** con**tra**ry"; (2) the *double-rise* (˘ ´ ˘ ´) as in "With **silver bells** | and **cock**le **shells**;" (3) the *rise-and-fall* (˘ ´ ´ ˘) as in "the **two gray** kits"; (4) the *rise-and-descend* (˘ ´ ´ •) as in "**My Maid Ma**ry"; (5) the *fall-and-ascend* (´ ´ ˘ •) as in "**To woo** the *owl*", and (6) the *descend-and-rise* (´ ´ ˘ ´) as in "**Hark! Hark!** the **lark!**"

There are, however, many more rhythmic variations possible. Two others are quite common: (7) the *short rocking foot* (´ ˘ ´) as in "**See** them **jump** | **up** and **down**!" This is called the *amphimacer* (*cretic*) in accentual-syllabic verse, where it is in fact never found in English language poetry written in that prosody. There are also (8) the *long rocking foot* (´ ˘ ˘ ´) as in "**Hip**pety-**hop**, | **hip**pety-**hop**!"; (9) the *long rise* (˘ ˘ ´ ´) as in "And a **one-two**, and a **three-four**"—Harvey Gross in his book *Sound and Form in Modern Poetry* (see Bibliography) calls this rhythm the *double iamb* and discovers it frequently in *accentual-syllabic verse*, where it substitutes for two iambic feet—and (10) the *long fall* (´ ´ ˘ ˘) as in "**Come jump** with me," which in accentual-syllabic prosody would be the *double trochee*.

The nineteenth-century British poet Gerard Manley Hopkins, in his *variable accentual prosody,* which he called *sprung rhythm,* likewise paid no attention to keeping only a certain number of stresses to the line, but he overstressed his heavily accented lines with all sorts of sonic devices including *alliteration*, *assonance*, *rhyme* (notice that this poem has *endrhyme*; that is, rhyming at the ends of the lines), *repetition*, and *vocalic* and *consonantal echo*; in fact, if it had been written in iambic pentameter lines, it would have been a *sonnet*:

God's Grandeur
The world is charged with the grandeur of God.
   It will flame out, like shining from shook foil;

It gathers to a greatness, like the ooze of oil
Crushed. Why do men then now not reck his rod?
Generations have trod, have trod, have trod;
   And all is seared with trade; bleared, smeared with toil;
   And wears man's smudge and shares man's smell: the soil
Is bare now, nor can foot feel, being shod.
And for all this, nature is never spent;
   There lives the dearest freshness deep down things;
And though the last lights off the black West went
   Oh, morning, at the brown brink eastward, springs—
Because the Holy Ghost over the bent
   World broods with warm breast and with ah! bright wings.
                   —Gerard Manley Hopkins

Through overstressing, Hopkins managed to get more than two contiguous accented syllables in a row quite often, though the English language normally will not allow three stressed vowels in a row without demoting one of them to secondary stress.

A native American form of *variable accentuals* is the *triversen stanza*, which was developed by William Carlos Williams. Essentially, a *triversen* ("triple verse sentence") stanza is partly *grammatic* in prosody: **One stanza equals one sentence**. This *sentence* is broken into three parts, each part becoming a **line composed of approximately one phrase**. Thus, **three lines** (three phrases**) are equal to one stanza** (one sentence or independent clause). Williams, in attempting to explain this prosody, spoke of the *breath pause*—all that this meant, finally, was the process of breaking the sentence or independent clause into phrasal lines, what has here been called "*line-phrasing*" or *lineating*, but there is a traditional term: The *verset* is a surge of language equal to one full breath.

Williams also spoke of the *variable foot*, and by this he meant the accentual element of the prosody: **Each line could vary in length**, carrying from one to four stressed (not necessarily alliterated) syllables, but generally two to four. He used this stanza quite often. See the later discussion of Williams for further insight into his method. Here is an unpunctuated triversen:

On Gay Wallpaper

The green–blue ground
is ruled with silver lines
to say the sun is shining

And on this moral sea
of grass or dreams lie flowers
or baskets of desires

Heaven knows what they are
between cerulean shapes
laid regularly round

Mat roses and tridentate
leaves of gold
threes, threes and threes

Three roses and three stems
the basket floating
standing in the horns of blue

Repeated to the ceiling
to the windows
where the day

Blows in
the scalloped curtains to
the sound of rain
    —William Carlos Williams

Accentual–Syllabic Prosody

These distinctions ought to be reviewed before *accentual-syllabic prosody* is considered: *Rhythm* is the movement of *cadences* in language; *prosody* is a system of poetic composition; and *meter* is a particular system of prosody that counts syllables in verse according to a pattern. Accentual-syllabic prosody is a metrical system that counts the *number of syllables in a line of verse*, both stressed and unstressed, and **then** the *number of stressed syllables in the line*. Moreover, in accentual-syllabic prosody the stressed syllables alternate more or less regularly with *unstressed syllables* to form *verse feet*. Therefore, **three things** are actually being counted in accentual-syllabic prosody: **first**, *all syllables*; **second**, *stressed syllables*; **third**, *verse feet* (unstressed syllables are **not** counted, for they may vary in number, to a degree).

It is important to note at this point that the terms used to designate verse feet in English are adopted from the classical Greek. These *Greek* (or *Attic*) terms are not, in fact, appropriate to English-language poetry, for *Greek prosody* was *quantitative* (that is, like musical notes, syllables were assigned "lengths"—full note, half note, quarter note, etc.), and English prosody is heavily dependent simply on three "weights" for syllables: *heavy accent (strong stress)* indicated by an *ictus* (´) or a *macron* (‾) placed over the *stressed vowel*; *light accent (secondary stress)* indicated by a *dot* (˙) placed over the *stressed vowel*, and *unstressed*, indicated by a *breve* or *mora* (˘) placed over the *atonic* (unstressed) *syllable (arsis)*; **nota bene**: the term "arsis" in English prosody, as distinguished from the Greek, is generally (and confusingly) applied to the *stressed syllable*.

Every word in English **two syllables in length** or longer **will have one strongly stressed syllable at least**. Every student of poetry ought to have a *pronouncing dictionary* so that he or she can check to see where the stress is placed in the ordinary pronunciation of an unfamiliar word being used in a poem. The general rule for stressing words of a single syllable is this: *Verbs* and *nouns* generally take a stress because they are important words in the sentence—action words, subjects, or objects; exceptions are those verbs that we generally *elide*: "Have" ("*I've* gone downtown"), "are" ("*You're* looking good today"), "am" ("*I'm* leaving town"), and so forth. Words of a single syllable that are not generally stressed are *articles* (*a, the*), *prepositions* (*of, to, on, in*, etc.), *coordinating conjunctions* (*and, but, or, nor, for*), and certain pronouns such as

"I" and sometimes "you," which we tend either to use in an elision or merely to slide over, even though they are important words ("I **wish** you **were** my **hon**eybun"). But *context*—the situation of the word in the line—will often dictate whether an unimportant one-syllable will take a stress: ("If **I** were **you** I'd **run** a**way**"). Here are those last two lines laid out schematically:

   ᵕ ´   ᵕ   ´   ᵕ   ᵕ   ´ ´

I wish you were my honeybun—

   ᵕ ´ ´   ´   ᵕ   ´ ᵕ ´

If I were you I'd run away.

There are four standard feet in English prosody: The *iamb* is a *verse foot* (*proceleusmaticus*) of two syllables, the second of which is stressed (ᵕ ´); the *anapest* has three syllables, the third of which is stressed (ᵕ ᵕ ´); the *trochee* has two syllables, the first of which is stressed (´ ᵕ)—a reverse iamb—and the *dactyl* has three syllables, the first of which is stressed (´ ᵕ ᵕ)—a reverse anapest. The standard prefixes attached to the word *meter* will indicate the kind and length of the line: The *couplet* just shown is written in *iambic tetrameter* verse (ᵕ ´ ᵕ ´ ᵕ ´ ᵕ ´). There are several *minor verse feet* in English prosody, usually used as variations only: The *headless iamb* is a foot of one stressed syllable (´), as is the *tailless trochee* (´). One can tell these two feet apart only from their position in a line of verse. They occur, for instance, when the unstressed first syllable of an iamb is dropped in order to vary the rhythm of a line of verse, or when the unstressed second syllable of a trochee is dropped for the same reason; the example given next is a line from an iambic tetrameter poem:

  [ᵕ]   ´ | ᵕ   ´ | ᵕ   ´ | ᵕ   ´

[Oh,] won't you be my honeybun?

Or consider this, from a trochaic tetrameter poem:

   ´   ᵕ | ´   ᵕ | ´ ᵕ | ´ [ᵕ]

Won't you be my honeybun[ny]?

In an iambic poem this line would still be an iambic tetrameter line, except that it begins with a headless iamb ([˘] ´ | ˘ ´ | ˘ ´ | ˘ ´). However, if this line were to be found in the context of a trochaic poem, then it would end with a tailless trochee (´ ˘ | ´ ˘ | ´ ˘ | ´ [˘]).

The *spondee* (*distributed stress, hovering accent*) is a verse foot of two syllables, both of which are accented (´´). (The iamb, trochee, and spondee are *double meters*: verse feet made up of two syllables.) The *amphibrach* is a *rocking foot* of three syllables, only the second of which is stressed (˘ ´ ˘); the second unstressed syllable in this foot would have been considered by Gerard Manley Hopkins as an *outride*—that is, an extra unstressed syllable attached to a verse foot, in this case, an iamb. The anapest, dactyl, and amphibrach are *triple meters*: verse feet made up of three syllables. The *double iamb* is a foot of four syllables, the first two unstressed and the second two stressed (˘ ˘ ´ ´). It equals two iambs in a line of verse. Classical prosodists would say that the double iamb is a combination of two shorter feet, the *pyrrhic* or *dibrach* (˘ ˘) and the *spondee*. The pyrrhic, however, does not seem to appear elsewhere in English prosody, unless as a variation in a trochaic poem that reverses the double iamb and would substitute for two trochees and perhaps best be identified as a *double trochee* (´ ´ ˘ ˘):

  ´ ˘ | ´   ´   ˘ ˘ | ´ ˘ | ´ ˘
Over there where the despairing children
  ´ ˘ | •   ˘ | ´   ´   ˘ ˘ | ´ ˘
Wander in the dark streets of uncaring.

Other classical Greek verse feet do not apply to English prosody in any way. An *amphimacer* (´ ˘ ´) is either a headless iamb and an iamb, or a trochee and a tailless trochee. The *antispast* is an iamb followed by a trochee (˘ ´ ´ ˘). We know that the *tribrach*—three unstressed syllables (˘ ˘ ˘) cannot exist, for the English language dislikes three unstressed syllables in a row, and the central syllable is almost always *promoted* to *secondary stress* in a line of verse (˘ • ˘), where the secondary accent takes the place of a full stress and counts as one. Annie Finch objects that in the phrase, "It is the star," the first three syllables are a tribrach, but in fact the middle syllable of the first three is a promotion,

⌣ • | ⌣ ´
"It is the star,"

and these are two iambs. The proof is in the listening: If one reads the phrase into a tape recorder and plays it back, one will hear the secondary stress on *is*. The reverse occurs in the case of the *molossus*, a foot of three stressed syllables, for English equally dislikes three stressed syllables in a row (except in strong-stress prosody), and the central syllable is almost always *demoted* to secondary stress in a line of accentual-syllabic verse (´•´), where the secondary accent takes the place of an unstressed syllable and counts as one. In the phrase Ms. Finch adduces as an example of a molossus,

´ | •   ´ |⌣   ´ |⌣ ´
Knock, breathe, shine, and seek to read,

there is not a strong stress on *breathe*, but a demotion to secondary stress, and reading the passage aloud will discover a headless iamb followed by three iambs, not a molossus and two iambs. The *bacchic* (⌣´´) would be an iamb and a tailless trochee, and the *antibacchius* or *antibacchic* (´´⌣) is a headless iamb and a trochee. The *choriamb* consists of a trochee (*choree*) followed by an iamb (´⌣⌣´). The *epitrite* is any one of four verse feet, each composed of four syllables, one unstressed and three stressed (⌣´´´, ´⌣´´, ´´⌣´, or ´´´⌣); the first is two iambs, third syllable demoted; the second is a trochee and a spondee, the third is a spondee and an iamb; and the last is two trochees, second syllable demoted. The *pæon* is the opposite: a foot containing one stressed syllable, and three unstressed, in any order (´⌣⌣⌣, ⌣´⌣⌣, ⌣⌣´⌣, ⌣⌣⌣´); depending on its location in the line, in English verse each of these would be transformed in some way into other things—for instance, in the first case the central syllable in the series of three unstressed syllables would be promoted, and the "pæon" would actually be two trochees (ˊ˘•˘).

Accentual-syllabics is a rhythm system that alternates stressed and unstressed syllables according to some *normative pattern*. The word "normative" is important, for the true accentual-syllabic poet knows that it is *variation* **against the pattern**, and not strict adherence to the pattern, that delights the ear. A *poetaster*, or unskilled *versifier*, memorizes a pattern and works with it, often producing *doggerel*, crude verse, but more often *garden-club verse*, which is typical of the production of "little old ladies in tennis shoes," of both sexes. A *poet* or *bard*, on the other hand, understands a pattern and works against it, for a metronome is boring; *counterpoint* or *modulation*—rhythm against a beat—is interesting; see *quality* and *substitution*.

The Rules of Scansion

Scansion is the process of isolating the accented or unaccented syllables in language. The rules of thumb regarding stressing are simple and few:

1. In every word of the English language of two or more syllables, at least one syllable will take a stress. If one cannot at first hear the stressing, then one may consult a pronouncing dictionary.

2. Important single-syllable words, particularly *verbs* and *nouns*, generally take strong stresses.

3. Unimportant single-syllable words in the sentence, such as *articles*, *prepositions*, and *pronouns* (except *demonstrative pronouns*), do not take strong stresses, though they may take *secondary stresses* through *promotion* or *demotion*, depending on their position in the sentence or the line of verse.

4. In any series of three unstressed syllables in a line of verse, one of them, generally the middle syllable, will take a *secondary stress* through *promotion* and will be counted as a *stressed* syllable.

5. In any series of three stressed syllables in a line of verse, one

of them, generally the middle syllable, will take a *secondary stress* through *demotion* and will be counted as an *unstressed* syllable.

6. *Any* syllable may be *rhetorically stressed* by means of italics or some other typographical ploy, as has just *now* been done.

The strong stresses of the English language usually coincide with the *long vowel sounds* rather than the short ones:

´ ˘ ´   ˘   ´ ˘ ´   ´   ˘   ´ ˘ ´ ˘ • ˘
Any language can be scanned. One could scan a novel, if one
´   ˘ ´   ˘   ˘ ´ ˘   ´   ´ ˘   ˘ ´ ˘   ˘
wished, and one could distinguish verse feet in the novel. But
´ ˘   ´   ˘ ´ ´ ˘ ´ ˘ ´   ˘ ˘ ´   ´
scanning prose does not turn it into verse. It remains prose
˘ ´   ˘ ´ ˘ • ˘   ´ • ´ ˘ ´   ˘ ´ ˘
because the syllables are not laid out in lines containing
´ ˘ ´   ˘ ˘ ´   ˘ ´ ˘   ´ ˘ • ˘ ´
certain numbers of stressed and unstressed syllables per verse.

´   ˘ ´   ´ ˘
Nor does line-phrasing
´   ´ • ˘ ´
turn prose into verse.   [3rd syllable demoted here]
˘ ˘ ´   ´   ˘ ´
It remains prose because
˘ ´ ˘ • ˘   ´
the syllables are not
•   ´ ˘ ´
laid out in lines
˘ ´ ˘   ´ ˘   ´   ˘
containing certain numbers
˘   ´   ˘   ´   ˘   ´ ˘ • ˘ ´
of stressed and unstressed syllables per verse.

Quality is a term that covers the *substitution* of one kind of verse foot for another: specifically, substitution of a verse foot that differs from the *normative meter* of the line. Substitution may take place anywhere in the line without changing its metrical length. For instance, taking a line of iambic pentameter verse (each "x" equals one syllable):

```
  ˘ ́ ˘ ́ ˘ ́ ˘ ́ ˘ ́
  xx xx xx xx xx
```

one may substitute a spondee in the first foot without harming the meter of the line (adding a stressed syllable anywhere in the line, **except** when a spondee is substituted for one normative foot, will lengthen the line):

```
  ́ ́ ˘ ́ ˘ ́ ˘ ́ ˘ ́
  xx xx xx xx xx
```

or one may substitute an anapest in the second foot:

```
  ˘ ́ ˘ ˘ ́ ˘ ́ ˘ ́ ˘ ́
  xx xxx xx xx xx
```

or one may substitute a trochee in the third foot:

```
  ˘ ́ ˘ ́ ́ ˘ ˘ ́ ˘ ́
  xx xx xx xx xx
```

or one may substitute an amphibrach in the fifth foot,

```
  ˘ ́ ˘ ́ ˘ ́ ˘ ́ ˘ ́ ˘
  xx xx xx xx xxx
```

and the line remains iambic pentameter. One may even substitute two verse feet in a five-foot line without changing the normative meter, but if one substitutes three feet in a pentameter line, the meter is changed:

```
  ˘ ́ | ́ ˘ | ́ ˘ ˘ | ˘ ́ | ˘ ́ ˘
  xx xx xxx xx xxx
```

It is impossible to identify the meter of this line except in the context of a whole poem that has a normative meter. *Acatalexis* is a term that designates a perfect line of accentual-syllabic verse. For instance, in an iambic tetrameter poem an *acatalectic* line will have eight syllables and four stresses, with the unaccented syllables alternating regularly with the accented syllables:

ᵕ⁄ ᵕ⁄ ᵕ⁄ ᵕ⁄
xx xx xx xx

Catalexis. A line is made *catalectic* (tailless) by dropping an unaccented syllable at the end of the line, as in a trochaic tetrameter poem:

⁄ᵕ ⁄ᵕ ⁄ᵕ ⁄[ᵕ]
xx xx xx x[x]

This line is now trochaic tetrameter with a tailless trochee substituted in the fourth foot. Dropping an accented syllable will shorten the line, as in an iambic pentameter poem:

ᵕ⁄ ᵕ⁄ ᵕ⁄ ᵕ⁄ ᵕ[⁄]
xx xx xx xx x[x]

This line is now iambic tetrameter with an amphibrach substituted in the fourth foot.

Brachycatalexis. Dropping more than one unaccented syllable at the end of the line makes it *brachycatalectic*, as in a dactylic pentameter poem.

⁄ᵕᵕ ⁄ᵕᵕ ⁄ᵕᵕ ⁄ᵕᵕ ⁄[ᵕᵕ]
xxx xxx xxx xxx x[xx]

This line is now dactylic pentameter with a trochee substitution in the fourth foot and an iamb substitution in the fifth foot.

Hypercatalexis. A line is made *hypercatalectic* (*hypermetrical*) by adding an unaccented syllable at the end of the line, as in an iambic tetrameter poem:

    ◡ ╱ ◡ ╱ ◡ ╱ ◡ ╱ ◡
    xx xx xx xxx

This line is now iambic tetrameter with an amphimacer substituted in the fourth foot. Adding an accented syllable will lengthen the line:

    ◡ ╱ | ◡ ╱ | ◡ ╱ | ◡ ╱ | ╱
    xx xx xx xx   x

This line is now an iambic pentameter line with a tailless trochee substituted in the fifth foot.

Acephalexis. A line is made *acephalous* (headless) by dropping unaccented syllables from the beginning of the line, as in an iambic pentameter poem:

    [◡] ╱ | ◡ ╱ | ◡ ╱ | ◡ ╱ | ◡ ╱
    [x]x xx xx xx xx

This line is now iambic pentameter with a headless iamb substituted in the first foot. Dropping a stressed syllable from the beginning of a line will shorten it, as in a trochaic trimeter poem:

    [╱]◡ ╱ ◡ ╱ ◡
    [x]x xx xx

The line is now unidentifiable as to meter (except in the context of a poem). All one can say of it is that it is dimeter, either an iamb followed by an amphibrach, or an amphibrach followed by a trochee; there is no running foot.

Epiploce. This is a term used to describe a situation when, in scansion, a line of verse may be viewed in either of two ways, that is, as a catalectic trochaic tetrameter line (╱ ◡ | ╱ ◡ | ╱ ◡ | ╱) , or as an acephalous iambic tetrameter line (ˊ|˘ˊ|˘ˊ|˘ˊ). Generally, the matter can be settled by a scansion of the rest of the poem to determine the normative meter.

Anacrusis. The line is made anacrustic by adding unaccented syllables to the beginning of the line, as in an iambic pentameter poem:

˘˘ˊ ˘ˊ ˘ˊ ˘ˊ ˘ˊ
xxx xx xx xx xx

This line is now iambic pentameter with an anapest substituted in the first foot.

Wordsworth's famous "Ode: Intimations of Immortality . . ." is *alloeostrophic* or *polyrhythmic*—that is, an example of *variable accentual-syllabic verse*. There is a running foot, just as in normative accentual-syllabics, but the line lengths vary and the rhymes are random. Here is the first stanza scanned with *dividers* inserted to separate the verse feet:

   ˊ   ˘|˘ ˊ | ˘ ˊ|˘ ˊ |˘ ˊ
There was a time when meadow, grove, and stream,

  ˘ ˊ | ˘ ˊ|˘ ˊ | ˘ ˊ
The earth, and every common sight,

˘ ˊ |• ˊ
To me did seem

˘ ˊ| ˘ • |˘ˊ˘ |ˊ
Appareled in celestial light,

˘ ˊ|˘ • | ˘ ˊ |˘ •|˘ ˊ
The glory and the freshness of a dream.

˘ ˘ ˊ ˊ |˘ ˘ ˊ ˊ | ˘ ˊ   [iambic pentameter:
It is not now as it hath been of yore   2 double iambs]

        ́   ́| ∪ ́ |∪ ́
Turn whereso'er I may,

    ∪ ́ | ∪   ́
By night or day,

    ∪   ́ | ∪ •| ∪   ́ | ∪ ́| ∪   ́ | • ́
The things which I have seen I now can see no more.

One can see that iambs predominate—in fact, there are very few substitutions: a trochee in the first foot of line one; a double iamb in the first two and the second two feet of line six; a spondee in the first foot of line seven. For the rest of it, the variations are primarily promotions and a demotion or two. The line lengths of this stanza range from *dimeter* (lines three and eight) to *hexameter* (line nine), but the lower and upper limits for the rest of the poem are *monometer* to *heptameter*.

Phrasing

Grammatic enjambment is the running-on of a sentence, without pause, from one line or stanza to the next, as between lines three and four of Wordsworth's "Ode," just shown. *Metrical enjambment* takes place when, in effect, half of a verse foot belonging to a following line occurs at the end of the preceding line, as in these lines from section eight of Wordsworth's poem:

      ́ ́|∪   ́ | ∪ ́   ∪ ́ ∪∪̲̲̲̲̲̲̲̲̲̲ ̲̲̲̲̲́   ∪ ́
Thou, over whom thy Immortality /Broods like the day . . .

where a double iamb is in effect substituted for syllables nine and ten of the first line and syllables one and two of the next. The reverse may also take place—metrical enjambment occurs when half of a verse foot belonging to a preceding line is added to the beginning of the following line.

The opposite of enjambment is *cloture* (*end-stopping*); which is a full stop (a *period*, *exclamation point*, *question mark*, or a *semicolon*) at the end of a *stich* (an *end-stopped line*, as in the *refrain* second stanza), couplet (a *closed couplet*, as in the first two lines), or larger stanzaic unit (a *closed stanza*, as in the third strophe) of "Wulf and Eadwacer," which follows. *Semicloture* takes place when the end of the line coincides with the end of a phrase or clause, as in lines five, nine, and fourteen of this next piece, which is an anonymous Old English poem in *Anglo-Saxon prosody* written from the woman's viewpoint; it is a fragment. A few liberties have been taken here to give it the appearance of completeness; that is, Eadwacer's name has been inserted into strophe three (not counting the *refrain* line, "We are undone!") where it did not appear in the original, and the refrain has been repeated at the end of the poem where, it seems likely, it ought to have reappeared with greatly increased dramatic irony. The refrain is a very unusual feature of early British verse.

Wulf and Eadwacer

The carls of my clan would catch him like prey;
Should he come to camp, they will slay him quickly.

We are undone!

Wulf is enisled, as I am elsewhere.
My isle is a fastness girdled by fens,
Defended by the fiercest of folk.
Should he come to camp they will kill him surely.

We are undone!

It was wet weather; I wept at the hearth,
Wondering of Wulf and his wandering afar;
Eadwacer, a chief, chafed and embraced me—
He made me glad, but I grieved as well.

Wulf, my Wulf, my wanting you
Made me heartsick, your seldom coming,
The cave of my breast, not thigh-hunger!

Do you hearken, Eadwacer?—our whelp Wulf
Shall take to the forest! What was never fettered
Is soon untwined, our loins together!

We are undone!
                    —Anonymous Anglo-Saxon

Normative accentual-syllabic meters have nothing whatever to
do with *quantitative accentual-syllabics*. The meters of quantitative
verse, which are Classical Greek in origin, are **prescribed**. For instance, in the Greek form called *Sapphics* the *Sapphic line* is composed of two trochees, a dactyl, and two trochees, in that order, although certain substitutions are allowed at prescribed places. This
is a Sapphic line: ´ ⌣ ´ ⌣ ´ ⌣ ⌣ ´ ⌣ ´ ⌣. The *Sapphic stanza* is made up of
three such lines plus a line called an *adonic*, which is a dactyl and a
trochee, in that order: ´ ⌣ ⌣ ´ ⌣. It is an unrhymed (*blank*) quatrain.

There are exactly eleven syllables in each Sapphic line (because
of the three-syllable dactyl), and it contains five verse feet, so it is a
pentameter line. While it is true that trochees predominate, since
their positions in the line are prescribed, they are not normative.
Likewise, the adonic contains five syllables and two verse feet—it
is dimeter, but not normative. No verse foot even predominates in
the adonic line.

The first stanza of the following poem has been scanned:

Sapphic Stanzas in Falling Measures

    ´   ⌣ | ´ ⌣ | ´ ⌣ ⌣ | ´ ⌣ | ´ ⌣
Now the frost is falling in all our gardens.
    ´ ⌣ | ´   ⌣ | ´ ⌣   ⌣ | ´ ⌣ | ´ ⌣
Fall has rimed itself with the call of autumn.
    ´   ⌣ | ´ ⌣ | ´ ⌣ ⌣ | ´   ⌣ | ´ ⌣
Now that frost, in crystals and webs, is falling
    ´ ⌣ ⌣ | ´   ⌣
Out of the dawn in

All our gardens, summer has fallen out of
Rime in crystals, webs, and the dawn in voices

Calling on the westerly winds of changing
    Weathers and climates.

Now the frost—in tentative webs and crystals
Falling from the dawning to all our gardens
Vined and gourded—has rimed itself with
    Calls of the fliers

Gliding on the westerlies. Changing weathers
Send our northern sojourners on their searches
After other climates, for now that autumn
    Falls in a rime of

Crystal webs on all of our summer gardens
Vined and gourded, riming itself with sounding
Calls of fliers gliding upon the western
    Winds in these changing

Weathers, dawns will shatter in all our climates:
South, the flocks of sojourners fall and settle
Out of early light in a hoarfrost made of
    Springtime and summer.

In this poem the technique of *prolepsis* (*q.v.*) has also been used—
see *The Book of Literary Terms* for a full discussion.

Contraction

Elision is concerned with the blending of two or more syllable
sounds so that they become one syllable sound. Robert Bridges
(see Bibliography) has discussed various ways of eliding, and Donald Justice (*q.v.*) has expanded upon them. *Vocalic elision,* as Justice
writes, occurs "When two vowel sounds come together[;] then if
the first of the two has a tail-glide (a y-glide or a w-glide), there
may be elision." (Some examples of y-glide are fl*y*ing, so b*e i*t, th*e*
*o*thers, th*ee a*nd sh*e a*nd all, glor*y a*bove, ri*o*t. Some examples of w-

glide are ru*i*nous, s*o o*ften, c*oo*perate, als*o i*n, foll*ow*ers [foll'wers], shad*ow*y [shad'wy], grad*ua*l, and infl*ue*nce.) In *semivocalic elision,* Justice says, "If two unstressed vowels be separated by **r**, there may be elision"; adding, "This applies also to **l** and **n** and perhaps may be extended to **m**." (Some examples are mur*mur*ing [murm'ring], pill*ar o*f state [pillar 'f state], car*o*ler [car'ler], begot*ten a*nd reared [begott'n and]).

Consonantal silence. "H is often considered as no letter," writes Justice, as in **ought to have** [ought to 'ave or to've], where the following vowel is also suppressed (I've, you've—see *vocalic suppression* described later). Other consonants are sometimes silenced as well, as in "often" (o*f 'e*n or o*f 'n*, although recently many people seem to be going out of their way to reinsert the **t** in the word, pronouncing it "off-ten"). The poetic diction of the nineteenth century dropped the en entirely, inserted the tee, and pronounced the word "oft," rhyming with "croft." For *consonantal suppression,* Justice says, "Final m and n are very frequently not counted any-how, as chasm [not chasum] or heaven [heav'n]."

Vocalic suppression, Justice continues, "The words evil [ev'l] and spirit [spir't] have also been taken in English verse to have but one syllable." Vocalic suppression sometimes takes place after a silent consonant as well, as in ought to've and of'n, mentioned earlier. There is also *counterelision (hiatus)*, where "In contrast," Justice says, "fire [fi-yer] often is counted as two [syllables in length]." The same is true of other words (hire, mire, lyre); in many dialects words will be pronounced as though they had more syllables than usual, as in repair (repay-er). In Maine words like this, ending in *ar*, are pronounced, "repay-ah." Another variant is *option*: "Elision in most of these words," Justice says, "is optional; that is, the word need not be elided each time it occurs, even if it occurs twice in the same line."

Overt elision. In everyday language we often use overt elision, indicating the spot of eliding with an *apostrophe* (you've, I've, we've, they're, you're), but in certain kinds of *poetic diction* overt elision will occur where the writer will indicate with an apostrophe where he or she wishes for elision to occur, as in "e'er" for ever, "o'er" for over, or "heav'n" (shown earlier). Wordsworth's poem is practically a paradigm—that is, a model—of nineteenth-century *Romantic poetic diction* and *period style*: Note the elisions, many of them overt ("whereso'er"), *archaic usages* ("hath"), and *syntactic inversions* for the sake of rhyme ("to me did seem").

Quantity

In normative accentual-syllabic English-language prosody, syllables are not prescribed as to "length" of sound in any way except that certain vowels are considered "short," as in the short **i** sound of, for instance, "**in**," or the long **o** sound of "**o**ver." Quantity in English, then, is not conventionalized as it apparently was in classical Greek poetry, when each syllable had its own length in the same fashion that a whole note may in music equal four beats, a half-note two beats, a quarter-note one beat, an eighth note a half-beat, and so forth. Thus, in order to compose a line of verse, the Greek poet would fill it out in the same manner that a composer today fills out a bar of music, choosing those words that not only made sense, but that also had the requisite number of beats to fill out the quantitative meter with which the poet was working. Although such quantitative systems have been attempted in English, they have never adapted themselves to the language, which is at root and heart strong-stress. The closest we can come is to say that the norm of a line of English verse often establishes that the *long syllable sound* coincides with the accented syllable:

　´　　　　´　　　　´　　　´　　　´

Over and over he spoke to me of doom.

When, in context, the meter of the line of verse demands that a normally unaccented syllable take a stress, the result is *recessive stress*:

　´　　　　´　　　•　　　•　　　´

Over and over he asked of us his doom.

Chime

Lines that have like endings exhibit *tail rhyme*. *True rhyme* has to do with the identical sound, in two or more words, of an accented vowel sound (oˊ-oaˊ-owˊ) together with all sounds following that vowel (oˊne-oaˊn-owˊn), while the consonant **sounds** immediately preceding the vowel differ in each word (**b**oˊne-**l**oaˊn-**gr**owˊn).

Single rhymes are chimes of one syllable (**morn-born**); *double rhymes*, chimes of two syllables (**singing-ringing**); and *triple rhymes*, chimes of three syllables (**carrying-tarrying**).

End-rhyme chimes line-endings:

Charm for a Thorn-Prick
Happy man that Christ was born,
He was crowned with a thorn;
He was pierced through the skin,
For to let the poison in:
But his five wounds, so they say,
Closed before he passed away;
In with healing, out with thorn;
Happy man that Christ was born.
—Anonymous

Head-rhyme (*initial rhyme*) chimes the beginnings of lines. It is very rare in English, but a passage or two of Sidney Lanier's long poem titled "The Symphony" uses it (though it also uses end-rhyme):

We weave in the mills and heave in the kilns,
We sieve mine-meshes under the hills,
And thieve much gold from the Devil's bank tills,
To relieve, O God, what manner of ills?—

Sometimes "head-rhyme" is construed to be *head-alliteration*, as in this love lyric by the fourteenth-century Welsh poet Dafydd ap Gwilym. The original poem had each line beginning with the letter H; this modern English version keeps the aitches and casts the poem into the form of a variant of the bardic meter *cywydd deuair hyrion, q.v.*

Love in Exile

Her grace has charmed away my
Heart—Morfudd, godchild of May.
Hail her, give her good morrow:
Hapless I lie the night through.
Here the wild sower has sown
Her seed to break my breastbone.
Hurt will bloom and heartwail blame
Hours trystless, bleak as henbane.
Heavenly being of grace,
Haunting voice, face, enchantress—
How I plead, without avail,
Hunger inconsolable.

Haply, lore might find a way
Hope can win my fair lady;
However, into exile
Hurled, I shun her domicile.
Heaped within my breast, yearning
Hurkles and writhes the night long:
Higher than waves on the shore
Hurtles the lust I bear her.
Heart to beauty has been chained,
Haft to fettering fastened.
Hard and bright as gold is she—
Hushed love creeps slow toward me.
Hale, long life is my wandream:
How can water flow upstream?
Hearthchild of Ynr—life were
Harder than death without her!
                    —Dafydd ap Gwilym

Linked rhyme (or "*chain rhyme*") chimes the last syllable or syllables of a line with the first syllable or syllables of the following line, as in this modern version of a Medieval Irish poem:

The Charm of Eire

Charmed be this, the land of Eire,
Fair isle of the fruitful sea;
Trees be laden on the green hill,
Filled with fruit be the rainy wood;
Moody with rain be the cascade,
Made of falls be the lake of tarns,
Tarn-deep be the tor-top well.
Well-met be the moot of clans,
Plain-spoken be the chiefs of Tara.
Temair shall be a mount of folk,
Yoked among the scions of Mil,
Mil of the coracles, Mil of the barks.
Harken! Let the lofty isle
Sail the ocean; let it be
Sea-born on the dark wave's song,
Tongue of craft, charm of cunning,
Canny and wise as the wives of Bres,
Brazen as Bres, the women of Buaigne.
A woman of might be the isle of Erin;
Eremon hath enthralled her,
Ir and Eber enchanted her.
Hear my charm for Erin the charmed!
                                    —Amergin

Falling rhyme is the chiming of lines of verse that utilize falling rhythms (or "feminine" endings), such as **fall**ing/**call**ing, as in stanza two of "The Ruin." Falling rhythms are those that begin with an accented syllable and end with an unaccented syllable. Dactyls and trochees are falling meters—see the Sapphic poem given earlier.

Rising rhyme is the rhyming of lines of verse that utilize rising rhythms (or "*masculine*" *endings*), such as a**rise**, de**spise**, **prize**, as in stanza four of "The Ruin." Rising rhythms are those that end with an accented syllable. Anapests and iambs are rising meters.

Light rhyme rhymes a falling ending with a rising ending (fall-**ing**, **ring**), as in this poem, which is attributed to Taliesin, who, with Aneirin, is one of the earliest Welsh poets whose work has survived. The version here has been cast into the bardic meter cywydd deuair hyrion. The lines rhyme *aa*:

Lament for Owain ab Urien

Owain ab Urien's soul
May the Lord keep immortal.
Lordly to praise Rheged's lord,
Greatly burdened by greensward,
Laid low, this far-bruited king,
His lances wings of dawning.
To none other was he thrall,
No other was his equal,
Reaper of foes, ravener,
Son, father, and grandfather.
When Owain scythed down Fflamddwyn
It was no more than nodding.
Sleeping are the Anglemen,
Light in their sockets open,
And those who but shortly fled
Were bolder than they needed—
Owain put them to the sack:
Sheep before the wolf-pack.
Grand in colored armament,
Well he horsed the suppliant:
For his soul's sake Owain shared
The treasure that he hoarded.
Owain ab Urien's soul
May the Lord keep immortal.

—Taliesin

Internal rhyme chimes the ending of a line with a word in the center of the same line, usually with a syllable just before the caesura (the song is **sung**, and the bell is **rung**), or as in stanza ten, line one of "The Ruin" in *casbairdne*, described later. (Homes were **sealed**, the ring-tank **walled**). *Interlaced rhyme* chimes a syllable or syllables in the center of a line with a syllable or syllables also in the center of a preceding or following line (The song is **sung**, and the bell is heard / It is **flung** upon the air), or as in stanza two, lines one and two of "The Ruin" (Rime scoiled gate-keeps; the **mortar** / Shattered, slate shower-shields **moulder**). *Cross-rhyme* chimes an ending with a sound at the center of a preceding or following line (The bell is heard, and the song is **sung**; / The sound is **flung** on the morning air), or as in stanza eight, lines one and two of "The Ruin" (There once many a mood-glad **wight**, / Garnished gold-**bright**, in wine-pride) and in many other lines of the same poem.

Apocopated rhyme drops one or more syllables from the ending of one of a pair of rhyming words (The bells were ringing on the **morn**- / ing that our present king was **born**). *Enjambed rhyme* uses the first consonant of a following line to complete the sound of the rhyme (He found the stair, and **he** / **d**escended to find the **seed**).

Compound rhyme treats groups of words as though they were one-word rhymes as in "call work"—"maid-of-all-work" in this portion of a song from Gilbert and Sullivan's *The Pirates of Penzance*:

Song

A nurserymaid is not afraid of what you people call work,
So I made up my mind to go as a kind of piratical maid-of-all-
    work.
And that is how you find me now, a member of your vile lot,
Which you wouldn't have found, had he been bound apprentice
    to a pilot.

Mosaic rhyme uses one compound ending and one normal ending in a rhyme, as in "vile lot" and "pilot" in the preceding song.

Omoioteleton is the term that covers the various types of rhyme other than true rhyme. *Identical rhyme* is really a form of *repetition*. It has identity of sound in the consonants immediately preceding the accented vowel as well as in the following sounds (**cy´st**, persi´**st**, insi´**st**). *Consonance* seems to have more synonyms than any other literary term. It means "similar sounds" and is not to be confused with a wholly different word with the same pronunciation, "consonants." Consonance assumes that all vowel sounds are interchangeable, as are certain related consonant sounds, as the soft g in "gou**g**e" and "ra**g**e," the harder dg of "bri**dg**e" and "he**dg**e," and the zh sound of "rou**g**e." The verb is "to consonate"—many lines in "The Ruin" and "A Charm for Eire" shown earlier consonate rather than rhyme.

Echo

Echo is the reappearance of identical sounds in poetry, or the appearance of similar sounds. *Parimion* is the classical term for *alliteration*, which has already been discussed to some extent. We noted in the section on strong stress prosody that alliteration is the repetition of initial stressed consonant sounds. There are six ways in which the stich of Anglo-Saxon prosody may alliterate: (1) The two center-stressed syllables can alliterate, as in stich 12 of "The Morbid Man Singing," shown later, under *Cynghanedd*; (2) the first three stressed syllables can alliterate, as in stich seven; (3) the last three stressed syllables can alliterate, as in stich eight; (4) all four syllables may (but usually do not) alliterate, as in stich five; (5) sometimes the alliteration continues into the following stich, and sometimes there is cross-alliteration between stichs, as in stichs ten and eleven; and (6) on occasion, what is alliterated is the absence of consonants—that is, any vowel may "alliterate" (actually, consonate) with any other, or with itself (assonate), as in stich six (note in this last example the vowel sounds of "at" and "martyr" are not the same).

Other devices involving repeated sounds are found under "Repetitional Schemes" in the chapter "The Genres of Nonfiction" in the companion volume of this book, *The Book of Literary Terms.*

The Sensory Level

"*Figures of speech*" (*imagery*) or *tropes* are word pictures; they are to be found on the *sensory level* of poetry, and they are intended to evoke the senses of taste, touch, sight, smell, hearing, together with the inner "sense" of feelings. There are four basic kinds of tropes: *descriptions, similes, metaphors,* and *rhetorical tropes.*

Descriptions and Similes

Description utilizes *adjectives* or *adjective phrases* to modify nouns (**green** morning, tons **of love**), or *adverbs* and *adverbial phrases* to modify adjectives (**very** green morning), verbs (swim **swiftly**), or other adverbs (swim **really** swiftly). Many of those who are newly come to poetry don't understand that *figurative language* (as distinguished from *literal language*—that is, having to do with actuality) uses few *modifiers*, but many tropes. As a result, new writers tend to fill up lines with adjectives, adverbs, and other modifiers through descriptions. In the following poem the descriptions—that is, the modifiers of other words—are printed in italics or boldface:

> *Grief*
> I tell you, **hopeless** grief is **passionless**;
> That only men *incredulous* **of despair**,
> *Half-taught* **in anguish**, **through the midnight air**
> Beat **upward** *to* **God's** *throne* **in loud** *access*
> **Of shrieking and reproach**. **Full** desertness,
> **In souls** as [in] countries lieth **silent-bare**
> *Under* the **blanching**, **vertical** *eye-glare*
> *Of the* **absolute** *Heavens*. **Deep-hearted** man, express

Grief **for thy Dead** *in silence* like to death—
Most like a **monumental** statue set
In everlasting watch and [in] **moveless woe**
Till itself crumble *to the dust* **beneath**.
Touch it; the **marble** eyelids are **not wet**.
If it could weep, it could arise and go.
                                              —Elizabeth Barrett Browning

This poem operates almost entirely on the level of description.
There are few more complex tropes in it, but there are some similes: In line nine, "like to death" is a comparison with "silence";
that is, one should "express grief for [the] dead in silence" that is
like . . . death" itself. There is a second simile in the following
line, "like a monumental statue." Although similes cannot always
be identified by finding the words "as" or "like," here (as in most
cases) those words are, indeed, the tip-off.

Omiosis means examination of different things by *comparison*—
"Her smile was like the sun, / As warm as morning light upon the
rose"—and by *contrast*: "But her eyes were cold as the lumen of
the moon." *Analogy* is the means by which *simile* proceeds, com-
paring things that are not identical ("He stood as if he were an oak
/ Braced against the winter wind"). Several similes were pointed
out in Elizabeth Barrett Browning's "Grief" just given.

The first half of the first stanza of Cynddelw Brydedd Mawr's
twelfth-century Welsh lyric "To a Girl" is a description; the second half—after the colon—is a simile. The form used in this
modern version is an official bardic meter, cyhydedd hir:

To a Girl

I saw on the face
Of a haughty lass
A look with no trace
Of love—cold, still:
The cresting spume-glow
Upon the billow
Of the sea's face, flow
And ebb of chill.

She sends her respects
To me, harshly, vexed—
The candle rejects,
Cuts shadow dead,
And now I must hoard
Disgrace's great hurt—
She's trod on my heart,
Sought Greeneye's bed!
—Cynddelw Brydedd Mawr

The second stanza is a trope: an *implied* or *subdued metaphor,* the woman is a candle, the suitor is darkness, which is "cut dead" by her light. In Mawr's poem, on the symbolic level, there are all sorts of implications or overtone in the image about the candle and shadow. "Light" is never mentioned, yet it is that which the candle gives off that dispels the darkness of shadow. On the narrative level, the suitor is "cut dead"—he is no more than a shadow lying flat on the floor, and then he is not even that as he is dismissed. Mawr does no more with this image—that is, he does not extend it throughout the second stanza but goes into other images of a more mundane kind: His mistress tramples on his feelings and chooses another lover, significantly "Greeneye," another image that refers to jealousy—but it is the speaker who is jealous.

Not all similes are mere "weaker metaphors," for some similes cannot be made into metaphors without destroying the validity of the comparison. A *subdued simile* is one that looks like a metaphor because the words "like" or "as" have been left out, but they are understood to be intended, as in, "You pearl of the heavens." *Subdued similes* are analogies rather than equations (see *metaphor*).

An *epic simile* or *extended simile* compares a complex action or series of things with an equally complex action or series. A greatly extended simile may become *formulated allegory,* which is *metaphysical* in structure (see *conceit*), as in "The Ecstasy" by John Donne, which begins:

The Ecstasy
Where, like a pillow on a bed,
A pregnant bank swelled up, to rest

The violet's reclining head,
Sat we two, one another's best.

Donne's analogy is between a "bank" of earth, the *text* of his
simile, and "a pillow on a bed," his *analogue*. He intends the *context*
of this simile to allow the *overtone* of sexuality, which is proved by
his *description* of the bank as a "pregnant bank." Would it be going
too far to note that the poet's choice of *b* rhymes, "rest" and
"best," suggests the *subliminal rhyme*, "breast"? There is another
simile in the next four lines, though it is not tipped-off by the
words "like" or "as":

Our hands were firmly cemented
By a fast balm which thence did spring;
Our eye-beams twisted, and did thread
Our eyes upon one double string.

The *epithetic compound* "eye-beams" is a reference to the presci-
entific notion that people see by means of invisible beams that are
projected by the eyes upon the object that is being perceived (exactly the opposite of what actually happens, for light reflected
from the perceived object is sensed by the organ of sight, the eye).
So when the lovers' "eye-beams" encounter one another, they
become intertwined in one filament which "did thread / Our
eyes upon one double string." The simile is this: that eyes are like
beads strung upon the "double string" of the lovers' tangled "eye-
beams."

So to engraft our hands, as yet
Was all the means to make us one;
And pictures in our eyes to get
Was all our propagation.

The first two lines here hark back to the lovers' hands, which
"were firmly cemented / by a fast balm," a kind of glue of the
heart, perhaps; that is to say, all they have done so far is to hold

hands: "So to engraft our hands, as yet / Was all the means to make us one;" the only "propagation," that is, reproduction, that has taken place so far is rather innocent: each lover's image is re- produced in the other's eyes. Then there is another simile:

> As 'twixt two equal armies Fate
> Suspends uncertain victory,
> Our souls—which to advance their state
> Were gone out—hung 'twixt her and me.

What we have here is a stalemate, "As [between] two equal ar- mies." The analogy now is with a contest, and the context allows the implication that the contest is aggressive, but the war of the sexes has been suspended for the nonce while the opposing sides silently negotiate and Fate holds the outcome of the battle of wills in suspense:

> And whilst our souls negotiate there,
> We like sepulchral statues lay;
> All day the same our postures were,
> And we did nothing, all the day.

Here is a fourth simile: the lovers "lay / all day" "like sepulchral statues," that is, like the sculptures on a tomb.

> If any, so by love refined,
> That he soul's language understood,
> And by good love were grown all mind
> Within convenient distance stood,
> He (though he knew not which soul spake,
> Because both meant, both spake the same)
> Might thence a new concoction take,
> And part far purer than he came.

That is to say, if a sensitive and invisible bystander could have seen and sensed what was going on, he would have realized that these

two lovers were soul mates, not sex partners, and he or she would
have left a better person for having observed the tryst.

> This Ecstasy doth unperplex
> (We said) and tell us what we love,
> We see by this, it was not sex,
> We see, we saw not what did move:
> But as all several souls contain
> Mixture of things, they know not what,
> Love, these mixed souls doth mix again,
> And makes both one, each this and that.

The stalemate is about to be broken, because each soul ("all several souls" is an old-fashioned way of saying "every single soul") is
a combination of elements, and the lovers' mingled souls, making
one "super-soul," so to speak, after a while must separate into its
elements, and some of those elements are our corporeal bodies.
Later in the poem, after a good deal of metaphysics, Donne wrote,

> As our blood labours to beget
> Spirits, as like souls as it can,
> Because such fingers need to knit
> That subtle knot, which makes us man:
> So must pure lovers' souls descend
> To affections, and to faculties,
> Which sense may reach and apprehend,
> Else a great Prince in prison lies.

Like it or not, we are but human, flesh and bone and blood, and
we must come down from the ethereal realms of love to simple af-
fections and senses ("faculties"), or "a great Prince in prison lies,"
no doubt the ruler of these senses and faculties, the person himself.

> To our bodies turn we then, that so
> Weak men on love revealed may look;
> Love's mysteries in souls do grow,
> But yet the body is his book.

And if some lover, such as we,
Have heard this dialogue of one,
Let him still mark us [that is, take note of the lovers, for] he shall
    see
Small change, when we are to bodies gone.

Metaphors

The difference between simile and metaphor is the difference between analogy and *allegory*. Similes show the likenesses between things, but no matter how much one modifies a *substantive* or *verb*, it will remain essentially unchanged. How does one change a word essentially? The answer is, the poet makes it equivalent, equal to, something else, as Mawr did in the second stanza of his poem cited earlier: "The candle" = the woman; "shadow" = the suitor. The nature of allegory is to speak about one *subject* in terms of another, allowing the subject to become new again, making it clearer and sharper. The heart of allegory is metaphor. Metaphors go one step further and equate two dissimilar things: $A = B$. There is no hedging: "The sun is a coin"—the sun is the *tenor* or subject of the metaphor, and the coin is the *vehicle* of the metaphor, the *predicate nominative* that bears the weight of the *language equation*. Here, the obvious point of *similarity* is the roundness of both coin and sun. *Ambiguity* is the allowance of *overtone* and *connotation* by *context*. Some tropes are inherently *inclusive*, as for instance *synesthesia*, which means talking about one of the senses in terms of another—"Monday morning smells blue" (scent-sight), "I could taste her sweet whispers" (taste-hearing), "He touched me with his mind" (thought-touch).

An *allegory* is a story told on two levels simultaneously, the *narrative level* and the *symbolic level*. At each point in the story on the narrative level, there must be a corresponding point on the symbolic level. For instance, if one were to employ a *conceit*—an *extended metaphor*—one might begin with a metaphor by saying that "The old professor is a sphinx," as in this poem.

The Old Professor and the Sphinx

It is a dry word in a dry book
drying out my ear. I squat and swallow
my tongue here in this chair,
the desert of my desk, summer bare, spreading
like a brown horizon into regions grown arid
with erudition. A caravan of books treks

stolidly across my eyes while I,
the Sphinx, a phoenix nesting in my skull,
pry into inkwells and
gluepots seeking the universal solvent.
There is none. The pages as I turn them sound like sand
rattling in the sec temples of a beast gone to

earth with the sun. I lie caught in my
creaking dune, shifting with the wind of the
pharaohs, wondering if,
somewhere, I have not missed my valley. Upon
the walls of my office there are Oriental prints
hanging stiff as papyrus, whispering their brown

images into the silent air.
I know the poems on my shelves speak with
one another in an
ancient language I have somehow forgotten.
If there is rainfall, I recall, the desert blossoms—
but I have somewhere lost the natural prayer

and instinctual rites of the blood
which can conjure clouds in seasons of drought.
There is but ritual
remaining; no honey is in the lion's
hide; my temples have mumbled to ruin: they endure
disuse and despair. An archaeologist of

cabinets and drawers, I exhume
paperclip skeletons, the artifacts

of millennia: red
ball-point pens with nothing in their veins, pencils
like broken lances, and notebook citadels empty
of citizens—the crusader has squandered his

talents on bawds, grown hoary in their
service. The town is sacked: the bawds are gone
to tame younger legions.
Look into my sarcophagus: the tapes are
sunken over my hollow sockets. Slowly the waste
swallows my oasis like a froth of spittle.

In this poem the *implied metaphor*—that "academe is a desert,"
which is its *motif*—is developed and expanded from the first line to
the last. There are many images of various kinds: *simile* ("the desert
of my desk . . . spreading **like** a . . . horizon"); *subdued metaphor*
("A caravan of books"); *allusion* ("Sphinx," "phoenix"); *description*
("brown horizon," "caravan of books"); *synesthesia* ("whispering
their brown images"); *puns* (my **temples** have mumbled to ruin,"
"squandered his talents on bawds, grown **hoary**"—here, **talents** is
simultaneously a pun and an allusion to an old Palestinian mone-
tary unit called a "talent"); *oxymoron* ("instinctual rites"); *denotation*
and *connotation* ("temples" = parts of the head denotatively; con-
notatively the word means places of ritual and prayer; the *implicit
statement* in this poem's *context* is that the mind should be a place
for instinctual ritual and prayer); *symbol* (a **beast** gone to earth
with the sun," "crusader"); *personification* ("paperclip skeletons");
onomatopoeia ("A caravan of books treks stolidly"); *abstraction* ("mil-
lenia"); *hyperbole, parallelism,* and *repetition* ("It is a dry word in a
dry book drying out my ear"); *ambiguity* of various kinds, like the
"temples" passage cited; and *concretions* throughout the poem in all
of the tropes. The entire poem is an *allegory* in which a teacher is a
crusader, perhaps a Knight Templar, whose crusade has worn him
out and seen him grow old and cynical.

An *abstract noun* is one that is open to broad and various *definition*, such as "soul," "truth," "love," "beauty," "justice," and "God";

a *concrete noun* is any term that may be conventionally defined (that is, individuals will agree with the definition): "table," "brick," "rug," "tree," "elephant," "house." One may make an *anchored abstraction* by equating an abstraction with a concretion: "Her soul is a brick," "Love is a fuzzy puppy," or "God is an elephant."

An *unanchored abstraction* is an abstract noun that is equated with another abstract noun, as in the "Ode on a Grecian Urn" by John Keats: "'Beauty is truth, truth beauty,—that is all / Ye know on earth, and all ye need to know.'" But in fact one doesn't "know" anything at all about what Keats has said, for he has not defined what it is he is talking about, although the context of the rest of the poem may give the clue. Many abstract nouns are *cues*, meant to elicit automatic *stock responses* in the reader or the listener. Society has conditioned its members to respond in knee-jerk fashion to certain words, much as the Russian scientist Pavlov conditioned his dogs to salivate at the sound of a bell by ringing one every time he fed them. After a while, he did not need to feed them at all to make them drool, simply ring the bell. Just so, we are meant to respond without thinking to terms such as "motherhood," "Old Glory," "evil," "love," "soul," "God," and so forth.

Likewise, writers often have stock responses to certain terms, as for instance the term "sonnet." "The sonnet is dead" is a frequent claim, but it cannot die, for it is merely an abstract pattern and was never alive. What one usually means when one makes such a claim is that nobody can write a sonnet anymore because the *form* has been done to death. It is not the form that is dead, however; it is the *burden of tradition* that lies upon the sonnet that stifles the would-be sonneteer. When one thinks "sonnet" one doesn't think merely of the form, one thinks of all the sonnets one has read, and when one goes to write, one **still** thinks of all those sonnets. As a result, one often winds up writing a sonnet like Shakespeare, or John Milton, Elizabeth Barrett Browning, or Edna St. Vincent Millay (1892–1950), and thinking, "I want to write like **me**, not like somebody else," and one grunts in disgust, crumples the paper, and tosses it into a wastebasket. But if one can unburden oneself of the weight of tradition, the form remains to be used in a new way, for it is neutral and merely waits for a poet to breathe new life into it.

On the other hand, it is quite possible to use a metaphor that has been so often used before that it is trite, a *dead metaphor* or *dead simile*: "Her eyes were as big as saucers." "I'm so hungry I could eat a horse." "He was as big as a house."

A *denotation* is the primary meaning or dictionary definition of a word; a *connotation* is an ancillary or secondary meaning of a word. Connotations of "heart" are "courage," as in "He has great heart"; "love," as in "An affair of the heart"; and "essence," as in "He is pure of heart." *Context* is the *environment* surrounding a word situated in a phrase, clause, or larger grammatic unit. This environment limits the denotations and connotations of the word. In "His heart beat strongly in battle," the context of the word "heart" allows the denotation "a bodily organ that circulates the blood" and the connotation "courage," while it eliminates the other connotations of love or essence.

Overtone. The allowance of connotations by context is called overtone. William Carlos Williams enunciated the *doctrine* that there ought to be "No ideas but in things," which means that, if one can choose the appropriate object, one need not even mention the actual subject one is writing on, for the subject will be contained in the object. Ezra Pound's "In a Station of the Metro" is an imagist poem; it is printed here as it originally appeared in 1913 in *Poetry*, complete with examples of *sight pause* or *eye-pause*;—that is, *spatial caesuras*:

> In a Station of the Metro
>
> The apparition   of these faces   in the crowd;
> Petals   on a wet, black   bough.
>
> —Ezra Pound

This is a *mote* (*motto, device, posie*): a one-sentence poem written in two lines. The *subject* of the sentence is "apparition," and the verb "is" is understood at the point of the semicolon or, if one wishes, one can imagine an equals sign at that point:

The apparition of these faces in the crowd = petals on a wet, black bough.

The first line consists of the subject and two *descriptions* in the form of *prepositional phrases*, the first acting as an *adjective* modifying the subject, and the second as an *adverbial phrase* modifying the adjective. The reader is told in what the apparition consists ("of these faces") and where they are to be seen ("in the crowd"), but one does not wish to forget the title, which is actually a third line and another prepositional phrase, which tells us that "the crowd" is in the Paris subway, for the French call their subway system the Metro.

The denotation of "apparition" is *appearance*, which is a *synonym* for apparition, but Pound chose not to use the former because he wanted the overtones, the connotation of "apparition," which is "ghost" or "phantom." Thus, the faces of the people standing in the underground station are wraithlike, evanescent.

The second half of the sentence consists of a *predicate nominative*, "petals," and another prepositional phrase acting as a modifier; the phrase contains two adjectives, "wet" and "black" modifying "bough," so the whole *predicate* is merely a *compound description*. But these simple tropes give the reader a wealth of information. First, there is a *seasonal element* (as in the *haiku*), for petals are seen on trees only in the spring. The tree is very likely a fruit tree (perhaps cherry or plum, traditional in Japanese haiku poetry), and the bough is black probably because it is wet—it has been raining. Finally, one must consider how long petals last—they are short-lived, and soon give way to developing fruit, so they are as delicate and evanescent as the faces in the crowd. The whole poem appears to be a metaphor that says, "People are as transitory as fruit petals in the spring," but the theme is *implicit*, for nowhere has Pound mentioned an explicit theme. It has arisen out of the image.

The *pathetic fallacy* is absurd or overstated *personification* (*prosopopœia*)—that is, the endowment of objects or animals with human qualities (*anthropomorphism*), often through *cues* ("motherhood," "Old Glory," "apple pie") that are meant to induce automatic sentimental responses in the reader. A distinction is to be made between the terms *sentiment* and *sentimentality*. The former is a feeling of tenderness, whereas sentimentality is an excess of sentiment, overstated *sympathy*. For instance, in the phrase, "The little white cloud that cried," **little**, **cloud**, and **cried** are cues.

Similarly, in Joyce Kilmer's "Trees," which is a series of rhymed *aphorisms* rather than a poem, the uncritical reader will see the tree as, simultaneously, a mother-figure ("A nest of robins in her hair"), an infant-figure ("whose mouth is pressed / Against the earth's sweet-flowing breast"), and an orant—that is, a praying figure ("that looks at God all day"). A bit of thought, however, will combine the images and piece together a monster that has hair for leaves, eyes tangled in the hair, its mouth at the bottom of an elongated head whose mouth is buried in the earth, and so forth.

If Western poets try to become one with the object of their perception, as Asian Zen poets do, their work is likely to appear to be self-indulgent and egocentric unless they apply T. S. Eliot's theory of the *objective correlative*: The poet must choose that object that will be the idea, not merely the symbol of the idea. The objective correlative is nothing more than the *vehicle of the metaphor* of the poem, the figure of speech that carries the weight of the identification of one object with another, dissimilar, object.

Rhetorical Tropes

Rhetoric is the art of effective speaking and writing; it creates an effect in the listener and affects him or her as well. Some tropes are called *rhetorical tropes* because they create their effects through nonmetaphorical figures of speech. A complete disquisition on the subject of rhetoric and rhetorical tropes is to be found in the companion volume to this text, *The Book of Literary Terms*.

The Ideational Level

A poem is an artifice of thought as well as of typography, sonics, and tropes, and there is no thought except in symbols, in forms. Every element of language is a form of some kind. The letters of the alphabet are forms—*conventions*, the meanings of which we have agreed upon in order to communicate. Syllables are forms, as are words, phrases, and sentences. The poet is interested in all of these forms, since his or her medium is language. On the ideational level a writer deals with the subject of words, specifically in their grammatic and syntactic forms, which are called *schemes* or *schemas*. There are *orthographical schemes, constructional schemes* (which have much to do with *syntax* or word order in a sentence), *exclusive, inclusive, substitutive*, and *repetitive schemes, diction*, and *voice*. All of these subjects are covered at length in the companion volume to this text, *The Book of Literary Terms*, but many applicable terms are explained in the glossary.

Chapter Glossary

Italicized terms are defined elsewhere within this glossary. Terms discussed in the text but not glossed here (and therefore not italicized) may be found in the index. For fuller definition of many of these terms, see *The Book of Literary Terms*.

ABSTRACT POETRY. See *abstract syntax*.

ABSTRACT SYNTAX. "[S]yntax is [*abstract*] or *musical* when its function is to please us by the fidelity with which it follows a 'form of thought' through the [writer's] mind but without defining that thought" (Donald Davie). The idea behind what is here called "abstract syntax," what Edith Sitwell called *abstract poetry*, and what Donald Davie calls "*musical syntax*" is the same idea as that which is behind "abstract art," which is to approach the condition of music in language or in painting. Music is the most abstract of the arts in that there are no "meanings" attached to notes or musical phrases. There may be a kind of general feeling attached to some aspects of music; for instance, minor keys "feel" sad whereas major keys don't; fast music feels happy, but slow music feels moody. Aside from that sort of thing, no meanings inhere in music, yet we enjoy it because we can perceive musical structures and progressions, harmonies, dissonances, counterpoint, and so forth. If painting, let's say, wants to approach the abstract condition of music, one must get rid of identifiable representations, of figures, in one's work. The same thing must be done in language, as well, if one is going to write using abstract syntax:

The Harper of Stillness
   The lawn is full of south
   and the odours tangle,

and I hear today for the first
   the river in the tree.

The cricket in the root
has found a note to cast
upon the pool of eventide,
   of shadow welling from

a coast of pines. Swiftly
now he comes, the harper
of stillness, lifting up his strings
   to net the western fire

shoaling the upper limbs,
the rooves of our houses
swept by a wave of daylight lost
   in the depths of summer.
            —Emily Dickinson/
               Lewis Turco

ALLUSION. A reference to something outside the text, as when Tennyson says in his poem "Summer Night," "Now lies the Earth all Danae to the stars, / And all thy heart lies open unto me." Unless one knows the allusion, the analogy will be obscure: In Greek mythology Danae was a maiden who became pregnant with a son, Perseus, after Zeus, in the guise of a golden shower, came down to her. An *echo allusion* is a reference to something in a changed way: "Tibia, or not tibia. That is the bone," rather than "To be, or not to be, that is the question."

AMBIGUITY. The allowance of extra (connotative) meanings to a word in the context of a sentence or larger literary construct. William Empson (see Bibliography) listed ambiguities that can add to the inclusive quality of a poem:

First type ambiguities arise when a detail is effective in several ways at once, e.g., by comparisons with several points of likeness, antitheses with several points of difference, "comparative" adjectives, subdued metaphors, and extra meanings suggested by rhythm.

Second type ambiguities arise when two or more alternative meanings are fully resolved into one.

Third type ambiguities arise when two apparently unconnected meanings are given simultaneously.

Fourth type ambiguities arise when the alternative meanings combine to make clear a complicated state of mind in the author.

Fifth type ambiguities arise when [there is] a fortunate confusion, as when the author is discovering his idea in the act of writing . . . or not holding it all at once.

Sixth type ambiguities arise when what is said is contradictory or irrelevant and the reader is forced to invent interpretations [This, in fact, is *obscurity*, not ambiguity. Meanings are blocked, not amplified.]

Seventh type ambiguities [occur when there is] full contradiction, marking a division in the author's mind.

AMPHISBAENIA, AMPHISBAENIC RHYME. "Backward" rhyme (later-retail; stop-pots; pets-instep).

ANACHRONISM. Placing something historically out of its time, as in Mark Twain's novel *A Connecticut Yankee in King Arthur's Court.*

ANALYZED RHYME. A system that Edward Davison described (see Bibliography). He said that one

takes two such words as *soon* and *hide* but separates the vowel from the consonantal sounds before looking for his rhymes. The **oo** of *soon* is united with the **d** of *hide*; and the **i** of *hide* with the **n** of *soon*. This simple analysis produces the [four] rhyming sounds

oon	**ine**
ide	**ood**

as a basis for new sets of words. Thus, by means of analyzed rhyme, an absolute sound relationship can be established among words that have hitherto seemed alien to each other.

This lyric is a *free meter*, an approximation of Welsh prosody: heptasyllabic lines and analyzed rhyme:

Winter

The wind keens on the bare hill;
The ford is froar, and the lake

Is hoar-crusted. A man's ilk
Might stand on a single stalk.

Comber after comber comes
To cover the shore. The gale
Hovers over the hill: owls
Crying. One cannot stand tall.

The bed of the fish is cold
In the ice where they shelter.
Reeds are bearded; the stag, starved.
Trees bow in the early dusk.

Snow falls, and the earth is pale.
Warriors sit near their fires.
The lake is a dim defile:
No warmth is in its color.

Snow falls; the hoarfrost is white;
The shield is idle upon
The old man's shoulder. The wind
Freezes the grass with its whine.

Snow falls on top of the ice.
Wind sweeps the crest of the trees
Standing close. On his shoulder
The brave fighter's fine shield shines.
                    —Anonymous Welsh

ANATHEMA. Invective.

ANTEPENULTIMATE SYLLABLE. See *ultimate syllable.*

ANTHOLOGY. A collection of literary pieces by various authors. See *epos.*

APHORISM. Sententia. See *pompous language.*

APPROXIMATE RHYME. See *consonance.*

AUREATE. Describes language that is highly ornamented.

BABBLE, BABEL. In "the tower of Babel" of the Bible, there were speakers of many tongues; written with a small initial letter, babel means a chaos of voices.

BACKBITER. See *calumny*.

BANTER. See *persiflage*.

BARD, BARDD TEULU. See *license*.

BILLINGSGATE. See *cacemphaton*.

BRAGGADOCIO. See *rant*.

BROKEN RHYME. See *apocopated rhyme* (in text).

CACEMPHATON. The use of foul speech or vulgarities, also termed "Billingsgate," after the sort of abuse to be heard in London in the old fishmarket of the same name.

CACOPHONY. An unpleasant mixture of sounds, both the euphonious and dissonant.

CALUMNY. Slander or disparagement (diminutio), defamation of one's character by an opponent or backbiter. If it is written down or printed and disseminated, it is libel and may be actionable in a court of law.

CANT. Like claptrap, cant is trite, excessively platitudinous, and often hypocritical speech, as for instance "the cant of politicians."

CATCH-WORD, CATCH-PHRASE. See *slogan*.

CHRONOGRAPHIA. The description of time, including such things as the times of day, day of the week, of the month, of the seasons, and so forth.

CLICHÉ. An overused expression.

CONFESSIONAL POETRY. Contemporary egopoetry, generally written in the mode of phrased prose, in which the poet speaks about very personal subjects.

CONSONANCE. Treated in the section on Chime in the text. Consonance has also been called diphthong rhyme, embryonic rhyme, imperfect rhyme, slant rhyme, off-rhyme, approximate rhyme, oblique rhyme, near-rhyme, paraphone, and pararhyme, and it substitutes similar sounds for identical sounds, as in the consonants and vowels of **brídge, hédge, goúge, roúge**.

CONSONANTAL ECHO. Repetition of consonant sounds, whether stressed or unstressed, anywhere among the words of poems.

CONTRARIUM. See *contrast*.

CONTRAST. Examines dissimilar things, pointing out their differences rather than their likenesses.

COWBOY POETRY. Contemporary rhymed, generally narrative verse in the tradition of country music and the western ballad.

CYNGHANEDD. Described by H. Idris Bell and David Bell, in their translation of the poet Dafydd ap Gwilym (see Bibliography), as the group of Medieval bardic sonic devices associated with Medieval Welsh syllabic verse but whose effects are similar to those found in association with Anglo-Saxon strong-stress prosody, as in "The Morbid Man Singing." There are four main types of cynghanedd: (1) "In *Cynghanedd Groes* there is an exact correspondence between the consonants in the first half of the line and those in the second, so that every consonant in the first finds its [consonantal echo] in the second, and there is no consonant unaccounted for in the scheme, with the exception of the final syllable in each half" as in stich one of "The Morbid Man Singing," which follows; (2) "In *Cynghanedd Draws* the same system is apparent, except that there is, as it were, an island in the centre of the line in which the consonants are in isolation and are not echoed elsewhere," as in stich four; (3) "In *Cynghanedd Lusg* the penultimate [next-to-last] stressed syllable is rhymed with a syllable in the first part of the line," as in stich ten; (4) and "*Cynghanedd Sain* has an internal rhyme together with [consonantal echo] between the second rhyming word and the last word in the line," as in stich two:

The Morbid Man Singing

1 23´4 5 ´   1 23´4 5 ´
This tone is his, the stone's song
´ ´   12´   12´
no other than brother of his breath,
´   ´˘   ´   ´
fang of water, tongue of the air.

1   2 3ʹ4 5 6ʹ7   1 2 3ʹ45 6ʹ7
He is life's fool, and his leaf's fall
   ʹ   ʹ   ʹ   ʹ

looms as the last laugh at last   5
 ʹ   ʹ   ʹ   ʹ

at this martyr and at his art.
     ʹ   ʹ   ʹ

But the leaf shall lie lightly upon him,
    ʹ   ʹ   ʹ   ʹ

its unique symmetry the summit of song
     ʹ   ʹ ˘   ʹ   .   ʹ ˘

which he will enter leaf-fall and winter—
    ʹ   ʹ   ʹ   ʹ

his blood sprung from rung rock   10
   ʹ   ʹ   ʹ   ʹ

till the long rain of time shall spill
ʹ   ʹ   ʹ   ʹ

over the stars, stunning their fires.   12

In this example also note the use of internal falling consonance in stich nine (**ent̲e̲r̲-win̲t̲e̲r̲**); of internal light consonance in stich three (**wat̲e̲r̲-air**); *vocalic echo*, and *consonantal echo*.

DEFAMATION. See *calumny*.

DESECRATION. Invective.

DIALECT RHYME. Often difficult to distinguish from sight rhyme. People from different places or from different eras (in this case it may be called historical rhyme) might pronounce the same word differently; for instance, one person might pronounce "again" so that it rhymes with **pain**, but someone else might rhyme it with **pen**.

DIMINUTIO. See *calumny*.

DIPHTHONG RHYME. See *consonance*.

DISPARAGEMENT. See *calumny*.

DISSONANCE. A mingling of unpleasant sounds, usually hard consonants.

DISTANCE. See *proportion by situation of rhyme*.

DOUBLETALK. Deliberately nonsensical language that is meant to fool the listener into believing that something is actually being said that makes sense.

DRAMATIC SYNTAX. "[S]yntax is dramatic," Donald Davie wrote (see Bibliography), "when its function is to please us by the fidelity with which it follows the 'form of thought' in some mind other than the [writer's], which the [writer] imagines." This word order is the same as in subjective syntax, in effect, except that it tells the reader not what is in the mind of the writer, but what is in the mind of an imaginary character—the thoughts of a persona or, sometimes, personae (see discussion of dramatis personae in the chapter on The Genres of Drama in *The Book of Literary Terms*)—more than one persona. The persona speaking in the following poem is a character named Pocoangelini; he is having a conversation with Mr. Earth, who has nothing to say:

Pocoangelini 7
POCOANGELINI: Sir. Your head. It is stuck into the sand.

MR. EARTH:

POCOANGELINI: I'm not sure I understand. You hear me,
don't you, even with both your earholes squat
up against those furrows? I say, YOUR HEAD
IS STUCK IN A BRAIN'S HARROWING. There's dirt
up your nose and ants are crawling about
your neck. YOUR HEAD'S STUCK IN THE FILTHY SAND!

MR. EARTH:

POCOANGELINI: The moon is out. It's playing with your spine.
The shafts of starfire are sticking in your

shoulderblades, making you appear to be
a sort of celestial porcupine. What
are you looking for? What color is the
inside? Have you found whether stones push each
other when they are together alone?

MR. EARTH:

POCOANGELINI: Look, I'll scoop you out so we can talk like
human beings. It's a cold night. Your thoughts
must be chilly. This is no hour for such
silver. I'll dig. Now pull, and tell me. . . .

MR. EARTH:

POCOANGELINI: Oh!

ECHO ALLUSION. See *allusion*.

EFFICTIO. See *icon*.

EGOPOETIC SYNTAX. See *subjective syntax*.

EGOPOETRY. See *confessional poetry*.

ELEVATED LANGUAGE. At least language that has been heightened
through enargia, the language music of poems, or through the
use of phanopoiea, that is, imagery, such as metaphor and symbol; at most, elevated language is a poetic diction.

EMBRYONIC RHYME. See *consonance*.

ENARGIA. See *elevated language*.

ENCOMIUM. See *epideictic*.

ENIGMA. A deliberately obscure description, as in a riddle—see "A
Riddle" (under "riddle" in Part III).

EPIDEICTIC. Laudatory language as in the encomium, a formal expression of approval; the paean, a joyous song of praise; the eulogy, high praise, especially at a funeral: or a panegyric (see under "occasional poetry" in Part III).

EPOS. A gathering or *anthology* of poems, not united in a formal manner, that treat of a heroic theme, as the Norse verse and prose eddas.

EQUIVOCATION. Language that is deliberately misleading and ambivalent; the equivoque is a pun that is meant to deceive.

EQUIVOQUE. See *equivocation*.

ETHOPOEIA. The portrayal of ethical character, of a person's moral nature.

EULOGY. Praise for a dead person; similar to the elegy. See *epideictic*. See also under "occasional poetry" in Part III.

EUPHONY. A mingling of pleasant sounds, usually including all vowels and certain consonants: soft **cee**, **eff**, soft **gee**, **aitch**, **jay**, **el**, **em**, **en**, **ar**, **ess**, **vee**, **double-yoo**, **wye**, and **zee** (**zed**).

EXECRATION. Invective.

EXHORTATION. Language that calls to action, political rhetoric.

FALSE RHYME. Omoioteleton; rime riche or rich rhyme; identical rhyme. For example, "sport," "disport," "transport" all have "port" in them, a false rhyme; whereas true rhyme would be "sport" and "court," where the consonant preceding the accented vowel is different but all succeeding sounds are the same. False rhyme does not include any other sort of rhyming effect such as *consonance* or slant rhyme. See also *homographic rhyme; homonymic rhyme; homophonic rhyme*.

FEMININE RHYME. Falling rhyme.

FIRST DISTANCE. Couplet rhyme. See *proportion by situation of rhyme*.

FOURTH DISTANCE. See *proportion by situation of rhyme*; *quintet envelope*.

FUSTIAN. Ordinary or trite content delivered in an overblown style.

GASCONADE. See *rant*.

GLOSSOLALIA. "Speaking in tongues," ununderstandable language, nonsense; or babble.

GRAND MANNER. See *pompous language.*

HISTORICAL RHYME. See *dialect rhyme.*

HOMOEOTELUTON. See *tail rhyme.*

HOMOGRAPHIC RHYME, HOMOMORPHIC RHYME. A form of rich rhyme, that is, repetition. See *false rhyme.*

HOMONYM. Homonyms are words that sound alike, but that are spelled differently and have different meanings: **bear–bare, time–thyme.**

HOMONYMIC RHYME. A form of repetition or rich rhyme. See also false rhyme.

HOMOPHONIC RHYME. Words that are pronounced alike but that have different spellings and meanings: **I, eye, aye**. It is a form of rich rhyme. See also *false rhyme.*

HYPOTIPOSIS. The *description* of reality, of actual objects.

ICON. The description of real people (as distinguished from invented characters).

IDENTICAL RHYME. See *false rhyme; homophonic rhyme.*

IMAGO. Comparison.

IMPERFECT RHYME. See *consonance.*

INTERNAL FALLING CONSONANCE. See *Cynghanedd.*

INTERNAL LIGHT CONSONANCE. See *Cynghanedd.*

KEENING. Mournful wailing. Both aureate language and a paean are in Swinburne's translation of lines from Aristophanes' "The Grand Chorus of Birds," to be found under "paean," in Part III.

LEONINE RHYME. Internal rhyme.

LETTRISME. Attempts have indeed been made to get rid of theme as well as the other elements of fiction and drama, even of poetry, as in the system called *Lettrisme*, a French movement of the 1940s based on the thesis that poems may be written with meaningless letters only, making with those letters words without sense—nonsense. The only rule, apparently, was that no agglomeration of letters might look like a word in any known language on earth. One might write very formally—sonnets and villanelles, perhaps, which might rhyme and meter, but the "poem" must not make *sense*, and if it made no sense at all, of course, it was themeless. Lettrisme disappeared completely, unlike the similar, earlier French movement called Dadaism, because the latter had as its point the satire of contemporary traditional art, morals, and religion; the former bore no significance to anyone. It amounted to nothing more than a trick or a game, and a trick is finally boring once one has seen it a certain number of times. Mankind insists upon entertainment at the very least, if not meaning, and Lettrisme was entertaining only to the composer of the "poem," but to no one else. Dadaism was at least able to shock the sensibilities of the middle classes.

LIBEL. See *calumny*.

LICENSE, LICENTIO. Bold speech. Poetic license is taking liberties with the language; however, it may also mean an actual license to practice, as among the medieval Welsh bardic orders. H. Idris Bell and David Bell point out in the introduction to their book *Dafydd ap Gwilym: Fifty Poems* (see Bibliography):

> The two higher classes into which the bards were divided, known respectively as *pencerdd* and *bardd teulu*, were, under the native princes, public officials and subject to strict regulation, both by the Welsh laws and by the rules of the bardic order itself. The *penceirddiaid*, whose work alone would seem to have been preserved, were limited to a very narrow range of themes, chiefly elegies and eulogies on the members of the princely houses and religious poems, and even their treatment of these was regulated by minute prescriptions.

This would seem to be a prison, but the Bells also point out, "It is . . . a curious paradox in literature, that often the most binding tradition and form are an incentive to spontaneity of expression rather than a hindrance." Many of the poems of the Welsh bards are included in this volume in modern versions. For many years poetic licenses were issued as documents by the

Ancient Order of Bards in America through its outlet in the Program in Writing Arts at the State University of New York at Oswego.

LOGORRHEA. The use of too many words; overwriting.

LYON RHYME. This isn't really rhyme at all, though it is a form of repetition. It is a grammatic trick, so it should more properly be considered a constructional scheme. One writes some verses that, when read backward—word for word, beginning with the last word—say exactly the opposite of what the verses originally said:

One in heat can love cool.
Believe, and remain her fool.

Fool her. Remain, and believe
Cool love can heat in one.

MAGNUM OPUS. A masterpiece or "great work."

MASCULINE RHYME. Rising rhyme.

MASTERPIECE. See *magnum opus*.

MELOPOEIA. Synonym for lyrics; lyrical poetry.

MINOR SUBGENRES. The minor subgenres of poetry include bucolics, didactics, forensics, liturgics, occasionals, and satirics. Current popular subgenres are *confessional poetry*, *rap poetry*, *cowboy poetry*, and *performance poetry*.

MIXED METAPHOR. The use of words inappropriate to the thing being described, as in "The sun and moon are baby buggies," where the vehicle is inappropriate to the tenor, or as in "Keep your nose to the grindstone, your shoulder to the wheel, and an eye peeled for trouble," where the vehicle itself is made up of inappropriate elements.

MONORHYME. The use of one rhyme sound through a whole stanza or poem. See qasida (in text).

MUSICAL SYNTAX. See *abstract syntax*.

NARRATIVE SYNTAX. See objective syntax.

NEAR-RHYME. See *consonance*.

NOMINATIO. Synonym for *onomatopoeia*.

NOTATIO. Synonym for *ethopoeia*.

OBJECTIVE SYNTAX. Donald Davie (see Bibliography) wrote that "syntax is objective [or narrative] when the function is to please us by the fidelity with which [word order] follows a 'form of action,' a movement not through any mind, but in the world at large." Objective syntax is narration. This following anonymous plaint (complaint) is from the Middle English. The original form has been adhered to. It is a variant of *short particular measure* in that each line is one foot shorter, but the rhyme scheme is the same.

The Maid's Complaint

The other day
I heard a fey
Maid piteously complain.
She said for aye,
Without allay,
Her heart was full of pain.

She said, alas!
It came to pass
Her dear heart was untrue.
"In every place
I know he has
Forsaken me for a new.

"Since he, untrue,
Hath chosen anew,
And thinks with her to rest,
And will not rue,
And I so true,
Therefore my heart will burst.

"Now that I may
In no manner or way
Obtain that which I sue,

So ever and aye,
Without deny,
Mine own sweetheart, adieu!

"Adieu, darling,
Adieu, sweeting,
Adieu, all my welfare!
Adieu each thing
To God pertaining!
Christ keep you for my care!

"Adieu, full sweet,
Adieu, right meet
To be a lady's heir!"
Her eyes replete
With salt tears wet,
She said, "Adieu, my dear!

"Adieu, farewell,
Adieu, *le bel*,
Adieu, thou friend and foe!
I cannot tell
Where I shall dwell,
My heart doth grieve me so."

And as she spoke,
At but a stroke
Her dear heart came a-near;
He said, "Good maid,
Be not dismayed,
My love, my darling dear!"

His arms he lent,
To him she went.
In voiding care and moan,
That day they spent
To their content
In the wilderness, alone.
                    —Anonymous

OBLIQUE RHYME. See *consonance*.

OFF-RHYME. See *consonance*.

ONOMATOPOEIA. A "description" of something through sound, the sonics of the verse being an imitation of the subject ("The seashore roared from the seashell's horn").

ORTHOGRAPHICAL RHYME. See *sight rhyme*.

OTIOSE LANGUAGE. See *pompous language*.

PAEAN. Occasional poetry written to celebrate a particular person. See *epideictic*.

PARABOLA. Discusses one thing in terms of something else that is totally different, as in Yeats's "Crazy Jane and the Bishop" when Crazy Jane says, "But a birch-tree stood my Jack: / The solid man and the coxcomb."

PARAPHONE, PARARHYME. See *consonance*.

PATTER VERSE. Verse uttered in a quick, glib manner. See *rap poetry*.

PENCEIRDD, PENCEIRDDIAID. See *license*.

PENULTIMATE SYLLABLE. See *ultimate syllable*.

PERFORMANCE POETRY. Poetry written to be presented in public, an extreme version of which is *slam poetry*, in which poets compete for the audience's votes. See *rhapsode*.

PERSIFLAGE. Banter—good-natured, jesting conversation.

PHANOPOIEA. See *elevated language*.

PLEONASM. The use of excessive words, as in the ending of Walt Whitman's "I Hear America Singing," which ends, "Singing with open mouths their strong melodious songs." It would be difficult for anyone to sing with closed mouths; therefore, "with open mouths" is a pleonasm.

PLURISIGNATION. Multiple or polysemous meaning. See *ambiguity*.

POETIC DICTION. See *elevated language* and *poetic language*.

POETIC LANGUAGE. or WRITING. Even in prose mode, this will display insistent rhythms and figures of speech. See *elevated language*; for an antonym, see *prosaic language*.

POETIC LICENSE. See *license*.

POLITICAL RHETORIC. See *exhortation*.

POLYSEMOUS MEANING. See *ambiguity*.

POMPOUS LANGUAGE. Bombastic in tone and sententious in expression, in a word, otiose. It is full of aphorisms and moralizing (sententia), delivered often in the grand manner, meaning emotively, with gestures.

PRAGMATOGRAPHIA. The description of actions.

PRAISE. See *epideictic*.

PROFANITY. Invective, execration, desecration.

PROPORTION BY SITUATION OF MEASURES. This has to do with variations in lengths of lines in a stanza; that is, the patterns of arrangement of long and short lines, as in, for instance, the stanza called *standard habbie* ("*Burns stanza*"), where the lines are sometimes of four feet, sometimes of two feet ($a^4a^4a^4b^2a^4b^2$— the numerals here indicate length of line).

PROPORTION BY SITUATION OF RHYME. This has to do with the arrangement of rhymes in a stanza by distance. First distance is couplet rhyme (*aa*); second distance is triplet rhyme (*aba*); third distance is envelope stanza quatrain (*abba*); fourth distance is quintet envelope, where the rhyme overlaps three lines of *b* rhyme (*abbba*) or a third rhyme is introduced centrally (*abcba*).

PROSAIC LANGUAGE OR WRITING. Does not display metrical rhythm, or is ordinary and unimaginative, straightforward, lacking in imagery. See *poetic language*.

PROSOPOGRAPHIA. The description of people one has not actually met or known—imaginative portraiture.

PRUNING. What the poet does when he or she writes echo verse.

PURE POETRY. *Lyric poetry*.

QUINTET ENVELOPE. An "envelope" is a rhyme enclosing other lines that don't rhyme with the envelope lines. First distance is couplet rhyme (*aa*, **not** an envelope). Second distance is triplet rhyme (*aaa, aba,* only the second of these is an envelope). Third distance is quatrain rhyme (*abba,* an envelope), fourth distance is quintet rhyme (*abcba, abbba,* etc., both of these being envelopes). This can go on forever. Dylan Thomas once did a 100-line envelope, which was ninety-ninth distance. See also *proportion by situation of rhyme*.

RABBETING. See *pruning*.

RALLYING CRY. See *slogan*.

RANT. Violent and bloated speech; rodomontade is gasconade, blustery braggadocio, vain boasting, derived from the character Braggadocchio who was the manifestation of vanity and conceit in *The Faery Queene* by Edmund Spenser (1552?–1599). See brag and backwoods boast (in text).

RAP POETRY. Contemporary stylized rhymed *patter verse* in the African-American "bebop" tradition of jazz.

RHAPSODE. One who is a professional reciter of poetry. The term may also be extended to include a lecturer on the subject. See *performance poetry*.

RHYMED PROSE. Rhyme is a sonic device usually, but not always, associated with metrical poetry. Prose, too, may be rhymed, as in the "Nasher," a form of satirical poetry.

RICH RHYME. Synonym for rime riche, *false rhyme*, identical rhyme. Includes *homographic rhyme, homonymic rhyme, homophonic rhyme*.

RIDDLE. See *enigma*.

RIME RICHE. See *false rhyme*.

RODOMONTADE. See *rant*.

SACRILEGE. Invective.

SECOND DISTANCE. See *proportion by situation of rhyme* and triplet rhyme (in text).

SENTENTIA. See *pompous language*.

SIGHT RHYME. Sight-rhymed words are spelled alike but sound unlike (**eight–sleight**; **ties–homilies**). See *dialect rhyme*.

SIGMATISM. The overuse of sibilances ("The **s**even **s**illy **s**i**s**ters **s**ang a **s**ong at **S**unday **s**chool").

SIMILITER CADENS. Rising rhyme.

SIMILITER DESINENS. See *perfect rhyme* and *tail rhyme*.

SIMILITUDO. See *analogy*.

SLAM POETRY. See *performance poetry* and *rhapsode*.

SLANDER. See *calumny*.

SLANT RHYME. See *consonance*.

SLOGAN. Slogans are mottos that serve as rallying cries or points of reference in campaigns of one sort or another—political, advertising, and so forth; catch-words or catch-phrases.

SUBJECTIVE SYNTAX. Donald Davie wrote (see Bibliography) that "syntax is subjective when its function is to please us by the fidelity with which [word order] follows the 'form of thought' in the [writer's] mind." In other words, the writer chooses a word order that tells the reader exactly what he or she is thinking. Subjective syntax is personal opinion:

On the Death of a Particular Friend

As those we love decay, we die in part,
String after string is severed from the heart
Till loosened life, at last but breathing clay,
Without one pang is glad to fall away.
Unhappy he who latest feels the blow!
Whose eyes have wept o'er every friend laid low,
Dragged lingering on from partial death to death
Till, dying, all he can resign is breath.
                                    —James Thomson

SYNTACTIC FORMS. Syntax is word order in a sentence. This general subject is treated at length in the Introduction at the beginning of this book. Donald Davie in his book *Articulate Energy* (see Bibliography) discussed the various types of syntax to be found in literature. They include *subjective* (egopoetic) *syntax*, *objective* (narrative) *syntax*, *dramatic syntax*, and *abstract* (musical) *syntax*.

TAIL RHYME. Rhyme at the ends of lines; homoeoteluton.

TELESCOPED METAPHOR. Extended metaphor, conceit.

THIRD DISTANCE. Envelope stanza quatrain (*abba*); see *proportion by situation of rhyme*.

TOPOGRAPHIA. The description of actual places.

TOPOGRAPHICAL VERSE. Retrospective, meditative verse written on the subject of a particular locale.

TRANSLATIO. Metaphor.

TRITE RHYME. The rhyming of words that have been overused for rhymes. Joyce Kilmer's "Trees" is a model for many of the trite rhymes in the English language; about the only ones he misses are **"love-above"** and **"June-moon."**

ULTIMATE SYLLABLE. The final syllable in a series is the ultimate syllable; the second-to-last is the penultimate syllable; the third-to-last is the antepenultimate syllable.

VERSE PARAGRAPH. Distinguished from the paragraph of a prose poem in that the verse paragraph is a unit of lines in a metrical poem that is analogous to a paragraph because it deals with matters that have logical relationships with one another and a common focus, but verse paragraphs need not be set off as units—like stanzas—as prose paragraphs are set off by indentations.

VERSE PROSODY. If, in writing poetry, one is counting merely syllables, measuring out a certain number to a line, then one is using syllabic prosody, and one is writing syllabic verse, as the ancient Irish and Welsh poets did. If one is counting only those syllables which, for some reason, are more heavily emphasized than others, then one is using accentual prosody, and one is writing accentual verse, as the Medieval Anglo-Saxon poets did. If one is counting not only all the syllables in the line, but all the stressed syllables as well, and arranging them in an alternating pattern of some kind, then one is using accentual-syllabic prosody, and one is writing accentual-syllabic verse, as Geoffrey Chaucer and William Shakespeare did. However, if, in writing poetry, one is not counting syllables at all, but instead is organizing according to the balance of sentence structures, then one is using the prosody called grammatical parallelism, and one is writing prose poetry, as the ancient Hebraic writers of the Bible did.

VITUPERATION. Invective.

VOCALIC ECHO. Repetition of vowel sounds, whether stressed or unstressed, anywhere among the words of poems.

WRENCHED RHYME. As much pun as anything else. It twists words in order to make rhymes, as in the beginning of Ogden Nash's prose poem:

Kindly Unhitch That Star, Buddy

I hardly suppose I know anybody who wouldn't rather be a success than a failure,

Just as I suppose every piece of crabgrass in the garden would much rather be an azalea,

And in celestial circles all the run-of-the-mill angels would rather be archangels or at least cherubim and seraphim,

And in the legal world all the little process-servers hope to grow up into great big bailiffim and sheriffim.

—Ogden Nash

Part II   Form-Finder Index

Introduction

Every element of language is a form of some kind, as has been suggested elsewhere in these pages, but there are certain structures that have traditionally been associated with the genre of poetry, and these will be the subject of the rest of this volume. Over seven hundred *traditional verse forms* are listed here. To identify the form of a poem, the reader should first determine its *meter*; second, determine its *rhyme scheme*; third, count the lines in one *stanza* (if looking for a *stanza form*) or the lines in the whole poem (if looking for a *poem form*). When these elements have been determined, the reader should look under the appropriate heading of the following Form-Finder: If the form is irregular, look under *General Forms*; if the form is regular, look under *Specific Forms* and then under the appropriate subheading ("One-Line Forms" through "Two-Hundred-Ten-Line Forms"). Under these headings are the lists of forms. Definitions of all these forms are listed alphabetically in the next chapter. The poem in question can be compared with the appropriate definitions until the form of that poem or stanza has been found.

One final note: Many poems are "regular," that is, traditionally formal, but the specific combinations of stanza pattern, line lengths, rhyme schemes, and meters have sometimes been created by the poet for that specific poem. Such patterns are called *nonce forms*.

Specific Forms

Cross-references are to the three alphabetical listings in the following chapter. Exact locations may be found in the index.

One-Line Forms

adonic (see SAPPHICS)
Alexandrine (see POULTER'S
  MEASURE)
Anglo-Saxon prosody
blank verse (see SONICS and
  HEROICS)
choriambics
classical hexameter (see
  ELEGIACS)
classical pentameter
cyhydedd naw ban
fourteener (see POULTER'S
  MEASURE)
grammatical parallelism (see
  PROSE PROSODIES)
    antithetical parallel
    climactic parallel
    synonymous parallel

synthetic parallel (For a
  complete disquisition
  on parallelism see the
  companion volume of
  this text, *The Book of
  Literary Terms*.)
hendecasyllabics
heroic line (see HEROICS)
hudibrastics (see SATIRICS)
mondo (see KATAUTA)
mote
rhupunt
Sapphic line (see SAPPHICS)
septenary (see POULTER'S
  MEASURE)
tawddgyrch cadwynog (see
  RHUPUNT)

Two-Line Forms

barzeletta
carol texte
choka
couplet
    Alexandrine couplet

cyhydedd fer
cywydd deuair fyrion
cywydd deuair hirion
Nashers
qasida

short couplet
    split couplet
elegiacs
ghazal
heroic couplet (see HEROICS)
Hudibrastics (see SATIRICS)

Nasher (see SATIRICS)
poulter's measure
primer couplet (see
    DIDACTICS)
tanka couplet (see TANKA)
toddaid byr

Three-Line Forms

blues stanza
haiku
    hokku
    senryu
katauta
tercet
    enclosed tercet
    Sicilian tercet

terza rima
    capitolo
triplet
    enclosed triplet
    englyn milwr
    englyn penfyr
    Sicilian triplet
triversen stanza

Four-Line Forms

ae freislighe
alcaics
awdl gywydd
ballad stanza
ballade envoy
    double refrain ballad envoy
byr a thoddaid
carol stanza
casbairdne
Clerihew
common measure
    hymnal stanza
    long hymnal stanza
    long measure
    short hymnal stanza
    short measure
deibhidhe

double dactyl
edda measures
    old story measure
    song measure
    speech measure
englyn cyrch (see ENGLYNS)
    englyn lleddfbroest
    englyn proest dalgron
    englyn proest gadwynog
    englyn unodl crwca
    englyn unodl union
gwawdodyn
heroic stanza (see HEROICS)
kyrielle
pantoum
quatrain
    envelope stanza

Five-Line Forms

Six-Line Forms

Seven-Line Forms

Eight-Line Forms

ballade stanza
   double ballade stanza
   double refrain ballade
     stanza
   huitain
common octave (see COMMON
   MEASURE)
   hymnal octave
   long hymnal octave
   long octave
   short hymnal octave
   short octave
cyhydedd hir

cyrch a chwta
double dactyl
lai nouveau (see LAI)
madrigal
octave
   Italian octave
   Sicilian octave
   strambotto
ottava rima
rispetto
   heroic octave
   heroic rispetto
triolet

Nine-Line Forms

lai
   virelai
Ronsardian ode stanza

rubliw
Spenserian stanza
triad (see TERCET)

Ten-Line Forms

ballade supreme stanza
   dizain
   double ballade supreme
     stanza

decastich
English ode stanza (see ODE)
madrigal

Eleven-Line Forms

chant royal stanza
madrigal

roundel

Twelve-Line Forms

rondine

Thirteen-Line Forms

madrigal   rondel

Fourteen-Line Forms

blues sonnet (see BLUES STANZA)   English sonnet
bref double   Italian sonnet
   quatorzain   Sicilian sonnet
rondel prime (see RONDEL)   Spenserian sonnet
sonetto rispetto (see RISPETTO)   terza rima sonnet (see TERZA
sonnet   RIMA)

Fifteen-Line Forms

rondeau

Eighteen-Line Forms

heroic sonnet (see SONNET)   triversen

Nineteen-Line Forms

terzanelle   villanelle

Twenty-Line Forms

caudate sonnet

Twenty-Four-Line Forms

roundelay

Twenty-Five-Line Forms

rondeau redoubled (see RONDEAU)

Twenty-Eight-Line Forms

ballade
   double refrain ballade

Thirty-Line Forms
English ode (see ODE)

Thirty-Five-Line Forms
ballade supreme (see BALLADE)

Thirty-Nine-Line Forms
sestina

Forty-Eight-Line Forms
double ballade (see BALLADE)

Sixty-Line Forms
chant royal

double ballade supreme (see BALLADE)

Ninety-Eight-Line Forms
crown of sonnets (see SONNET)

Two-Hundred-Ten-Line Forms
sonnet redoubled (see SONNET)

General Forms

Cross-references are to the three alphabetical listings in the following chapter. Exact locations may be found in the index.

abecedarius

acrostic

    double acrostic

    telestich

alba

allegory

alphabestiary

amphigory

anacreontics

anagram

antiphon

aubade

backwoods boast

balada

    dansa

ballad

barzeletta

beast epic

bestiary

blessing

blues

brag

bucolics

burlesque

caccia

calligramme

cancione

canso

canticle

canto

canzo

canzone

carol

catalog poem

catch

cento

chanso

chanson de geste

chant

chante-fable

chantey

charms

choral ode

cobla

commiato

complaint

coronach

curse

débat

    debate

descort

didactics

    alphabestiary

    barzeletta

    bestiary

    epistle

georgics
riddle
diminishing verse
dirge
dit
dithyramb
ditty
double acrostic
double forms
dramatics
   dialogue
   eclogue
   monologue
   soliloquy
dream allegory
dream vision
droighneach
echo verse
eclogue
eclogue débat
elegy
envoi
envoy
epic
epicedium
epigram
epilogue
epistle
epitaph
epithalamion, epithalamium
epyllion
evensong
fable, fabliau
flyting
forensics
   debat

pregunta
requesta
respuesta
genethliacum
georgics
geste
glee
glose
grammatical parallels
   catalog
   parenthetics
   polyphonic prose
   prose poem
haibun
heroics
hokku
homostrophic ode (see ODE)
Horatian ode (see ODE)
idyll
incantation
interlude
irregular ode (see ODE)
katauta
lament
lay
litany
liturgics
   antiphon
   blessing
   canticle
   carol
   chant
   curse
   dirge
   evensong
   hymn

liturgics (*continued*)
- incantation
- litany
- morningsong
- nightsong
- obsequy
- prayer
- sermon

lyrics
- alba (aubade)
- amphigory (amphigoury)
- anacreontics
- balada
- blues
- caccia, catch
- canso, canzo, canzone
- carol
- chantey
- complaint
- dithyramb
- ditty
- elegy (coronach, dirge, monody, threnody)
- encomium
- epithalamion
- epithalamium
- hymn
- lament
- lay
- madrigal
- madsong
- nonsense verse
- nursery rhyme
- paean
- panegyric
- pastoral (idyll)
- pastoral elegy
- prothalamion
- prothalamium
- reveille
- romance
- roundelay
- rune
- serenade
- sirvente

madrigal
madsong
mask, masque
metrical romance
miracle play
mondo
monody
monologue
morality play
morningsong
mote
mystery play

narratives
- ballad
- beast epic
- chanson de geste
- epic
- epyllion
- exemplum
- fabliau
- metrical romance
- romance

nightsong
noh play (see DRAMATICS)
nonsense verse
nursery rhyme
obsequy

occasionals
  elegy
  encomium
  epithalamion
  epithalamium
  genethliacum
  obsequy
  ode
  palinode
  prothalamion
  prothalamium
  triumphal ode
ode
  homostrophic ode
  irregular (Cowleyan) ode
  Pindaric ode
palinode
panegyric
passion play
pastoral
pastorale
pastoral elegy
pastoral ode
pastourelle
pattern verse
picture poem
Pindaric ode (see ODE)
plampede
posie, posy

pregunta
prose poem
prothalamion
prothalamium
quaternion
reveille
riddle
rimas dissolutas
romance
rune
satirics
  epigram
  epitaph
  sirvente
  Skeltonics
serenade
sermon
sirima
sirvente
Skeltonics
song (see LYRICS)
spatials
  calligramme
  concrete poem
telestich
tragedy
tragicomedy
triad
tumbling verse

All these forms are described, ordered alphabetically, with cross-references, in the succeeding pages.

Notation has to do with shorthand noting of the rhyme schemes and line lengths of poems. *Rhyme scheme* is a system of rhyming, and its notation is simple: *Small letters* (**other than x**) stand for rhymes. *Capital letters* stand for *refrains*—repeated lines or sections of the poem. The first rhyme sound of a poem is always noted as *a*. The second rhyme is *b*, the third *c*, and so forth. The numerals above the small letters (a^4) indicate length-of-line (in this case, four verse feet).

When a line is used as a refrain, the first refrain will, if it is also the first rhyme, be noted with a capital letter *A*, the second refrain, if the second rhyme, will be capital *B*, and so on. If there are two refrains in the poem with the *same rhyme*, they are differentiated by numerals: A^1bA^2, as in the *villanelle*, for instance. Should one wish to indicate line lengths as well, a second numeral will indicate line length, the first indicating the refrain (A^{1-4}—see the *pantoum;* which is built entirely of repeated lines). In a poem containing two or more refrains that rhyme with one another, *superscript numerals* stand for the differentiation between those lines.

A particular system of metrical notation was developed for, and copyrighted in, the first edition of *The Book of Forms* (New York, 1968), and it is retained here. The schematic diagrams that appear beneath most of the prose descriptions of the various poetic forms, lines, and stanza patterns are designed to present visually (1) the number of syllables in each line of verse; (2) the number of accents in each line; (3) the rhyme schemes; and (4) the positions of rhymed and unrhymed refrains and repetitions. For these reasons the traditional method of scansion is not often used, and the following symbols should be noted:

> x —Small x stands for an unrhymed syllable that is either unaccented or whose accent is unimportant. Please note that the *breve* (˘) symbol is not necessary under these circumstances, and it is not often used.
>
> ´ —Stands for an accent (stress).
>
> x́ —Stands for an unrhymed, stressed syllable.
>
> a, b, c —Small letters other than x stand for rhymes.
>
> á, b́, ć —Small accented lettters other than x stand for stressed rhymed syllables.

A, B, C —1. In the Welsh and Irish forms, capital letters stand for *main* rhymes.

—2. In the French forms, capital letters (except R) indicate *rhymed refrains that are whole lines or repetons.*

R —In some French forms, R indicates a *refrain that consists of only a part of a line.*

$A^1B^1A^2B^2$ —Numbered capital letters indicate *sequence of refrains*; the example of the *pantoum.*

or —In certain Welsh forms "*or*" indicates a single syllable or word that *consonates* (off-rhymes or slant-rhymes).

oe, ay, ei —In certain Welsh forms, grouped letters (other than *exes* and *or*) indicate *diphthong rhymes.*

c, xc, bc —In certain Irish forms, a small *c* used alone or grouped with other letters indicates *consonance*, not rhyme.

xx, xax, xxxb —Otherwise, grouped letters indicate a *word* consisting of that many syllables.

x x a x x —In the Welsh and Irish forms, *italicized syllables* indicate *possible positions* for rhymes, cross-rhymes, assonances, or alliterations.

Although these symbols might seem confusing out of context, they will become immediately clear when one consults the schematic diagrams themselves. There are certain exceptions to these notation rules, but in each case the exceptions are apparent and are stated in the heading for each form.

Part III   Traditional Verse Forms

Dramatic Poetry

The forms of dramatic poetry are those of drama itself: *tragedy, comedy, tragicomedy*, the *monologue, dialogue, soliloquy*. For a complete discussion of all these forms, see the chapter "The Genres of Drama" in *The Book of Literary Terms*.

These are some of the shorter forms:

A DIALOGUE is a conversation among characters.

The Age of Philosophy

A Play in Ballad Form

Characters: Frank, a gay young lord
                 Lloyd, a sober young lord
                 David, the gardener, an old man

Scene: The garden of a manor. It is raining and the foggy night lies heavily upon the manor and its surroundings. Lloyd stands leaning against a statue of Venus near the terrace. The sounds of a dance may be heard emanating from the ballroom which is located directly behind the terrace. Frank steps out of the ballroom through French doors and walks over to the edge of the terrace to stand behind Lloyd.

FRANK: Know this well, friend, and end
        your windy, wet lament:
        Love owns its laughter and
        A zephyr's supple scent—
        So fling away the chords
        of lachrymose discords!

Beyond those whipping vines
snapped by nocturnal squalls
lie cellars filled with wines
and boulder-bolstered halls
wherein ladies and lords
know no tears or discords.

A violon lies low
beneath the tempest beat;
no slippered heel or toe
arches upon retreat.
The dancers tread the boards
and trample their discords.

Come on! Come join the dance!
Give raindrops back to earth.
Love's but a game of chance—
toast it before the hearth,
admit that it affords
the gambler his discords!

LLOYD: You seek release through song;
I do not wish release.
I deem your method wrong—
true love has no surcease,
yet I must bow to fate—
love owns no potentate.

Beyond the edge of night,
far past the spark of day,
I know there lies a flight
of swans upon the bay,
of which, I'm glad to state,
I *am* the potentate!

Then let me lie upon
my hillock here and raise

the image of a swan
to rest upon the haze
of my lethargic state . . . ,
let me play potentate!

The storm has passed. My flock
lies smoothing ruffled wings.
I am content to mock
the song your minstrel sings
and merely cogitate,
as should a potentate.

David, who has been lingering unseen in the shadow of a nearby
pillar, now emerges into the light spilling from the windows of the
ballroom and addresses the two young men.

DAVID: But even swans must leave
the gentlest of lagoons
to bring forth eggs and weave
their nests. Summer monsoons,
though you be swan or goose,
may interrupt your views.

Dancing is fine, and so
is dreaming . . . now and then.
But neither can bestow
a chick upon the hen.
Whichever one you choose,
rectify your views.

FRANK: Old man, keep out of this!

LLOYD: We are philosophers!
Be it chaste tear or kiss

FRANK: (whichever one prefers)

LLOYD: we'll never change or lose
        our well-considered views!

FRANK: I'll dip and sway till dawn—

LLOYD: And I will fly beyond
        in the manner of a swan
        to find the night's still pond.

BOTH: Though this may come as news,
        we *like* our diverse views!

Envoi

DAVID: Then join your dancing hordes,
        or, weeping, contemplate
        the gander's sterile hues!
        Melodies breed discords
        and life is potentate
        over our youthful views.

        Where youth and love contend, the stage
        is set to enact a wiser age.

Exit David back into the shadows. The young lords exchange
angry looks, then shrug their shoulders. Frank cocks his head to listen to the music, then abruptly turns and reenters the ballroom.
Lloyd resumes his pose against the statue of Venus.

CURTAIN

—Wesli Court

For a discussion of the various dramatic and narrative techniques
used in this poem, see *The Book of Literary Terms*.

  The ECLOGUE DÉBAT is both a form of dialogue and a form of
pastoral (see *eclogue* among the *pastoral poetry* that follows). It is an

argument between pastoral sweethearts. Robert Henryson wrote the following example in *hymnal octave*, a doubling of *hymnal quatrain* which has, in lines 1 and 3, four iambic feet, and in lines 2 and 4, three iambic feet. Hymnal octave rhymes *abababab*—it should not be confused with Sicilian octave, which is written in iambic pentameter. The original form has been kept for this modern version.

The prosody of Chaucer (1340?–1400) was kept alive for a hundred years, until the English Renaissance, by the Scots poets like Robert Henryson (1430?–1506), who, though they were Celts, also kept Middle English alive, for modern Scots is in effect still Middle English. Elsewhere, on the Scottish border and in England itself, the poets backslid into accentual verse and wrote in podic "folk meters" instead of accentual-syllabics.

Robin and Makyn

Robin sat on a good green hill,
Keeping a flock was he,
Merry Makyn near him till,
"Robin, have ruth for me;
I have loved thee loud and still
For years now two or three,
Doleful in secret; unless thou will,
I fear I shall doubtless die."

Robin answered, "By the Rood,   [cross]
Nothing of love I know
But keeping my sheep under yon wood—
Lo! where they wander a-row:
What has marred thee in thy mood,
Makyn, I beg thou show;
Or what is love, or to be loved?
Fain would I learn that law."   [willingly]

"At love's lair, to learn its lore
Take here this a–b–c:

Be kind, courteous, and fair as fair,
Wise, generous, hearty
So that thou need not to endure
What hidden hurts may harm thee;
Fight thy pain with all thy power,
Have patience and be privy."   [private]

Robin answered her again,
"I know not what is love,
But I am marvelous uncertain
What makes thee thus to grieve:
The weather is fair, I have no pain,
My hale sheep climb above;
And should we play upon this plain,
We both would earn reproof."   [blame]

"Robin, pay heed unto my tale,
Work all as I have said,
And thou shalt have my heart all hale,
Aye, and my maidenhead.
Since God sends thee beauty for bale   [ugliness]
And mourning is remade,
I plead with thee, if I turn tail,
Doubtless I am but dead."

"Makyn, this morning it may betide,
While ye waylay me here,
My sheep may hap to stray aside
While we have lain full near;
I fret this moment as I bide
That they shall disappear—
What freights my heart I will not hide;
Makyn, be of good cheer."

"Robin, thou rob my ruth and rest;
I love but thee alone."
"Makyn, adieu, the sun goes west,

The day is nearly gone."
"Robin, I grieve; I am distressed
That love will be my bane."   [poison]
"Go love, Makyn, wherever thou list,   [wish]
For mistresses I want none."

"Robin, I stand in such a stall;
I sigh, and that full sore."
"Makyn, I have been here this while;
At home God grant I were."
"My honey, Robin, talk awhile,
If thou wilt do no more."
"Makyn, some other man beguile,
For homeward I will fare."

Upon his own way Robin went
Light as the leaf of a tree;
Makyn, spited of her intent,
Watched Robin across the lea   [meadow]
And vowed to spurn him without stint.
Then Makyn cried out on high,
"Now may thou sing, for I am spent!
What ails this love in me?"

Makyn went home and did not fail,
Weary of learning to weep.
Then Robin in a full-fair dale
Gathered together his sheep,
When some part of what made Makyn ail
Into his heart did creep;
He followed her fast till he could hale
And tell her, "Take good keep!

"Abide, abide, thou fair Makyn,
One word for anything;
For all my love, it shall be thine,
Without any departing.

O take my heart, for to have thine
Is all my coveting;
My sheep till morrow's hours nine
Will need of no keeping."

"Robin, thou hast heard sing and say
In gestes and stories old,
'The man that will not when he may
Shall have not when he would.'
I pray that Jesus every day
Increase their cares and cold
Who shall contend with thee to play
By firth, forest, or fold."

"Makyn, the night is soft and dry,
The weather is warm and fair,
And the greenwood is here nearby,
We may talk privily where
No gossips will be near to spy
Upon our trysting there;
Therein, Makyn, both ye and I,
Unseen we may repair."

"Robin, that world is all away
And quite brought to an end,
And never again after today
Shall I come as thou wend;
For of my pain thou made but play,
Vainly did my bough bend;
As thou hast done, so shall I say,
'Mourn on, *I* think to mend.'"

"Makyn, the hope of all my weal,
My heart on thee is set,
And ever to thee shall I kneel
While I have blood to let;
Never to fail, as others fail,
Whatever grace I get."

"Robin, with thee I will not deal;
Adieu, for thus we met."

Makyn went home, blithe anew,
Across the forest floor;
Robin mourned, and Makyn flew,
She sang, he sighed full sore;
And so she left him woe and rue
In care and in dolor,
Keeping his herd beside a sleugh   [bog]
Upon the forest floor.
     —Robert Henryson

INTERIOR MONOLOGUE—See *soliloquy.*

A MONOLOGUE is half of a conversation, a speech to a character who is presumed to be present, though a listener may not be evident to the audience.

A SOLILOQUY, sometimes called an INTERIOR MONOLOGUE, is differentiated from a monologue in that it is personal thoughts verbalized rather than half a conversation; it is "talking to oneself," for no other audience is present or assumed to be present. Here is a soliloquy by Robert Browning:

Porphyria's Lover

The rain set early in tonight;
The sullen wind was soon awake—
It tore the elm-tops down for spite,
And did its worst to vex the lake.
I listened with heart fit to break.
When glided in Porphyria; straight
She shut the cold out and the storm,
And kneeled and made the cheerless grate
Blaze up, and all the cottage warm;
Which done, she rose, and from her form
Withdrew the dripping cloak and shawl,
And laid her soiled gloves by, untied
Her hat and let the damp hair fall,

And, last, she sat down by my side
And called me. When no voice replied,
She put my arm about her waist,
And made her smooth white shoulder bare
And all her yellow hair displaced,
And, stooping, made my cheek lie there,
And spread, o'er all, her yellow hair,
Murmuring how she loved me—she
Too weak, for all her heart's endeavor,
To set its struggling passion free
From pride, and vainer ties dissever,
And give herself to me forever.
But passion sometimes would prevail,
Nor could tonight's gay feast restrain
A sudden thought of one so pale
For love of her, and all in vain;
So, she was come through wind and rain.
Be sure I looked up at her eyes
Happy and proud; at last I knew
Porphyria worshiped me; surprise
Made my heart swell, and still it grew
While I debated what to do.
That moment she was mine, mine, fair,
Perfectly pure and good; I found
A thing to do, and all her hair
In one long yellow string I wound
Three times her little throat around,
And strangled her. No pain felt she;
I am quite sure she felt no pain.
As a shut bud that holds a bee,
I warily oped her lids; again
Laughed the blue eyes without a stain.
And I untightened next the tress
About her neck; her cheek once more
Blushed bright beneath my burning kiss.
I propped her head up as before,
Only, this time my shoulder bore
Her head, which droops upon it still—
The smiling rosy little head,

So glad it has its utmost will,
That all it scorned at once is fled,
And I, its love, am gained instead!
Porphyria's love—she guessed not how
Her darling one wish would be heard.
And thus we sit together now,
And all night long we have not stirred,
And yet God has not said a word!

      —Robert Browning

Lyric Poetry

The problem of *voice* is discussed at length in "The Genres of Fiction" in *The Book of Literary Terms*, but often readers do not realize that in poetry there is also always a *narrator*. T. S. Eliot wrote, in *The Three Voices of Poetry* (1955):

I shall explain at once what I mean by the "Three Voices." The first is the poet talking to himself—or to nobody [the *subjective* or *egopoetic voice*]. The second is the voice of the poet addressing an audience, whether large or small [the *objective* or *narrative voice*]. The third is the voice of the poet when he attempts to create a dramatic character speaking in verse; when he is saying, not what he would say in his own person, but only what he can say within the limits of one imaginary character addressing another imaginary character [the *dramatic voice*]. The distinction between the first and the second voice, between the poet speaking to himself and the poet speaking to other people, points to the problem of poetic communication; the distinction between the poet addressing other people in either his own voice or an assumed voice, and the poet inventing speech in which imaginary characters address each other, points to the problem of the difference between dramatic, quasidramatic, and non-dramatic verse.(4)

Most *lyric poems* are written in the subjective voice; all *narrative poems* are written in the objective voice, and all *dramatic poems* are written in the dramatic voice. There may, of course, be combinations of these voices in various poems. For more on point-of-view (viewpoint), see *The Book of Literary Terms*.

Lyrics are *songs*, poems meant to be sung originally, and *melic poetry* was written with the intention that there be flute or lyre accompaniment; the term *lyrics* is still used to designate the words of songs. However, *literary lyrics* carry their own music, and no extraneous musical accompaniment is required. There are a great many traditional *lyric forms*:

For the ABECEDARIUS, see *acrostic*; see also *alphabestiary* (under *bestiary*), *primer* (under *didactic poetry*), and the companion volume, *The Book of Literary Terms*.

An ACROSTIC can be written in any verse prosody or in any form, but it is usually metered and rhymed as in the example given here, which is in the form of a *rondeau*. An acrostic is a poem whose *initial letters* of each line, when read down, give the letters of the alphabet (in which case it is called an abecedarius), a *name* or a *phrase,* or some other *word* or grammatical construct:

Virelai Avortée en Forme de Rondeau Acrostiche

Anagram: "Ring a Virile Lady."

V irelai, won't you come? Just so,
I t will have to be the rondeau
R ising to love. Nor will you spurt,
G alloping response to the quirt
I n my hand. You will merely go
N ag on me, like that bland "No!"
I n my lady's lips. You will grow
A trifle testy if I flirt.

L ai, won't you?

R ing a virile lady and blow
A s you will, winding to and fro,
D iking up happiness and hurt.
L eman, once more before I squirt,
E asing off this sheet . . . yes, I know:
Y ou won't lai.
                        —Wesli Court

A *telestich* accomplishes this same effect with the *ultimate* (last) *letters* only; the *double acrostic* duplicates the feat with both initial and ultimate letters; the *compound acrostic* is similar, except that different words are spelled out down the left-hand and right-hand margins, and the *mesostich* does the trick with middle letters.

The ADONIC LINE is a dactyl and a trochee, in that order: ´ ˘ ˘ ´ ˘. A consideration of it is found in the earlier discussion of *Sapphics*. See also *Sapphics*, discussed later.

AE FREISLIGHE (*ay fresh-lee*) is an Irish syllabic stanza form. Since this is the first Celtic one to be encounted here, a note is in order. Almost all the Irish and Welsh forms are complex systems of rhyme, alliteration, and consonance (see *cynghanedd*). For the practical purpose of versification in English, it should be understoood that the systems are most difficult to reproduce accurately in our language. It would therefore be as well for the poet attempting these forms to pay attention only to the rhyme scheme and syllabification. Thus, ae freislighe, simplified, is a *quatrain stanza* of seven-syllable lines. Lines one and three rhyme in triple rhymes; lines two and four rhyme in double rhymes. The *poem* (not the stanza) should end with the same first syllable, word, or line with which it begins. The technical term for this ending is *dunadh*, and it occurs in all the Gaelic forms. The diagram looks like this:

lines	*syllables and rhymes*
1.	x x x x (*xxa*)
2.	x x x x x (*xb*)
3.	x x x x (*xxa*)
4.	x x x x x (*xb*)

Love Curse

What's love but a bobolink
Beating its voice on the air,
A morningsong robawink,
Wrack of sleep beyond repair?

What's love but a nematode,
The worm that gnaws its wee hole,
A minuscule episode
Restless to become the whole?

Love, love, let me mock you thrice

With catspaw, rue, and foxglove.
Basilisk and cockatrice
Know how to answer, "What's love?"
                    —Wesli Court

The ALBA (or *aubade*) is a love song sung at dawn:

Dawn Song

> *". . . world of the first rose, and the first lark's song."*
>   *—Margaret Mead*

I am the first to know dawn for the dawn—
it breaks across my mind as across the eyes
of the beast I was, of the beasts from whom I come,
and the swift sun slows, and I know it for the sun
in the world of the first rose, and the first lark's song.

I am the first to see the sharp sun dawn,
breaking across my terror and my surprise;
to know that I am the beast who knows his name:
Beast of the Sun, beast of the spinning sun
of the world of the first rose, and the first lark's song.

I am the first to see stone for a stone,
to heft it in my hand, to feel its weight
and know what it may do to the brittle bone
of the beasts of the sun, in the morning of the sun,
in the world of the first rose, and the first lark's song.

I see, and my sight is hard, hard as the stone
held in my hand, and this stone will be my fate.
The beast is my brother—beast is his only name.
He is the child of dust. I am stone's son,
born of the first rose and the first lark's song.

A *morningsong* (*matins*) is a *prayer* sung at daybreak. The *reveille* is
described later. Also see the *serenade*.

ALCAICS is a quantitative accentual–syllabic Greek *quatrain* stanza *form.* The first two lines are made up of an *acephalous* (headless) iamb (merely the accented syllable is left—the unaccented first syllable has been dropped), followed by two trochees and two dactyls, in that order. The third line is made up of an acephalous iamb followed by four trochees, and the last line of the stanza contains two dactyls followed by two trochees:

```
´|´ ∪|´ ∪|´ ∪ ∪|´ ∪ ∪
x  xx xx  xxx  xxx
´|´ ∪|´ ∪|´ ∪ ∪|´ ∪ ∪
x  xx xx  xxx  xxx
´|´ ∪|´ ∪|´ ∪|´ ∪
x  xx xx xx xx
´ ∪ ∪|´ ∪ ∪|´ ∪|´ ∪
xxx xxx xx xx
```

This is the first half of a poem; it is written in alcaics; the second half is written in *hendecasyllabics*, which is where it may be found:

Milton (Alcaics)

O mighty-mouth'd inventor of harmonies,
O skill'd to sing of Time or Eternity,
　　God-gifted organ-voice of England,
　　　　Milton, a name to resound for ages;
Whose Titan angels, Gabriel, Abdiel,
Starr'd from Jehovah's gorgeous armories,
　　Tower, as the deep-domed empyrean
　　　　Rings to the roar of an angel onset—
Me rather all that bowery loneliness,
The brooks of Eden mazily murmuring,
　　And bloom profuse and cedar arches
　　　　Charm, as a wanderer out in ocean,
Where some refulgent sunset of India
Streams o'er a rich ambrosial ocean isle,
　　And crimson-hued the stately palm-woods
　　　　Whisper in odorous heights of even.
　　　　　　　　　　　　—Alfred Tennyson

An ALEXANDRINE COUPLET is composed of two Alexandrine lines rhyming *aa*; it is often used as a *coda*. The ALEXANDRINE LINE will be found under Narrative Poetry and *poulter's measure*.

There are various entries for ALLEGORY. See also the *dream vision* under Narrative Poetry.

The ALPHABESTIARY is found under *bestiary*.

AMOEBEAN VERSE is poetic dialogue; see Dramatic Poetry.

AMPHIGORY or AMPHIGOURY is *nonsense verse*:

Partsong for Gorgonzola

My tongue is hanging out my head
And wetting down my empty bed,
My bellybutton sighs with grief
Because my thorax is a thief,
I'll have to jump along the floor
And throw my eyeball out the door—
   O waly waly waly O
   Cry how my noses want to blow!

I feel my nostril growing thick,
My earlobe's lowing like a tic,
My hangdog fingernail cuts glass—
I'll have to miss my social class.
Give me a good old kneecap cup,
Fill it with lymph and let me sup—
   O waly waly waly O
   Weep how my soul has wed my toe!

The atomy of molecules
Gives me the cheek to rise to stools,
The tear that falls along my chin
Turns all my whiskers into gin.
My legs are even as I sit,
And that's the long and short of it!
   Sing waly waly waly O
   My buttox follows as I go!
             —Wesli Court

See also the *madsong, nonsense verse,* and *nursery rhyme.*

ANACREONTICS are songs in praise of revelry and womankind sung in the style of the classic Greek poet Anacreon. For an English example see Robert Herrick's "Anacrontic Verse" under *qasida.*

The ANAGRAM transposes the letters of one word in order to make up another word, for example, Gerald Ford = forged lard. Popular in the seventeenth century and earlier, casting anagrams was a form of divining; that is, it was a means of foretelling the future of a person or of extracting the essence of his or her life or personality:

> *MARY*
> *ANA-   GRAM*
> *ARMY*

How well her name an *Army* doth present,
In whom the *Lord of Hosts* did pitch his tent!
                                        —George Herbert

The anagram is sometimes associated with the *acrostic,* and sometimes it serves as the *epigraph* of other kinds of poems.

The English ANGLO-SAXON LINE or *stich* is discussed in the section on The Sonic Level, under *accentual prosodies.* See also *edda measures.* For examples, see the anonymously written "The Wanderer" and "Wulf and Eadwacer," given earlier, and "The Magi Carol" under *bob and wheel.*

The poem forms ANTHEM and ANTIPHON are found under *liturgics.*

For the ANIMAL EPIC see beast epic and *fable* under Narrative Poetry.

The ANTITHETICAL PARALLEL, a line form, is found under the headings of *syntax* and *parallel structure.*

The AUBADE, a poem form, is discussed under the *alba.*

AWDL GYWYDD (*owdl gów-widd*) is a syllabic Welsh stanza form, a *quatrain* of seven-syllable lines. Lines two and four rhyme; lines one and three *cross-rhyme* into the third, fourth, or fifth syllable of lines two and four. Here is a possible scheme for two stanzas of awdl gywydd:

lines	*syllables and rhymes*
1.	x x x x x x a
2.	x x *a* x x x b
3.	x x x x x x c
4.	x x *x* x *c* x b
5.	x x x x x x d
6.	x x x *d* x x e
7.	x x x x x x f
8.	x x *x f* x x c

Here is a modern version of a medieval poem cast into awdl gywydd:

Spring Song
Earthspring, the sweetest season,
Loud the birdsong, sprouts ripple,
Plough in furrow, ox in yoke,
Sea like smoke, fields in stipple.

Yet when cuckoos call from trees
I drink the lees of sorrow;
Tongue bitter, I sleep with pain—
My kinsmen come not again.

On mountain, mead, seaborne land,
Wherever man wends his way,
What path he take boots not,
He shall not keep from Christ's eye.
　　　　　　　—Anonymous Welsh

The BACKWOODS BOAST: see the *brag*.

The BALADA is a lyric poem with an insistent *refrain* meant to be danced to. In this case the repeated line is an incremental refrain, for it changes slightly each time it appears:

Balada of Uncertain Age

"You see what we must all come to if we live."

Twenty was a handsome age.
I set my foot upon the stage

And donned both skullcap and tragic mask—
  What more could any poet ask
Than to be young and full of woe,
    Concerned with death and twining time?
I did not know enough to know
    One cannot blunt a scythe with rhyme.

When thirty years had rolled around
I thought that I had surely found
    A lucky charm to keep me young
    In all the sorrowing songs I'd sung.
I stood astonished to descry
    The fact that I was still in time.
But had I truly felt I'd die
    Before I'd learned to cope with rhyme?

Then forty took me by surprise,
Dropped the blinders from my eyes.
    Now I was but an aging man,
    A father with a father's plan
To see his children lettered well
    And launched upon the tide of time—
Therefore I wrote my songs to sell.
    I learned to merchandise my rhyme.

Now I've rolled up ten and two-score
Of years and masks, of songs and lore.
    My young are grown or on their way
    To tomorrow from yesterday,
And I have little left to do
    But play my angling games with time—
Cast lines, wind in my reel, renew
    The bait upon my hooks with rhyme

Envoy:
And find what sort of shape will rise
    Out of the crystal pool of time
To clear the cataracts from my eyes
    And show me all the depths of rhyme.

A *ditty* is any simple lyric meant to be sung. A *roundelay* (*round*) is any relatively simple, short lyric with an insistent refrain, like the longer *caccia* (*catch*) and *glee*, both of which are often put to music and sung with voices repeating the lines in an overlapping, rhythmically complex manner so that new meanings, often bawdy, appear as the lines are performed. For a set form of the roundelay, see the alphabetical entry, given later.

The BALLAD and BALLAD STANZA are discussed in the section on *podics* (chapter 1) and in Narrative Poetry (part III). For related forms, see *common measure*.

The French BALLADE was a poem originally written in syllabic prosody; its lines may be of any *single* length, such as decasyllabics or iambic tetrameter. The poem has three stanzas turning on three rhymes only—the rhymes do not change; these stanzas are *octaves* rhyming *ababbcbC*, with the capital letter indicating a *refrain*. Ordinarily, the concluding *envoy* is a half-stanza rhyming *bcbC*:

Stanzas 1 to 3		Envoy	
Line	Rhymes	Line	Rhymes
1.	a	25.	b
2.	b	26.	c
3.	a	27.	b
4.	b	28.	C—*refrain*
5.	b		
6.	c		
7.	b		
8.	C—*refrain*		

"To Rosemunde" is a French ballade without an envoy. The meter is iambic pentameter: Chaucer was one of the fourteenth-century inventors of accentual-syllabic prosody. Accentual-syllabics harmonized the Norman French syllabic prosody, which had been standard in England since the Norman conquest of 1066, with the ancestral accentual prosody of the Anglo-Saxons. Though the Celtic prosody of the Irish, Welsh, Manx, Cornish, and the continental Bretons was also syllabic, it had little effect on English poetry.

To Rosemunde

Madame, you be of all beauty the shrine
As far as is circled the Map-o'Munde,   [world map]
For as the crystal glorious you shine,
And like to rubies are your two cheeks round.
Therewith you be so merry and so jocund
That at a revel, when I see you dance,
It is an ointment then unto my wound,
Although you do not do me dalliance.

For, though I weep of sad tears full a tun,
Yet may that woe my heart never confound;
Your seemly voice, that you so small out-twine,
Makes all my thoughts in joy and bliss abound.
So courteously I go, in love enbound,
That to myself I say, in my penance,
"Suffice it me to love you, Rosemunde,
Although you do not do me dalliance."

Never was pike wallowed in galantine
As I in love am wallowed and enwound,
For which full oft I of myself divine
That I am truly Tristram the Second.
My love may not be cooled, nor may be drowned;
I burn aye in an amorous pleasance.
Do what you will, I shall your thrall be found,
Although you do not do me dalliance.
                                    —Geoffrey Chaucer

For another example, see the section on *light verse*.

The BALLADE SUPREME, another of the French family of forms, has three ten-line stanzas that rhyme *ababbccdcD* and a quintet envoy rhyming *ccdcD*, with the capital letters, as usual, indicating refrains. All lines are written in the same meter and are of the same length.

The *double ballade* and the *double ballade supreme* have twice as many stanzas as the ballade and the ballade supreme whose rhyme schemes they follow, respectively; they may or may not have envoys.

The *double refrain ballade* is made of three octaves that rhyme *abaBbcbC* plus a quatrain envoy, *bBcC*. Notice that it has two refrains, the first appearing as lines four, twelve, twenty, and twenty-six, the second appearing as lines eight, sixteen, twenty-four, and twenty-eight.

Will Somers

from Bordello

The sun shone all day
like a bright cock preening
for its hen. Making hay
lay over the greening
grass. There is no meaning
hidden for you to trace
in these wishes leaning
like moonlight on my face,

for I live as I may—
I, Will Somers—gleaning
in all weathers. I say,
"lay over the greening
world well, the wind keening
or soughing." Woman's grace
is but a night's dreaming,
like moonlight on my face:

a thing met with on the way,
taken without scheming.
I never married. Clay
lay over the greening
sap of my youth. Steaming
nights I spent alone; lace
fancies all went streaming
like moonlight on my face,

like sweat. Sweat, careening,
lay over the greening

fields. Now, I know love's place,
like moonlight on my face.

Also a member of the ballade family is the *grande ballade* or *chant royal*. A whole poem consisting of a single ballade stanza without a refrain (*ababbcbc*)is called a *huitain*. It is called *Monk's Tale* stanza if it is used to write long poems, as Chaucer did in "The Monk's Tale" from *The Canterbury Tales*. The *dizain* is a whole poem made of one ballade supreme stanza without the refrain (*ababbccdcd*). All lines in the stanzas of all these forms are of equal length.

The addition of an Alexandrine line to an iambic pentameter ballade stanza in order to make a final couplet gives rise to the *Spenserian stanza*, in which Edmund Spenser wrote *The Faery Queen*, $a^5b^5a^5b^5b^5c^5b^5c^5c^6$—notice that there is no refrain in this stanza. For an example of the form, see Narrative Poetry.

The Italian BARZELETTA is a poem written in *blank verse* pentameters, heptameters, or *hendecasyllabics* (*Phalacean verse*; eleven-syllable lines) that utilizes internal rhyme, witticisms, didacticisms, and aphorisms. For an example, see the "Barzeletta" of the "Canzone" in *canzone*.

The BEAST EPIC is a form of Narrative Poetry; see also the *fable*. BENISON—see *blessing*.

A BESTIARY is a collection of descriptions of fabulous creatures used as allegories of human nature. An *alphabestiary* is a didactic bestiary illustrating the alphabet. This is the letter *N* from a modern alphabestiary written in quantitative syllabics (8-5-5-5-5):

Ñ ASNAS

It must hop, having but one leg,
    but it does so swiftly.
    They say its flesh is sweet.
    It can give half a smile,
    but its laugh is grotesque,

so Nasnas snirtles instead, to
    keep its mouth as close as

may be; thus, it tries to
suppress its yawn as well.
If it winks with one eye,

 it is blind a moment and may
  be captured then. If one
  listens at its breast, to
  the half-beat of the heart's
  single chamber, one hears,

besides, the lone lung's suspiring.
  Its nostril flares in half-
  hearted anger. It can
  give but partial comfort.
  God knows how it makes love.

BLANK VERSE is any *unrhymed* accentual-syllabic verse. See *heroics*, *epic*, and *narrative poetry*. It is not to be confused with "free verse," which is prose broken into lines that may or may not rhyme—for rhyming prose, see the *Nasher*.

BLESSING—a *benison*, a form of *liturgical poetry*. For an example, see "A Blessing Upon Munster" under *droighneach*.

For the BLUES SONNET see *blues stanza*.

The BLUES STANZA is a *triplet* derived from the Afro-American tradition of lamentation or complaint in which line two is an *incremental repetition* of line one and the third line is a *climactic parallel*, *AAa*, *BBb*, etc.

The Shadowman

This is the year when everybody died—
This is the year when friends and neighbors died,
Took that short trip or ended the long slide.

Jim shot himself on Cemetery Road,
Left an ironic note beside the road.
No one heard his desperate heart explode.

Our frightened former next-door neighbor went—
Rita, the fearful widow from next-door went
To join her husband John in the firmament.

Paul's heart quit because his cough would not.
His life went up in smoke, for he could not
Stop smoking soon enough—so he would trot

Along our streets slower than folks could walk,
Jog the streets slower than we could walk
And slower than the shadowman can stalk.

Cooper's blood sluggishly turned to whey
In his pale veins—slowly turned to whey
Beneath the translucent skin now turned to clay.

Kermit and Dorothy lost this chilly spring
To the sickle and the crab—lost the spring
To the dim weather and the scorpion's sting.

And Mag, our neighbor on the other side,
Next door toward the lake on our north side,
Father of my son's best friend, has died

Because he loved his beer more than his life,
Loved his suds more than his very life,
Let alone his daughter, his son, his wife.

The shadowman comes tapping down the street,
His feet come stuttering along the street.
Nobodaddy's patrolling, walking his beat.

Hear him, townsmen, between the curbs of night,
Among our yards, towing the craft of night
Whether the hour is dusky or dark or light.

Listen to him breathing in the walls
Of all our houses, breathing in the walls,
In our kitchens and in the empty halls.

Stop when you listen and whisper to the dust,
"These are the names of neighbors scrawled in dust,
Whistled to shadow, scattered in a gust."

A *blues sonnet* is fourteen lines consisting of four *blues stanzas*
written in iambic pentameter meters and a *heroic couplet*: *AAa BBb
CCc DDd ee*. There is a *volta* after the last triplet.

Envoi
Just let me drop this note into the dark,
Yes, let me drop this note into the dark—
I'll light it with a match and watch it spark.

I'll sail it into night with fire and flare,
Fly it into darkness, see it flare
And wink out in those shadows circling there.

I'll watch it take its place among the stars,
Among the minor planets and the stars.
I'll hum the blues, not much—a couple bars—

Until the spark has died to inky ash,
And words have flickered into smoken ash.
Then I'll have me a sip of sour mash,

And lean against this marker made of stone
That will not last as long as ink or bone.
                                        —Wesli Court

BOB—see *bob and wheel*.

The English BOB AND WHEEL is an accentual-syllabic *quintet* ap-
pended as a *tail* (*cauda*, *coda*) on a stanza of *Anglo-Saxon prosody* in
certain poems, such as the anonymous Medieval *romance*, *Sir Gawain and the Green Knight*. The *bob* is a one- or two-foot line running on (*enjambed*) from the alliterative accentual stanza, and it is
continued by the *wheel*, a *quatrain* of short lines, generally of three
feet, rhyming *baba*. The whole quintet bob and wheel rhymes

ababa. The bob rhymes with lines two and four of the wheel; lines one and three of the wheel rhyme with each other. The following is a diagram of the structure of the entire bob and wheel:

lines   meters and rhymes

1.
   . . . xx xa—*bob*

2.
   xx xx xb

3.
   xx xx xa   } *wheel*

4.
   xx xx xb

5.
   xx xx xa

Sir Gawain and the Green Knight is too long to quote here, of course, but in the poem that follows, quatrains of Anglo-Saxon prosody precede the bobs and wheels, which, in this specific case, are *burdens*. Bobs and wheels are not ordinarily refrains:

The Magi Carol
Sheep of the fold,   fowls of the storm,
In chill the child,   chaste in His manger—
The kings are coming   to crown a King
And here are we   waiting to welcome
                     them together:
                       We wish you joy again,
                    Gale, oak and heather,
                       Mistletoe and pine,
                    In any winter weather.

Bearing gold,   gifts of myrrh,
Of frankincense—   seed of thyme,
Vervaine and thorn,   horn at the Gate—
The Magi move   among the snows
                    together:
                       We wish you joy again,

> Gale, oak and heather,
>   Mistletoe and pine,
>   In any winter weather.

Reap the heart   of the hoar oak
With a scythe of ore,   open the Gate
Of the golden Bough,   bend to dream
Before the stable,   the stall of fortune
>   all together:
>   We wish you joy again,
>   Gale, oak and heather,
>   Mistletoe and pine,
>   In any winter weather.

BOUTS-RIMÉS is a French verse-writing game played by various hands who write verses utilizing specific rhyme-words in a given form, usually that of the *sonnet*. For a similar form, see the *renga chain*, in the discussion of the *renga*.

The BRAG, an English tradition as old as *Beowulf*, was adopted by nineteenth-century America and transformed into what folklorists call "the backwoods boast." The American poet Robert Hayden was acquainted with the tradition and used it in his poem titled "Witch Doctor": "'He's / God's dictaphone of all-redeeming truth. / Oh he's the holyweight champeen who's come / to give the knockout lick to your bad luck; / I say he's the holyweight champeen who's here / to deal a knockout punch to your hard luck.'" See also *forensic poetry*.

The BREF DOUBLE is a French *quatorzain*—any fourteen-line poem or stanza other than a *sonnet*, such as the *blues sonnet*, *Sicilian sonnet*, *sonetto rispetto*, and the *terza rima sonnet*. There are only three rhymes in a bref double, but not every line is rhymed. There is no requirement as to meter, but all lines must be of equal length. The *a* and *b* rhymes must appear twice somewhere within each of the three quatrains and once in the concluding couplet; the *c* rhyme ends each quatrain. The example given here is also an example of *echo verse*:

Bref Double à l'Écho

Echo, speak—I expect no answers, though	*Though*
I address rock out of a cage—from this	*This*
Stalk of flesh, begotten of earth and sun.	*Son*
What may one do who has no wish to blaze?	*Blaze*
Through burning blood there move pure being's winds,	*Winds*
Mindless, augmenting chance's forging blow.	*Blow*
These simple facts! Do they apply to all?	*All*
In the balance, is there nothing else that weighs?	*Ways*
High and low are baffled—not queen nor nun	*None*
Knows why the womb leads to this maze. The May	*May*
Bee—it buzzes into heat, swarms to count	*Count*
Blossom and bloom for what, beyond mere daze?	*Days*
I ask you clear: Why are we? Do you know?	*No*
Why all our multitudes? What shall be won?	*One*

—Wesli Court

BUCOLICS, a minor subgenre of the genre of poetry, is intended to contrast simple modes with complex modes of life. Specifically, the subject matter of bucolics concerns the exaltation of the natural over the cultivated person, and of the country and rustic life over the life of the town and city. Bucolics are essentially romantic in content and viewpoint, often set in *Arcadia (Arcady)*, an idealized rural *locale*, after an idyllic and fabled region of ancient Greece, for bucolics have had a place in literature of the Western world from classic times to the present. The speeches of characters in such poems, or the language of such poems themselves, is sometimes *Doric*, after a province of ancient Greece, meaning "simple" or "unaffected." For further discussion of these terms, see the companion volume, *The Book of Literary Terms*.

Although there is no single set external form for the genre, several general forms have been associated with it. The *pastoral* or *idyl* is concerned, on its surface, with country ways, especially with the doings of shepherds or other rural people, but its allegorical level is concerned with more generally applicable topics.

The *eclogue* is a brief pastoral cast in the form of a dialogue or monologue spoken by country folk—see Philip Sidney's double sestina, "You Goat-Herd Gods," under *sestina*. The *pastoral elegy* combines elegy and bucolics, as the name of the form would indicate, as in such readily available examples as "Thanatopsis" by William Cullen Bryant and "Elegy Written in a Country Churchyard" by Thomas Gray. The *pastoral ode*, like the pastoral elegy, is a combination of the two forms, except that the ode is more specifically commemorative and may be set in one of the ode forms.

BURLESQUE is found under *satirical poetry*.

BURNS STANZA is discussed under *rime couée, standard habbie*, and *tail-rhyme stanza*.

BYR A THODDAID (bir a thód-deyed) is one of the 24 official Welsh "meters." It is a *quatrain stanza* that combines a *couplet* made of two octosyllabic lines rhyming *aa* with a *couplet* (called *toddaid byr*) made of one decasyllabic line and a hexasyllabic line. In the decasyllabic line the *main rhyme* is found before the end of the line, and the syllables that follow the main rhyme in this line must be linked by means of alliteration, assonance, or *secondary rhyme* with the early syllables of the first part of the hexasyllabic line. In this quatrain, either couplet can follow the other. Note that in this scheme, primary or main rhymes are in capital letters; alliteration, assonances, or secondary rhymes are indicated by means of small letters:

lines   syllables and rhymes

1.   x x x x x x x x A
2.   x x x x x x x x A
3.   x x x x x x x B x c
4.   *x c x* x x B

5.   x x x x x x x D x e
6.   *e x x* x x D
7.   x x x x x x x F
8.   x x x x x x x F

The CACCIA is discussed under *balada*.

A description of the CALLIGRAMME is found in the section on The Typographical Level and on Spatial Prosody.

The CANCIONE is a lyric laid out in any nonce stanzaic form, the lines of which are written in heptasyllabic (seven-syllable) or hendecasyllabic (eleven-syllable) lines. Like the *canso* (*canzo*, *canzone*), it is usually a song about beauty and love.

CANSO—see *cancione*.

The CANTICLE is found with the *liturgical* forms.

CANTO—a section of a longer poem, as for instance *The Cantos* of Ezra Pound. See *canzone*.

CANZO—see *canso* and *cancione*.

The CANZONE is an Italian form structured, like the *Pindaric ode*, in three *strophes* or *movements*. Each strophe is divided into three parts. The first two stanzas (*piedi*, "feet"; singular, *piede*, "foot") are structurally alike in each strophe; the third stanza in each strophe (the *sirima* or *cauda*) is structurally different from the piedi, but the structures of piedi and sirima are *nonce forms*: the poet's invention. The poem often closes with an *envoy*, a *commiato* or *valediction*:

Canzone

> "Whatever you set your mind to, your personal total obsession, this is what kills you. Poetry kills you if you're a poet, and so on. People choose their death whether they know it or not."   —DON DELILLO in *Libra*, p. 46.

Canto Uno. Obsessive Ottavi

It's said we choose the thing that will destroy us:
The plumber picks the scalding pipe that bursts.
We seize upon the obsession to employ us
All our days—the butcher among his wursts
Will gasp his last on the sausage he embraces,
The cobbler strangle in his own shoelaces.
The tease will die in a way that will annoy us,
The sweetie-pie in a manner sure to cloy us.

The fiddler will pass away in some vile inn
Between gigs on the road. The hypnotist

Will suffer stroke and spend a little while in
Staring into nothingness; the dentist
Will feel the drill slicing through his sinus,
The banker's columns add at last to minus.
The model shall come to end her days in style, in
Styli the engraver; the clerk shall file in.

Who makes these rules? One wishes it were so,
But only poets smother in their words
That spill like cottage cheese out of their vents
In swollen streams throughout their lives. Although
The words are for the world, the world says, "Hence!
Take back this whey, take back these pallid curds."
And so we eat our words all our lives long,
Stifling finally in a mound of song.

Canto Due. Terminal Capitolo

Why is it when we've worked our will and won,
Some goomba comes along and trips us up?
Just when we're on our toes he knocks us down.
The ewe's in place, and now here comes the tup—
The ram is blind! He misses by a mile!
Basta! It does no good to mope and gripe—

We ought to groan and berate with a snile;
We ought simply to turn the other cheek,
But when we do we're met with another snarl
And batted from today into next . . . month.
That's to the good! for there we'll find the sun
Filling the halcyon sky with light and warmth.

Basta! again—smoke rises between our toes!
Just when the eyes have it, so does the nose.

Canto Tre. Aria Gone Awry

Everything is gall and bile at last,
A dagger in the liver or the spleen,

A splash of acid from the acrid past,
A dash of bitters in life's chipped tureen.
No matter what we do it comes out wrong,
Our voices crack in the middle of the . . . aria.

The world is a martini mixed, not stirred,
Its twist of lemon sere as August's rind.
Search as one may to find the proper word,
A synonym will have to do: "behind"
Becomes arrears and smells a little strong,
And that's the short of it, the short and . . . interminable.

So, what to do? Drink up the curdled broth;
Quaff the quotidian cocktail at the sink;
Choke down the peel that tastes like pickled moth;
You'll never swallow finer food or drink—
For future food becomes what you have passed,
And everything is gall and bile . . . in the final analysis.

Commiato. Elegiac Barzeletta

No one can tell which way the wind is blowing
Unless it's snowing; then the eyes can wrinkle
And an inkling—just a hint—of the future
Lash its way beneath your eyelid. Your cornea
Will be abraded. You will be all but blinded.
You'll long for California, or perhaps you'll
Wish that you'd been born dead. You take my meaning?

The weather of the world's demeaning, *non e
Vero*? The temperature is zero even
On a summer evening: Here comes the sunset;
The azure of the heavens slowly deepens
To violet. The sun on the horizon
Cloaks itself in velvet mists. It is lovely . . . ,

Until the hailstones fall upon our foreheads
As we look up. The wind comes whistling meanly
Among the fuschias, knocking down the bluebirds'

Happy house. Outstanding among the headstones
We find our fortune: "He who lies here sleeping
Cares not for hail or gallstones, earth or ether,
Nor for songs of the plaining poet's making,
But for dreams that rise from a gravel pillow."

CAPITOLO is satirical *terza rima*. See the first two stanzas of "Canto Due" of the "Canzone" just shown.

The CAROL (CAROLE) is a joyous hymn of no particular pattern lately, but it originally had a more-or-less set form that consisted of a two-line *burden* or *texte couplet* that rhymed A^1A^2 (the *superscripts* indicate the fact that these are different refrains that rhyme with one another—see Notation at the end of the Form-Finder Index), and any number of quatrain stanzas rhyming *bbba* (or *c* or A^1 or A^2), *ccca* (or *d* or A^1 or A^2), etc. The last lines of these stanzas rhyme with the burden, or they echo or repeat one or the other of the burden lines. Usually the meter is short, trimeter/tripodic or tetrameter/tetrapodic, with no set verse foot, though whatever meter is chosen (if it is written in accentual-syllabic prosody) would be a *running meter*—that is, the lines would all be of the same length. The Christmas carol in France is called the *noël*. This poem, from the anonymous middle English, has been regularized to fit the original form:

The Shepherds' Carol
Terly terlow, terly terlow,
Merry the shepherds began to blow!

About the field they piped full right,
Round about the dark midnight,
When down from Heaven there came a light,
Terly terlow, terly terlow!

Of angels there came a company
With merry songs and melody;
The shepherds anon did them espy—
Merry the shepherds began to blow!

"Gloria in Excelsis!" the angels sung
And said that peace was come among
Everyman that to the faith clung,
Terly terlow, terly terlow!

The shepherds betook them to Bethlehem
To see that blessed sun abeam,
And there they found that glorious stream—
Merry the shepherds began to blow!

Now do we pray to that meek child
And to his mother that is so mild,
Never sullied, undefiled—
Terly terlow, terly terlow!

Terly terlow, terly terlow!
Merry the shepherds began to blow!
                    —Anonymous Middle English

For other forms that gloss the poem's initial phrase, see the *rondeau* and the *roundel*. For another example of the carol, see "The Magi Carol" in the section on the *bob and wheel*.

The Irish form CASBAIRDNE (coss-búyer-dne) is a bardic form that requires internal rhyming and thick texture. It is a quatrain stanza of heptasyllabic lines with trisyllabic endings. Lines two and four rhyme, and lines one and three consonate with them. There ought to be at least two *cross-rhymes* in each couplet. In the first couplet these need not be *true rhymes*. Two words alliterate in each line, the final word of line four alliterating with the preceding stressed word—here is a simplified scheme (note the consonances rather than rhymes):

lines   syllables and rhymes

1.   x *x b x* (x x ac)
2.   x *a x x* (x x bc)
3.   x *x x b* (x x dc)
4.   x *x c x* (x x bc)

The poem that follows is modified casbairdne—the trisyllabic line endings have not been adhered to. Alexander (see Bibliography) notes that this anonymous Old English poem is unique in its internal rhyming, concreteness of vocabulary, and use of unusual words. It appears here, then, not in Anglo-Saxon prosody, as in the original, but in a modern English version cast into a bardic form that requires internal rhyming and thick texture—the Irish form casbairdne.

Since this version is composed in quatrains and the original was composed in stichs, what appears here in each stanza is what appeared in the corresponding four lines of the original, but the translation is not line-by-line. Furthermore, because the original is a fragment in its last six lines (and elsewhere), this version is a more compact forty lines as compared with fifty. The last two lines of the original were not used because they trail off into nothingness; instead, the last quatrain is here rounded off and made into a definite ending. It has been suggested that this is an *elegy* written on the Roman ruins of the city of Bath by a wandering bard who stumbled across them and imagined that they had been built by mythical beings.

The Ruin

Well wrought, this wall that fate felled.
The fort failed, smoke cast its pall,
Snapped tall roofs: towers fallen
On the trollmen's stone-hard hall.

Rime scoiled gatekeeps; the mortar
Shattered, slate shower-shields moulder.
Age ate them, wright and wielder;
Earth-grip clasps builder, elder

And son, in grave-grasp lichen.
Kings fell often under stone
And storm, first slain by weapon:
Arch crashed, stricken, on bare bone.

To soil-crust sank works of skill:
A mood-quick mind bound the wall
All in iron—what wit and will!
Cunning wonders, well-fixed, fall.

Among these hearths ran hot springs;
In horn-gabled wings ran throngs;
Men filled meadhalls, long buildings.
Weird made silence of strong song.

There came days of death and pest;
The folk were lost, their flower snatched.
Where they fought, vetch carpets waste,
Ruins where they faced the Fetch.   [doppelgänger]

Henchmen who would build are cinched
In loam-clench under this arch
Breached and broken, wried and wrenched
Groundward from the roof-ridge reach.

There once many a mood-glad wight,
Garnished gold-bright, in wine-pride,
Gazed wide on gems, silver wrought
And fought for from tide to tide;

On wealth held, bared in a hoard
Where hoar now holds the brave, broad
Burg, here where the goodman stood
In amber hearing loud laud.

Homes were sealed, the ring-tank walled
Till time failed it, with it melled,
Stopped streams where they snelled and coiled,
Boiled to the baths that Fate felled.
                    —Anonymous Anglo-Saxon

The CATALOG POEM is outlined in the section on *constructional schemes* in The Sonic Level in chapter 1. See also the *prose poem* and the *antithetical parallel*, the *climactic parallel*, the *synonymous parallel*, and the *synthetic parallel*. For examples, see "The Mystery" by Amergin under *chant*, and "Cool Tombs" by Carl Sandburg under *polyphonic prose*.

For the CATCH see *balada*, *caccia* (under *balada*), and *roundelay*.

Types of CAUDA (*coda*, *tail*) are the *bob and wheel*, *caudate sonnet*, *coda*, and *envoy* (*envoi*). Also see the *canzone*.

The CAUDATE SONNET is not a "sonnet"; rather, it adds a pair of iambic trimeter tails and two *heroic couplets* to the *Italian sonnet*, and it rhymes *abbaabba cdecde e³fff³gg*; it is thus twenty lines long.

CAUTIONARY VERSE, a form of *didactic poetry*, is verse that warns. This anonymous Middle English *epigram* is clearly a dramatic poem in which the speaker addressing the reader is the *memento mori*, the skull that sat on the table of the medieval monk to remind him of the transience of the flesh. The version here follows the form of the original.

Memento Mori

You wretched ghost, with clay bedight,
Think on me here in this plight!
I was a man, with a man's fear—
You shall be such as I am here.

—Anonymous

The CENTO is a *pastiche* poem made up of lines from the work of an author. An example is "The Harper of Stillness," shown earlier, made from lines in Emily Dickinson's letters. In this case, the prose lines were cast into *quantitative syllabic prosody*.

There are various forms of CHAIN VERSE; see *chain rhyme*, *interlocking rubaiyat*, *pantoum*, *roundelay*, and *terza rima*.

The CHANSO is a syllabic French form written in five or six identically structured *nonce stanzas* and an *envoy* that mirrors the last half of the stanza pattern. No rhyme scheme or meter is prescribed, but it must be *homostrophic*, with the stanzas being identically rhymed and all lines of equal length.

The CHANSON is simply a song. For a discussion of the CHANSON DE GESTE, see the section on Narrative Poetry.

The CHANT is a repetitive liturgical song (see the section on *liturgical poetry*; see also the *chant royal*) intoned on one note. "The Mystery" is attributed to Amergin (ca. sixth century), reputedly the eldest Irish poet, if one excludes St. Patrick, who has been credited with poems as well as other sorts of writings. In *An Introduction to Irish Poetry*, Hoagland (see Bibliography) says, "The earliest form [of Irish-Gaelic poetry] was rhymeless, based upon alliteration." This modern version, therefore, has been cast in the form of *Anglo-Saxon prosody*.

"The Mystery" also exhibits parallel construction, for each line is an independent clause beginning with either "I am the" or "Who." *Grammatical parallelism*, whether used in verse or in prose composition, is the oldest prosody in the world, antedating accentual verse by many centuries, but used as often today as in ancient Chaldea.

The Mystery
I am the breeze breathed at sea,
I am the wave woven of ocean,
I am the soft sound of spume,
I am the bull of the seven battles,
I am the cormorant upon the cliff,
I am the spear of the sun striking,
I am the rose of the fairest rose.
I am the wild bull of war,
I am the salmon stroking the flood,
I am the mere upon the moor,
I am the rune of rare lore,
I am the tooth of the long lance,
I am He who fired the head.
Who emblazons the mountain-meeting?
Who heralds the moon's marches?
Who leads the sun to its lair?
I am the Word, I am the Eye.

—Amergin

The CHANTE-FABLE will be found in the section on Narrative Poetry.

A CHANTEY (SHANTY) is a nautical work song; for an example, see "Pirate Song," given in the listing for *children's poetry*.

The French CHANT ROYAL is a *grande ballade*. It has three eleven-line stanzas rhyming *ababccddedE* and a concluding *envoi* rhyming *ddedE*. The rhymes do not change, although the rhyme words must, and every line is the same length, usually tetrameter or pentameter.

Chant Royal for the Old Professor

"Put not a naked sword in a mad man's hand."

The day dawned when his scholar's armament
    Grew thin as rust. A crust of lacy mold
Lay thick upon his lectures in the tent,
    Weathered by lost crusades, that let the cold
Sigh in through rents and fissures. Now the mailed
Fist loosened, lost its grip. His standard swaled
    And fell in tatters to lie upon the green,
Abandoned sward that had been his demesne—
    The Groves of Academe. He would avoid
This final joust if some way might be seen;
    Alas! The old professor is destroyed.

He saw the horseman pale upon a bent
    And bony courser—as had been foretold
In many an ancient tome and document—
    Hover into view: Death held a rolled
Parchment summons. As he rode he flailed
The air with a crescent edge—the blade was tailed
    With a long, thin snath curved and serpentine.
The wind began to rise, to sough and keen.
    Steel must meet steel in combat unalloyed
By mettle that is base or in-between—
    Alas! The old professor is destroyed.

The spectres of the hosts that he had sent
    Into the world, girded with lore and bold
With youth, began to gather, each intent

Upon this field of combat, for he had doled
His learning out among them but regaled
None with tales of wisdom. Nor had he railed
    In passion at their phlegm, their lack of spleen,
    For he had aimed his point against their mean.
        His tun of ordinary mead had cloyed
    With age, become the Ambrosia-That-Might-Have-Been.
        Alas! The old professor is destroyed.

Now his lance is lowered; his sands are spent,
    Gone siling down the glass. His quivering hold
Upon the haft is weak. His lungs give vent
    To one last battlecry. He has cajoled
His steed of hours into a trot, assailed
The Knight of Darkness—at least he has not quailed
    Before his sure defeat: it is a clean
    Break with the flesh, this ultimate careen
        Against the foe that he could not avoid.
    He lifts his buckler and begins to lean—
        Alas! The old professor is destroyed.

Let us abandon tropes, say what is meant
    In clear, spare language so that we may hold
The old professor to the light. He went
    The way that all flesh goes; first, he told
Himself that he would seek the Grail. He failed.
He found preferments, tenure, and he nailed
    His sheepskin to the wall, then mailed a lean
    Listing of his honors to the Dean
        Who filed it in a folder labeled Void.
    That's all there was. He faded from the scene.
        At last the old professor is destroyed.

Envoi:

Here lies a man benighted. What may we glean
From his demise and tale? Alack! I ween
    There is but little here to be enjoyed—
We join the host of phantoms who convene
    To see the old professor is destroyed.

The CHARM will be found in the section on *liturgics*; see also the *anagram*. For an example, see "Charm for a Thorn-Prick" under *end-rhyme* in the section on Chime in chapter 1.

CHAUCERIAN STANZA is another name for *rime royal*.

CHILDREN'S POETRY is often *nonsense verse* or *nursery rhymes*—see both, plus *amphigory*. This poem will illustrate both an example of this genre and the *chantey*:

Pirate Song

By jingo, by Joe, by gee,
I think I'll go to sea.
    I'll set my sail
    Abaft of the rail,
A binnacle on my knee, by gee,
A binnacle on my knee.

By jingo, my gee, by Joe,
I think I'll go below.
    I'll stow my gold
    Down deep in the hold
Because of the winds that blow, by Joe,
Because of the winds that blow.
                            —Wesli Court

The Japanese CHOKA is a poem written in alternating 5-7-syllable lines. The conclusion of the choka would be, often, an *envoy* that doubled the last seven-syllable line, 5-7-7, or that consisted of two *choka couplets* with a doubled last line: 5-7-5-7-7—the *tanka*.

For a discussion of the CHORAL ODE, see the section on *tragedy* in The Genres of Drama in the companion volume of this text, *The Book of Literary Terms*. See also the *ode* under *occasional poetry*.

CHORIAMBICS is an unrhymed Greek *line* form consisting of two trochees, an iamb, a trochee, an iamb, a trochee, and two iambs, in that order: ´˘|´˘|˘´|´˘|˘´|´˘|˘´|˘´; there may be any number of such lines in a choriambic poem:

Falling **down** the re**paired lad**der, he **called loud**ly for **help** and **aid**.

A choriambus is a Greek four-syllable metrical foot that in English prosody would be a trochee and an iamb: ⁄ ⌣ ⌣ ⁄.

CHORIC SONG is any song sung by a chorus in a Greek play— see the *dithyramb* and the *choral ode* and *choriambics*. For a discussion of Greek drama, see companion volume, *The Book of Literary Terms*.

• The CINQUAIN is a twentieth-century American syllabic form invented by Adelaide Crapsey. Originally accentual-syllabic, her *quintet* form consisted, in the first line, of one iamb; in the second, of two iambs; in the third, of three; in the fourth, of four, and in the fifth, of one iamb again. It soon evolved into a syllabic form, somewhat analogous to the Japanese *tanka*, having line counts of 2-4-6-8-2 syllables, respectively.

This anonymous poem was originally written in Gaelic, but the form into which it is cast here is an anomaly and an anachronism. With next to no tampering, the poem fell into the form of the cinquain. One of the ancient Irish bardic devices we would today call the circle-back: a poem ended with the same word with which it began. This version keeps that requirement since it ends with the word "Devil," which contains the word "evil":

Evil It Is
Evil
It is to shun
The King of Righteousness
And to make a compact with the
Devil.
                         —Anonymous

The CLASSICAL HEXAMETER is discussed under *elegiacs*.
The CLASSICAL PENTAMETER is also found under *elegiacs*.
The CLERIHEW is described in the section on *satirical poetry*.
The CLIMACTIC PARALLEL, a line form, is found under the heading of Prose Prosodies in the section on The Sonic Level in chapter 1.

CLOGYRNACH (clog-ír-nach) is one of the twenty-four official Welsh "meters." It is a quantitative syllabic sestet stanza having line counts of 8-8-5-5-3-3 syllables, respectively. The two three-syllable lines may, if desired, be written as one six-syllable line. The stanza rhymes *aabbba*:

lines   syllables and rhymes

1.   x x x x x x x a
2.   x x x x x x x a
3.   x x x x b
4.   x x x x b
5.   x x b
6.   x x a

In Summer

Summer I love, stallions abroad,
Knights courageous before their lord;
The comber booming,
Apple tree blooming,
Shield shining, war-shouldered.

Longing, I went craving, alack—
The bowing of the slim hemlock,
In bright noon, dawn's sleight;
Fair frail form smooth, white,
Her step light on the stalk.

Silent is the small deer's footfall,
Scarcely older than she is tall.
Comely, beautiful
And bred bountiful,
Passion will heed her call,

But no vile word will pass her lips.
I pace, I plead—when shall we tryst?
When will you meet me?
Love drowns me deeply—
Christ keep me! He knows best.
                —Cynddelw Brydedd Mawr

The COBLA is merely the French term for a poem consisting of one stanza; see the *monostrophe*.

CODA—see *cauda*.

For a discussion of the COMMIATO and an example, see the *canzone*.

COMMON MEASURE, mentioned earlier under Podics in The Sonic Level, chapter 1, is an accentual-syllabic iambic quatrain rhyming $a^4b^3c^4b^3$. *Hymnal stanza* is nearly the same, but it rhymes *abab*. Other members of the common measure family are *short measure*, $a^3b^3c^4b^3$, and *short hymnal stanza*, $a^3b^3a^4b^3$:

The Elixir

　　Teach me, my God and King,
　　In all things thee to see,
And what I do in any thing,
　　To do it as for thee:

　　Not rudely, as a beast,
　　To run into an action;
But still to make thee prepossessed
　　And give it his perfection.

　　A man that looks on glass,
　　On it may stay his eye;
Or if he pleaseth, through it pass
　　And then the heaven espy.

　　All may of thee partake:
　　Nothing can be so mean,
Which with his tincture (for thy sake)
　　Will not grow bright and clean.

　　A servant with this clause
　　Makes drudgery divine:
Who sweeps a room, as for thy laws,
　　Makes that and the action fine.

This is the famous stone
That turneth all to gold:
For that which God doth touch and own
Cannot for less be sold.
                    —George Herbert

The lines of *long measure* rhyme *abcb*, whereas *long hymnal stanza* (both are quatrains) has iambic tetrameter lines that rhyme *abab*. This illustrative poem is a dramatic tour-de-force, inasmuch as it is told from the viewpoint of a hunted, in fact of a dead, animal:

The Mourning of the Hare

By a forest I began to fare,
Walking by myself alone,
When I heard the mourning of a hare—
Ruefully she made her moan:

"Dear worthy God, how shall I be living
And lead my life upon the land?
From dale to down am I driven;
Nowhere may I sit or stand!

"I may neither rest nor sleep
By any wallway ever so tall,
Nor no covert may me keep,
But ever I run from hole to hole.

"Hunters will not be remiss
In hope of hunting for to wend.
They leash their hounds more or less
And bring them to the far field's end;

"Anon, as they come up behind,
I look and sit full still and low;
That man who is the first to find
Me cries aloud, 'Ho! Tally-ho!'

"All winter in the deepest snow
Men seek about to find my trace,
And by my footprints I am known—
They follow me from place to place,

"And if I sit and crop the kale
Whenas the wife be in the way,
Shortly she swears, 'By the cock's soul,
There is a hare within my hay!'

"Ere ever I may start to flee,
The greyhounds run me to the grave;
My bowels they be thrown away,
And I am borne home on a stave."
                                    —Anonymous

All of these common measure forms may be doubled to make, respectively, *common octave, hymnal octave, short octave, short hymnal octave, long octave,* and *long hymnal octave,* an example of which is "Robin and Makyn" among the Dramatic Poetry. See also *short particular measure.*

The COMPANION POEM is one that, though it can stand alone, is paired with another poem, the two amplifying and complementing one another. Milton's "l'Allegro" and "il Penseroso" are companion poems. A *sequence* is a *cycle* of poems on a single topic, such as W. D. Snodgrass' "Heart's Needle" about his divorce. For set forms of the sequence, see the *crown of sonnets,* the *renga chain,* and the *sonnet redoubled.*

The COMPLAINT is a song of *lamentation,* a *jeremiad* (see the companion volume, *The Book of Literary Terms*). This poem by the Scots poet William Dunbar has a Latin refrain in the third line of each quatrain, which has been rendered here into English in the first quatrain only, keeping the rest of the poem in its original form: quatrains made of two *short couplets,* written in either iambic or trochaic tetrameter measures, rhyming *aa* but making a quatrain stanza with a refrain: *aabB, ccbB, ddbB,* and so forth. Dunbar's title was originally "Lament for the Makers" (Scots makirs), meaning "poets."

Lament for the Poets

I who was in health and gladness
Am troubled now with great sickness,
Enfeebled with infirmity;
Fear of death disturbeth me.

Our pleasance here is all vainglory,
This false world is but transitory,
The flesh is fragile, the Fiend is sly;
Timor mortis conturbat me.

The state of man does change and vary
Now sound, now sick; now blithe, now sorry,
Now dancing merry, now like to die;
Timor mortis conturbat me.

No state on earth here stands staunch.
As with the wind waves the branch,
So waves this world's vanity;
Timor mortis conturbat me.

Unto Death go all estates,
Princes, prelates, and potentates,
Both rich and poor, of each degree;
Timor mortis conturbat me.

He takes the knight in the field
Armed under helm and shield—
He is victor of the melee;
Timor mortis conturbat me.

That merciless and tyrant king
Takes, on the mother's breast suckling,
The babe full of benignity;
Timor mortis conturbat me.

He takes the champion of power,
The captain sheltered in his tower,
The embowered lady in her beauty;
Timor mortis conturbat me.

He spares no lord for his puissance,
Nor clerk for his intelligence;
His awful stroke may no man flee;
Timor mortis conturbat me.

Neither astrologers nor magicians,
Clerics, scholars, or logicians
Find help in their conclusions sly;
Timor mortis conturbat me.

Those most learned in medicines—
Leeches, surgeons, and physicians—
May not cure their mortality;
Timor mortis conturbat me.

I see that poets sing their sheaf,
Play their pageant, then go to grief;
Death does not spare their faculty;
Timor mortis conturbat me.

He had to impetuously devour
The noble Chaucer, the poets' flower;
The Monk of Bery, and Gower, all three;
Timor mortis conturbat me.

The good Sir Hugh of Eglinton
And also Heriot and Winton
He has torn from this country;
Timor mortis conturbat me.

That evil scorpion has brought to wreck
Master John Clarke and James Affleck
From ballad-making and tragedy;
Timor mortis conturbat me.

Holland and Barbour he has bereft;
Alas! that he could not have left
Sir Mungo Lockert of the Lee;
Timor mortis conturbat me.

Clark of Tranent, too, he's slain,
Who wrote The Adventures of Gawain;
Sir Gilbert Hay—ended has he;
Timor mortis conturbat me.

He has Blind Harry and Sandy Traill
Slain with his shower of mortal hail,
Which Patrick Johnston could not flee;
Timor mortis conturbat me.

He's taken Ralph of Aberdeen
And gentle Ralph of Corstophin—
Two better fellows may no man see;
Timor mortis conturbat me.

Now in Dumferlintown he's done
With Master Robert Henryson;
Sir John of Ross has bent his knee;
Timor mortis conturbat me.

And he has taken in his maw
Good, gentle Strobo and Quentin Shaw
On whom all creatures have pity;
Timor mortis conturbat me.

Good Master Walter Kennedy
In point of deed lies verily—
It were great ruth that such should be;
Timor mortis conturbat me.

Since all my brothers thus are gone,
He will not let me live alone;
I may perforce his next prey be;
Timor mortis conturbat me.

Since for the dead there is no cure,
We'd best prepare for what is sure
that we may live eternally;
Timor mortis conturbat me.
                    —William Dunbar

The COMPOUND ACROSTIC is discussed under *acrostic*.

CONSTRUCTIONAL SCHEMES—see the section on Prose Poetry under The Sonic Level.

The CORONACH is a *dirge*, discussed under *occasionals*.

There are many COUPLET forms, in particular the *heroic couplet*, which has its own description later. A couplet is any *distich* used as a unit, whether rhymed or unrhymed. The *short couplet* is written in either iambic or trochaic tetrameter lines and rhymes *aa*. The *split couplet* has lines of unequal length, with the first being iambic pentameter, the second iambic dimeter:

Lafe Grat

from Bordello

In this house I am not ugly—nowhere
else. Nor is there
a mirror in the room we use, my bought
bride and I. What
images are reflected in her eyes
I recognize
as in a dream only, my face redrawn
by night. Reborn
each evening of this woman, spared my name,
the cruel fame
of the publicly disfigured, I roar
with my old whore
like a whole man, transfigured for a time.
Sordid? I am
Lafe Grat. I work hard to make a living.
There's no giving
to a man who makes you think of darkness,

for my likeness
is found buried in everyone, hidden
till, unbidden,
it rises to gorge the beast in the blood.
So, out of mud
I am formed and rise each morning to stalk
where others walk
in a world of surfaces—till night when,
like other men,
I may purchase with coin my manhood, life—
a moment's wife.

COUPLET ENVELOPE—see *stave*.

A CROWN OF SONNETS is a series of seven *Italian sonnets*. The last line of each of the first six sonnets becomes the first line in each of the ensuing sonnets; the last line of the seventh sonnet is the first line of the first sonnet. Since the seven sonnets are considered to be one poem, no rhyme word can be reused except in the formally repeated lines, and new rhymes when they appear cannot be those used elsewhere in the poem. For another *sonnet sequence* see the *sonnet redoubled*.

CURSE—a *malison*; see *liturgical poetry*. This is an anonymous Old English dramatic (it is Death who speaks) curse in Anglo-Saxon prosody, as in the original, with added echoics. The stichs are split at the caesurae into hemistichs.

The Curse of Death

An abode was built ye
                              Ere you were born;
For ye a mold minted
                              Ere your mother made ye.
Its height is not scaled
                              Nor depth delved,
It is never locked,
                              Be it ever so long,
Until I fetch ye
                              Where you be fettered—

Fettered and measured
                    For sod and mould.
Nor be your house
                    High-timbered, nay—
It be unhigh and low;
                    When you be therein
Heel-ways are low,
                    Side-ways unhigh.
The roof is raised
                    Full nigh your breast:
Thus you in fell mould
                    Shall dwell full cold,
In dim and dark,
                    Your weal turned doleful.
That door is doorless
                    And dark it is within—
There you be fastled,
                    And Death keeps the keys;
Loathly is that earth-house,
                    Grim to dwell in,
Yet there shall you dwell
                    And worms deal with ye,
Thus you be laid
                    And lorn of your friends,
For you have no friend
                    Who will fare with ye,
None who will look to
                    Your house-liking
Nor ever undo
                    The latch of that door
And ask after ye,
                    For soon you be loathly
And ugsome to see.

                                —Anonymous

Also see "Ancient Music" by Ezra Pound in the section on the
madsong and the anonymous "The Blacksmiths" (see *curses*).

The CURTAL SONNET, so called, is not a sonnet but an eleven-line form invented by Gerard Manley Hopkins. The first ten lines are written in iambic pentameter meters, but the eleventh line is spondaic monometer (one spondee). The whole poem rhymes *abcabcdbcdc*:

lines   meters and rhymes

<pre>
        ′ ′ ′ ′ ′
 1. xx xx xx xx xa
        ′ ′ ′ ′ ′
 2. xx xx xx xx xb
        ′ ′ ′ ′ ′
 3. xx xx xx xx xc
        ′ ′ ′ ′ ′
 4. xx xx xx xx xa
        ′ ′ ′ ′ ′
 5. xx xx xx xx xb
        ′ ′ ′ ′ ′
 6. xx xx xx xx xc
        ′ ′ ′ ′ ′
 7. xx xx xx xx xd
        ′ ′ ′ ′ ′
 8. xx xx xx xx xb
        ′ ′ ′ ′ ′
 9. xx xx xx xx xc
        ′ ′ ′ ′ ′
10. xx xx xx xx xd
        ′
11. xc
</pre>

The CYCLE or *sequence* is a series of related poems—see *companion poem*.

CYHYDEDD FER (cuh-hée-dedd ver), one of the Welsh forms, is an octosyllabic *couplet*, x x x x x x x a / x x x x x x x a. For an example, see the last two lines of "Huntsong for a Small Son" under *toddaid*.

CYHYDEDD HIR (cuh-hée-dedd heer) is also an official Welsh bardic meter, an *octave* stanza comprised of two *quatrains*. The first three lines of each quatrain are *pentasyllabic* and the last is *tetrasyllabic*: 5-5-5-4-5-5-5-4. Each quatrain may be arranged, if desired, as a single 19-syllable line. The five-syllable lines in each quatrain rhyme with each other; the four-syllable lines carry the *main rhyme*: aaaBcccB / dddBeeeB, and so on. Strictly speaking, the stanzas need not be octave stanzas. Any number of quatrains may be used in a stanza and, technically, the meter will remain cyhydedd hir. However, within any stanza the short lines must carry the same rhyme. The diagram of two stanzas is this:

lines	syllables and rhymes	lines	syllables and rhymes
1.	x x x x a	9.	x x x x d
2.	x x x x a	10.	x x x x d
3.	x x x x a	11.	x x x x d
4.	x x x B	12.	x x x E
5.	x x x x c	13.	x x x x f
6.	x x x x c	14.	x x x x f
7.	x x x x c	15.	x x x x f
8.	x x x B	16.	x x x E

CYHYDEDD NAW BAN (cuh-hée-dedd naw ban) is a Welsh non-asyllabic *line* that must rhyme with at least one other line to form, minimally, a couplet, but it can continue to rhyme throughout the stanza, which can be of any length, provided only that all lines are nine syllables long:

In Praise of Owain Gwynedd

I hail a boonsman hearty in war,
Battlewolf, boastful, first to the fore—
I sing of serving him with fervor,
Sing his mead-fed and worthy power,
Sing his ardor, this wind-winged falcon,
Sing his thoughts, lofty as the welkin,   [sky]
Sing his dauntless deeds, lord of frayhounds,   [dogs of war]
Sing his praises—they may know no bounds,
Sing odes for my magnanimous thane;   [lord]
I sing paeans of praise for Owain.

Armed for Angles in Tegeingl's realms,
Blood's spouting streams, our blades' spating storms,
We met dragons, the warriors of Rome,
A prince's son—costly their winestream.   [blood]
Striving with the Dragon of the East
The western Dragon showed which was best.
Lusty our lord, his bright blade unsheathed—
The sword poured forth, the spear was strife-bathed,
Blade in hand and all hands hewing heads,
Hand on hilt and edge on Norman hordes—

At the sight of death, constant wailing
And swashbuckling and loud reveling,
Blood flowing from brave men's riven skulls—
I heard flesh pledged to the birds' bowels
In the fierce thrust of the sharp ash-haft,
In the raven-beckoning blood-path.
On corpses to feed a thousand shrikes
Brynnich's riders rode, Owain's war kites.
Carcasses, carrion by the bushels,
The taste of battle, killed men's entrails!

For his prize we fought, and for his praise,
Hosts and bards, for Owain's bounteous ways,
To Cadell Hiriell Hiriein's scion   [heir]
For reward, guardian of Coel's line,
Battlefield's lance-thrust, praise-lavishing,
Shield-carrying, eagle onrushing
Court's stalwart, vigilant defender—
Beware his thrusting, three-colored spear!
They harvested Aberteifi's spears
With battlecries, as at Badon Fawr.
I saw war-stags, corpses stiff and red—
We let the fierce wolf put them to bed;
They ran without arms—some without hands,
Mighty warriors under talons;
I saw their rout—three hundred were slain;
I saw bowels on thorns, the war won.

I saw the strife, heard the battleshout,
Saw knights belaboring troops in flight.

I saw men falling from the chalk heights,
The foe slaughtered among their redoubts;
I saw pikes blooming about a wall
And lances rushing at Owain's call—
I saw the charge make Saxon carnage
And princes reaping the day's courage.
Prince of princes! His battle is won,
Bought dearly—he is pursued by none.
I saw at Rhuddlan a ruddy tide,
A hero's host heroic in pride—
I saw in Penfro a prince peerless;
I saw in Penardd a lord fearless;
I saw their slaughter of the doughty
Borne by a brave land, the fern's bounty.
I saw men thronging and scurrying,
Heard alarums, saw troops hurrying,
Saw them taken, saw comrades in pain,
Saw strife near Caer and Coen Llywyfain.
Gwynedd's valor was proven again—
You were dauntless, shepherd of Britain!
                    —Cynddelw Brydedd Mawr

CYRCH A CHWTA (kirch a chóo-tah) is a syllabic Welsh *octave* stanza made up of six heptasyllabic lines rhyming *a*, plus a final couplet rhyming *ba*, the penultimate *b* line rhyming into the center of the last line:

lines   syllables and rhymes

1.   x x x x x x a
2.   x x x x x x a
3.   x x x x x x a
4.   x x x x x x a
5.   x x x x x x a
6.   x x x x x x a
7.   x x x x x x b
8.   x x *x* b x x a

Aberdovey Music

The bells of Aberdovey
Sound from a buried city
Sunken far under the sea,
Heard when the nights are stormy
And carried inland, faintly,
As far as Montgomery.
Hearken! Music of the lost
Haunts that coast, all shadowy.

And there could be voices there,
Leagues and fathoms down, a choir
Whose intoning reaches far
Out along that lonely shore
Up to ghostly cloud and air,
Cadences profound and pure,
Solemn choral, when the bell
Has tolled the knell of the hour.

As winds on earth go over,
Aeolian-wise, to stir
Response of harp or zither,
So, under ocean-water,
Currents deeper and stronger
Sweep strings of salt and silver
In their ultramarine room,
Break off, resume, and linger.
                    —Rolfe Humphries

The Welsh CYWYDD DEUAIR FYRION (ców-idd dye-ire vúhr-yon) is an octosyllabic rhymed or consonated *couplet* form. This example is a twelfth-century lyric cast into modern English:

My Choice

I choose a fair
Maid so slender,
Tall and silver,
Her gown of heather

Hue—I choose her,
Nature's daughter,
For the kind word
Dropped, scarcely heard,
And for my part
Take her to heart
For gift, for grace,
For her embrace.

I choose the wave,
The water's shade;
Witch of the shire,
Your Welsh tongue pure,
My choice you are,
And am I yours?
Why be silent
(Sweet your silence)?

I choose my course
Without remorse,
With a clear voice—
So clear a choice.
   —Hywel ab Owain Gwynedd

CYWYDD DEUAIR HYRION (ców-idd dyé-ire héer-yon) is a
Welsh light-rhyming seven-syllable couplet—that is, the first line
is "rising," ending on a stressed syllable, and the second is "falling," ending on an unstressed syllable. The lines rhyme aa. For an
example, see "Love in Exile" by Dafydd ap Gwilym, in the section on Chime in The Sonic Level.

CYWYDD LLOSGYRNOG (ców-idd llos-gr-nog) is a Welsh *sestet*
stanza whose respective lines have syllable counts of 8-8-7-8-8-7.
Lines one and two rhyme and cross-rhyme with the middle syllable of line three; lines four and five rhyme and cross-rhyme with
the middle syllable of line six; lines three and six rhyme with each
other. For an example, see the second version of "The Rule of
Three" under the *triad*, below.

DEACHNADH MOR is discussed under *rannaigheacht*.

The DÉBAT (*debate*) is found under the heading of *forensics*.

A DECASTICH is any whole poem of ten lines.

DEIBHIDHE (jay-vee), an Irish Celtic form, is a *quatrain* stanza light-rhyming in couplets. There is alliteration between two words in each line, the final word of line four alliterating with the preceding stressed word. There are at least two cross-rhymes between lines three and four, and every line is heptasyllabic:

lines   syllables, rhymes, stressed endings

1.   x x x x x x á

2.   x x x x x x á

3.   x b x x x x b́

4.   x x x b x x b́

The Death of Conain
The shining tides rise and swell,
Swing him in his coracle,   [small boat]
Break across the sandy strand:
Conain looks at the riband,

Then she whose white hair he grips—
Hair of spindrift, frigid lips—
Fleers and turns her phlegm to foam
On the tomb that was his home.
                    —Anonymous

The French DESCORT has only one requirement: Each line must be different from every other line in the poem in every way (discordant). It is a *nonce form* that mixes rimes, meters, line and stanza lengths, and itself may be of any length at all.

DIDACTIC POETRY is poetry that teaches, and some of these forms, such as the *bestiary*, the *epistle*, the *primer*, and the *riddle,* are discussed elsewhere in these pages. Another didactic form is *georgics*, a versified *handbook* in the trades, crafts, arts, or sciences. There are *verse essays*, as well, such as were written by Alexander Pope. For a fixed form, see the *rubliw*.

DIMINISHING VERSE is any metrical poem written in such a manner as to drop the last few words or syllables progressively from the ends of the lines so as to form new words or meanings. See *echo verse* and George Herbert's "Paradise" in that discussion.

The DIRGE is a death march; see *coronach*, *elegy*, *monody*, and *threnody* all discussed under *occasionals*. This example following is rendered from Middle English, as distinguished from Old English. This version strictly follows the form of the original. The prosody used, as in the original, is the accentual prosody called *podics*, or "*folk meters*," in which most nursery rhymes, madsongs, and Scots-English border ballads are written.

A Lie-Awake Dirge

This very night, this very night,
    Every night and all,
Fire and sleet and candle-light,
    And Christ receive your soul.

When you are passed away from here,
    Every night and all,
To Thorny Moor you come at last,
    And Christ receive your soul.

If ever you gave hose and shoes,
    Every night and all,
Sit ye down, put them to use,
    And Christ receive your soul.

If hose and shoes you gave to none,
    Every night and all,
The thorns shall prick you to the bare bone,
    And Christ receive your soul.

When from the Bridge of Dread you pass,
    Every night and all,
To Purgatory's fire you come at last,
    And Christ receive your soul.

If ever you gave meat or drink,
    Every night and all,
The fire shall never make you shrink,
    And Christ receive your soul.

If meat or drink you gave to none,
    Every night and all,
The fire will burn you to the bare bone,
    And Christ receive your soul.

This very night, this very night,
    Every night and all,
Fire and sleet and candle-light,
    And Christ receive your soul.

                —Anonymous

DIRUM, *dirae* (plural) are songs of *imprecation* delivered against enemies, *maledicta*, lyric curses.

For DISTICH, see *couplet* and *twime*.

A DIT is an *exemplum* (*example*). For a discussion of the exemplum, see the companion volume, *The Book of Literary Terms*.

The DITHYRAMB, a frenzied *choric song* (performed by a chorus) in honor of revelry and wine, honors the god Dionysus. Versions of this late middle English dithyramb have been ascribed to John Skelton (1450–1529) and to William Cornyshe, Jr., who scored it as a part-song. This piece is a blending of the versions. One or two liberties have been taken in the collation:

Jolly Rutterkin

Rutterkin has come to town—
    Hey! jolly Rutter, hey!
Without a cloak nor coat nor gown,

But a good green hood upon his crown
        Like a hoyden rutter!

Rutterkin has no English—
        Hey! jolly Rutter, hey!
His tongue runs on like butterfish
Smeared with grease upon his dish
        Like a hoyden rutter!

Kiss Rutterkin and change your luck—
        Hey! jolly Rutter, hey!
He takes his ale down at a suck
Till he be wiser than a duck
        Like a hoyden rutter!

When Rutterkin gets up from board—
        Hey! jolly Rutter, hey!
He'll piss a gallon in a gourd,
Then take the lasses like a lord,
        Like a hoyden rutter!
        —John Skelton/Wm. Cornyshe, Jr.

A DITTY is any simple song—see the *balada.*

The DIZAIN is explained under the *ballade.*

The DOUBLE ACROSTIC is found under the *acrostic.*

The DOUBLE BALLADE and the DOUBLE BALLADE SUPREME are found in the entry on the *ballade.*

The DOUBLE DACTYL is a light verse form championed by the American poet Anthony Hecht. It is a poem made up of two quatrains rhyming *abcd efgd*. Lines 1–3 of each stanza are dactylic dimeter lines (´ ˘ ˘ ´ ˘ ˘); the last line of each stanza is composed of an iamb and a trochee (´ ˘ ˘ ´). The first line of the first stanza is always "Higgledy-piggledy"; the second line is a name. The second line of the second stanza is a double dactyl modifier. Only the last lines of each stanza are required to rhyme, though there may be other rhymes of various kinds as well:

Emily

Higgledy-piggledy
Emily Dickinson
Lived in her bedroom and
Seldom came down

Into the parlor where
Hyperhermetical
Emily kept herself
Far from renown.

Hennery

Higgledy-piggledy
Hennery Longfellow
Wrote out his verses in
Meters and rhymes

One might describe as quite
Hiawathetical
If one were Minneha-
Ha-ing betimes.

          —Wesli Court

The DOUBLE REFRAIN BALLADE is found in the entry on the *ballade*.
DRAMATIC MONOLOGUE—see Dramatic Poetry.

The later bardic form called DROIGHNEACH (dráiy-nach) is a
loose Irish stanza form. The single line can consist of from nine to
thirteen syllables, and it always ends in a trisyllabic word, a requirement not always kept in this case. There is rhyming between
lines one and three, two and four, and so forth. There are at least
two *cross-rhymes* in each couplet, and *alliteration* in each line: Usually the final word of the line alliterates with the preceding *stressed
word*, and it always does so in the last line of each stanza. Stanzas
can consist of any number of quatrains.

lines   *syllables amd rhymes*

1.   x x b x x x x (x x a)
2.   x x x x a x x x (x x b)

3.   x x x x x b (x x a)
4.   x x x x a x x (x x b)

5.   x x x x x d x x (x x c)
6.   x x x c x x x x x x (x x d)
7.   x x d x x x x x x (x x c)
8.   x x x x c x (x x d)

This poem is reputedly by St. Patrick (c. 385–461), but the original of this version is probably from the seventh century.

A Blessing on Munster

God's blessing be invoked upon Munster now,
Upon its men and boys, its womenfolk;
Blessings be upon the land, peak and down,
That boons the flock fruit, root, stem and stalk.

A blessing upon all kinds of fruitfulness
That shall be borne upon this meadowland,
No neighbor going in want of helpfulness.
God place over Munster his healing hand!

A blessing be upon the high ridge,
Upon their cottages' bare flagstones;
A blessing upon heather, sedge, the sheer cliff edge;
A blessing upon lea and ledge, their gloaming glens!

Like sands of ocean under vessels
Be the numbers of their dwellings' hearthstones
Upon their downlands and their sloping hills,
Upon their crags and fells, their misty mountains!
                                        —Attr. St. Patrick

ECHO VERSE is any verse form written so that the last part of the line—a phrase, word, or syllable—forms a response to the line, such as, "Do you love me? Me! / Do you love me not? Not!" See the example given in the section on the *bref double*, "Bref Double à l'Écho." In that poem it is possible for the repeated words to be read as a separate poem that responds to the main poem as a whole, in addition to the individual lines.

Another type of echo verse is *diminishing verse,* in which a part of the repeated element is eliminated by *pruning* or *rabbeting* each time it reappears, as in this poem:

> *Paradise*
> I bless thee, lord, because I *grow*
> Among thy trees, which in a *row*
> To thee both fruit and order *owe.*
>
> What open force, or hidden *charm*
> Can blast my fruit, or bring me *harm,*
> While the inclosure is thine *arm*?
>
> Inclose me still for fear I *start.*
> Be to me rather sharp and *tart,*
> Than let me want thy hand and *art.*
>
> When thou dost greater judgements *spare,*
> And with thy knife but prune and *pare,*
> Even fruitful trees more fruitful *are.*
>
> Such sharpness shows the sweetest *friend,*
> Such cuttings rather heal than *rend*:
> And such beginnings touch their *end.*
> —George Herbert

An ECLOGUE is a short pastoral *monologue, dialogue,* or *soliloquy*; see Dramatic Poetry. For an example and discussion of the ECLOGUE DÉBAT, see Robert Henryson's "Robin and Makyn," in Dramatic Poetry. Also see *bucolics.*

There are three alliterative Norse EDDA MEASURES including OLD STORY MEASURE, which is a *quatrain* stanza. Each stich has four strong stresses, which, like *Anglo-Saxon prosody,* are divided by a medial *caesura* into two *hemistichs* containing two stresses each.

The third stressed syllable in each line alliterates with either or both of the first two stressed syllables, but the fourth syllable never does so; however, it may cross-alliterate with the following line. In each hemistich there are **two** or **three** unstressed syllables.

lines   stresses, alliterations, caesurae

```
        ′   ′      ′ ′
1.   b x b x • x b c x
       ′     ′     ′   ′
2.   d x x f • x d x g
        ′   ′   ′   ′
3.   x h x j • j x k x
        ′ ′     ′   ′
4.   x x k k • x k x l x
```

Speech measure is built in exactly the same way, except that in each hemistich there are **three** or **four** unstressed syllables.

lines   stresses, alliterations, caesurae

```
        ′     ′            ′ ′
1.   b x x c x • x c x x d x
         ′       ′      ′     ′
2.   x f x x g • x f x x h
       ′         ′      ′     ′
3.   h x x x m • x m x x h x
       ′     ′         ′     ′
4.   x m x m x • x m x x n x
```

The poem following is an abstract from *The Anglo-Saxon Chronicle* for the year 1083. In the *Chronicle* this story is a long prose entry. The poem tells the story of the "Normanizing" of one of the English monasteries after the English invasion of William the Conqueror in 1066. It has been cast here into Norse *song measure*: couplets consisting of one four-stress alliterative stich with a central caesura (dipods), as in Anglo-Saxon prosody, followed by a three-stress (tripodic) alliterative line:

lines   *stresses, alliterations, caesurae*

```
          ´        ´  ´       ´
1.   b  x  x  c • c  x  x  d  x
          ´        ´  ´
2.   x  f  x  x  f  g
          ´     ´    ´      ´
3.   x  h  x  j • h  x  k
          ´        ´   ´
4.   x  k  x  x  l  x  l
```

The Monks' Massacre

Those were dreary days and dire
  At the abbey of Glastonbury
When Thurstan came from Caen to become
  Abbot of the English monks.

But a little wit and less wisdom
  Had the Abbot Thurstan.
In many matters he misruled the monks—
  They suffered at first in stillness.

At last they complained in a kindly way,
  Asked him to rule them rightly;
They would be steadfast in all he asked
  If the abbot would but love them.

Thurstan would think no thoughts of the sort,
  But made them give up St. Gregory
And chant his French chansons instead—
  The foolish songs of Fécamp.

He treated them woefully, threatened worse
  Till one day he went into chapter
And spoke against them, swore to ill-treat them.
  He called for his layman knights

Who fell on the monks fully armed—
    The monks were stricken to stone,
Bewildered at first, fearful and helpless
    Before the furious onslaught.

At last they scattered—some of them fled
    From chapter into the church.
They heaved the doors hard-to behind them
    And shot the bolts in the locks.

The French knights followed the monks
    Into the monastery, meaning
To drag them forth, for they dared not go
    To face the abbot's henchmen.

But a heavy thing happened that day:
    The French forced the choir
And threw missiles at the monks below
    Gathered about the altar,

And some from above, in the upper storey,
    Shot arrows altarward
Where the wretched monks writhed
    Beneath the shaft-struck cross.

Some cried to God and crept beneath
    The altar, asking of Him
The mercy their fellow men denied them.
    Yet more fiercely the French

Shot their shafts and, shouting, broke
    Down the doors of the chapel,
Killed some monks and wounded more
    Till, spilling down

Out from under the altar of God,
    The blood of the brothers flowed
About the boots of the brave French
    And their thirsty abbot Thurstan.
            —Various Anonymous Authors

The ELEGIAC COUPLET (ELEGIAC DISTICH) is a Greek quantitative accentual-syllabic distich without rhyme. The first line is a *classical hexameter*: the *first four feet* are either spondees or dactyls, the fifth foot is a dactyl, and the sixth is a spondee. The second line of the couplet is a *classical pentameter* consisting, in this order, of two dactyls, a spondee, and two anapests. It can be rhymed or unrhymed. This is a possible scheme:

lines   meters

1.   ´ ´ ´ ´ ´ ´´
      xxx xxx xxx xxx xxx xx

2.   ´ ´ ´´ ´ ´
      xxx xxx xx xxx xxx

A Talisman

For Dave McLean, too late

Lead for this talisman. Pure, so that Saturn will live in it. Pure
                                                         lead.
  Both of its faces are rubbed smooth. On its front, in a star
pentagram, cut with a diamond burin a scythe so that Nabam,
  standing upon his demoniac pedestal Tau, shall be laid low—
old as he is—by Oriphiel, angel of Saturday. Jesus,
  nailed to a T, is the capstone of this coin made of lead,
though he will never appear in his person, but only as backdrop.
  Grave on the opposite face this, in a six-pointed star:
REMPHA, surrounding the head of a bull. Without witnesses carve
                                                         your
  talisman. Wear it in good health. It will keep you from death,
frighten the devil of cancer, leukemia—rot of the white bone.
  Marrow will redden. Wear this! It will save you and me.
Bear it—your talisman; wear it, my brother. Or carry this poem,
  Dies Saturni, to life's end. It is all I can do.

                                        —Wesli Court

For ELEGIACS see the ELEGIAC DISTICH, described earlier, and *elegy*, under *occasional poetry*.

ELEGY—see *occasional poetry*.

The ENCLOSED TERCET is described under *tercet*.

The ENCLOSED TRIPLET is described under *triplet*.

ENCOMIUM—see *occasional poetry*.

The ENGLISH ODE will be found with the *ode* under *occasional poetry*.

ENGLISH QUINTET—see the *quintet*.

The ENGLISH SONNET is described with the *sonnet*.

Among the eight Welsh bardic ENGLYN stanza forms, ENGLYN MILWR and ENGLYN PENFYR are listed with the entry on the *triplet*.

These lines following are from the anonymous Old English, lines 71 to 80 only, of the Anglo-Saxon *Gnomic Verses* cast here into the Welsh bardic form ENGLYN CYRCH (én-glin kirch), a quatrain stanza each line of which is heptasyllabic. Lines one, two, and four turn on a single rhyme; line three cross-rhymes into one of the three central syllables of line four. The lines selected here seemed to be all of a piece; succeeding lines went off in another direction entirely. Here is the schematic first:

lines   syllables and rhymes

1.   x x x x x x a
2.   x x x x x x a
3.   x x x x x x b
4.   x x x *x b x* a

Gnomic Verses

Frost shall freeze, fire will eat wood,
Ice will bridge and the earth brood.
Water shall wear winter's shield,
Yet the field will be renewed.

Frost's fetters shall free the grain,
Wonderlock will yield to rain,
And there shall be fair weather
When the winter goes to wane.

Sun-warmed summer! What was dumb
Shall find voice. The body, numb
When the deep wave was most dark,
Will feel when the lark has come.
—Anonymous Anglo-Saxon

Each line of ENGLYN LLEDDFBROEST (én-glin llédd-uhv-broyst) diphthong-rhymes with the others and has a count of seven syllables. In Welsh, the rhymes used were the for diphthongs *ae, oe, wy,* and *ei*. Since this structure is probably impossible to reproduce in English, any *similar diphthongs* can be substituted and can be considered to rhyme with one another. Here is a one-stanza diagram:

lines   *syllables and diphthong rhymes*
1.   x x x x x x oe
2.   x x x x x x wy
3.   x x x x x x ei
4.   x x x x x x ae

ENGLYN PROEST DALGRON (eń-glin proyst daĺ-gron) is a *quatrain* stanza of heptasyllabic lines, all of which consonate with one another on vowels or similar diphthongs. This lament is by the Welsh poet Dafydd Benfras (c. 1230–1260).

The Grave
Everyman comes to the dank earth.
Folk, forlorn and small, perish.
What wealth rears is wracked by death.
In an hour dirt devoureth.

Great maw, end of what I clutch,
What I loved you turn to filth.
Mine will be a chill stone hearth—
Life was not meant for a youth.

Each man's cold estate is death;
He walks alone on the heath

That will take him in its clinch,
Come at last to the cromlech.
                    —Dafydd Benfras

Each line of the quantitative syllabic, *quatrain* stanza ENGLYN
PROEST GADWYNOG (én-glin proyst ga-dóy-nog) is seven syllables
long. Lines one and three rhyme; lines two and four consonate
with lines one and three and with each other:

lines   syllables, consonances, and rhymes

  1.   x x x x x x r
  2.   x x x x x x or
  3.   x x x x x x r
  4.   x x x x x x or

ENGLYN UNODLE CRWCA has syllable counts of 7-7-10-6 syllables, in that order. Lines one, two, and four end with the *main
rhyme*, but in the third line the main rhyme is followed by one,
two, or three syllables that are echoed by assonance, alliteration, or
secondary rhyme in the first part of line four. In this rhyme
scheme the capital letters stand for the *main rhyme*, not a refrain.

lines   syllables, consonances, and rhymes

  1.   x x x x x x A
  2.   x x x x x x A
  3.   x x x x x x A x x b
  4.   *x b x* x x x A

ENGLYN UNODL UNION (én-glin éen-oddle éen-yon) simply
transposes the positions of the two couplets that comprise englyn
unodl crwca.

For discussions of the ENVELOPE, the ENVELOPE QUATRAIN, and
the ENVELOPE QUINTET, see the *quatrain* and *quintet*; for the ENVE-
LOPE SONNET, see the *sonnet*.

The ENVOI or ENVOY is discussed in various places throughout
the text; as the term suggests, the function of an envoy was tradi-

tionally to send the poem on its way to its destination, and not always to provide the *denouement* for what had been said in the body of the poem; for an example, see "Balada of Uncertain Age," under *balada*. Also see *cauda, coda, commiato, tail,* and *valediction*.

The EPICEDIUM is a *choric song*, an *elegy* for the dead delivered by a chorus—see the *obsequy*.

For the EPIGRAM see *satirical poetry*, and "Two Epigrams" under *rispetto*.

The EPILOG (EPILOGUE) is a short poem addressed directly to the audience following the conclusion of a drama, or it is a summation of occurrences that follow the main action of a play, story, or poem—see "The Death of the Astronaut" in Narrative Poetry.

The EPISTLE, a type of *didactic poetry*, is a *general form*, a letter to someone in particular or to mankind in general. However, Richard Wilbur invented a specific form in the late twentieth century, the nine-line *rubliw*:

For Lewis Turco

      Dear Lew,
     All hail to you,
   Old formalist, who through
  Your *Book of Forms* inform the new.
If you can name this bloody form, please do,
  before it disappears from view,
    For you're the one man who
     Might manage to.
      Adieu.

              —Richard Wilbur

For Richard Wilbur

      Dear Dick,
     It's quite a trick
    To name the form poetic
   You sent Sam Gwynn who, in the nick
Of time, included it in his panegyric

> Celebrating my arthritic
>   Remove from the academic,
>   But *rubliw*'s a quick
>   Kick.

—Lewis Turco

The form begins with a *salutation,* which sets the rhyme scheme (all *a* rhymes). The nine lines are iambic monometer, dimeter, trimeter, tetrameter, pentameter, tetrameter, trimeter, dimeter, and monometer again, in that order. Here is a description of the form in the form itself:

> *Rubliw for Dana Gioia*
>
>   Dear Dan–
>   a, in the main,
>   A *rubliw* is a skein
> Of monorhymes making a chain
> To this point that's formally a cinquain,
>   But then the lines, like a train
>   Losing cars, refrain
>   And start to wane
>   Again.

Here is the diagram:

lines   *meters and rhymes*

```
         ◡ ／
I.    xa
         ◡ ／ ◡ ／
2.    xx  xa
         ◡ ／ ◡ ／ ◡ ／
3.    xx  xx  xa
         ◡ ／ ◡ ／ ◡ ／ ◡ ／
4.    xx  xx  xx  xa
```

```
        ᴗ ⁄  ᴗ ⁄  ᴗ ⁄  ᴗ ⁄  ᴗ ⁄
5.      xx  xx  xx  xx  xa
        ᴗ ⁄  ᴗ ⁄  ᴗ ⁄  ᴗ ⁄
6.      xx  xx  xx  xa
        ᴗ ⁄  ᴗ ⁄  ᴗ ⁄
7.      xx  xx  xa
        ᴗ ⁄  ᴗ ⁄
8.      xx  xa
        ᴗ ⁄
9.      xa
```

For another epistolary form, see the *somonka*.

The EPITHALAMION or EPITHALAMIUM, a form of *occasional poetry*, is a wedding song:

Hornpipe Epithalamium

The sea blows high and the wind blows cold,
   The *Hornet* sails out to sting.
We bellbottom boys are bully and bold,
Young at the moment but growing old,
And it's no damn good that I bought Jean a ring,
   I bought pretty Jean a ring.

The Gunner's Apprentice is cute as a pin,
   The Yeoman can really swing.
Those almond-eyed girls all know how to sin
To make your eyes swivel and your head spin—
But I had to go buy Jeannie a ring,
   A yellowish diamond ring.

Davy Jones flirts with the mermaids below.
   Down there where Neptune is king
The seacows come swimming along in a row
With nothing more on than a green weed bow
While the drowned sailors gather around in a ring
   And dance till the fathoms ring,

For each wooed a maiden of iron and steel,
    Then took her out for a fling.
She had a pert hull and a lovely keel,
But one day she just wouldn't answer her wheel—
I wonder if Jeannie's still wearing her ring,
    That beautiful bargain ring.

The wind blows cold, the sea blows high;
    I stand here trying to sing,
But the salt spray rises to spit in my eye
Till I'm ready to kill and fit to die
While Jeannie sits home and stares at her ring,
    For I gave sweet Jean my ring.

                                        —Wesli Court

EVENSONG—see *liturgical poetry*.

For discussions of the FABLE and the FABLIAU, see *didactic poetry* and Narrative Poetry, respectively.

The FLYTING will be found listed under *forensic poetry*, following.

The FOLK BALLAD is discussed under Podics in The Sonic Level and in Narrative Poetry. See also the *ballad* and *ballad stanza*.

FORENSIC POETRY is poetry of argument and debate, as in the *eclogue débat* discussed in the section on *bucolics*. A set form of the debate is the Spanish *pregunta,* in which one poet grills another poet with a *requesta (question)*, and the second replies with a *respuesta (response)*:

Upon Love, by Way of Question and Answer

I bring ye love, *Quest*. What will love do?
        Ans. Like, and dislike ye;
I bring ye love, *Quest*. What will love do?
        Ans. Stroke ye to strike ye;
I bring ye love, *Quest*. What will love do?
        Ans. Love will befool ye;
I bring ye love, *Quest*. What will love do?
        Ans. Heat ye to cool ye;

I bring ye love, *Quest*. What will love do?
    Ans. Love gifts will send ye;
I bring ye love, *Quest*. What will love do?
    Ans. Stock ye to spend ye;
I bring ye love, *Quest*. What will love do?
    Ans. Love will fulfill ye;
I bring ye love, *Quest*. What will love do?
    Ans. Kiss ye to kill ye.
           —Robert Herrick

Another Western form of the *débat* (*debate*) is the Scottish *flyting*, in which two bards attempt to outdo one another with invective and insults. The *backwoods boast* and *brag* are similar. A Japanese form of this poetic cross-examination is the *katauta*.

A FOUND POEM is poetry discovered in a place where one would never expect it to be as, for instance, in an eighteenth-century *pharmacopoeia* or chemist's reference book:

Balsamum Apoplecticum★

From John Quincy's *Pharmacopoeia Officinalis Extemporanea, Or, A Complete English Dispensatory, in Four Parts.* London: Thomas Longman, at the Ship in Paternoster Row, 1742, pp. 504–505.

  "Take the distill'd Oil of Cinnamon,
    Cloves, Lavender, Lemons,
  Marjoram, Mint, Rue, Rosemary"
[if you would enjoy a calming down],

"Sage, Rhodium, and Wormwood, of each
    12 drops; of Amber, 6
  drops; Bitumen Judaicum,
2 drams; Oil of Nutmegs by Expression, 1

  ★Apoplexy, in the sense used here, is a fit of violent rage. Balsam is any of various aromatic resins, including balsam of Peru, containing measurable quantities of cinnamic and/or benzoic acid, or the esters thereof. The recipe is for a sedative.

"ounce; Balsam of *Peru*, as much as
        is sufficient to make
    all together into a smooth
Balsam" [if you would enjoy a coming

down]. "This warms and enlivens the Nerves
        being either smell'd to
    or rubbed upon the Temples, or
any other convenient Part" [or

convening Part, unlike the Temples];
        "it does much good also
    to paralytic Limbs, by rubbing
them well with it. It has been in

"mighty Esteem and Fashion to wear
        it in little Ivory Boxes
    and Cane Heads; but it has in such
respects given place to more modish

"Contrivances" [couches, capsules]. "In
        Distempers of the Head
    and Nerves it is likewise directed
to be given inwardly from

"3 to 6 drops in a Bole or an
        Electuary." [If,
    indeed, after Visions, Love and
Hours, you would enjoy a common Down.]

Here is a William Carlos Williams poem as it was originally
published in 1916:

Marriage
So different, this man
And this woman:
A stream flowing
In a field.

The original version of this poem is a prose sentence that has been line-phrased; that is to say, the sentence has been broken into phrases and each phrase has become a line (see *free verse*). However, if the lines of this prose sentence/poem are rearranged in syllabic lengths of 5-7-5, it becomes a perfect three-line "found" *senryu*, a Japanese form:

Marriage

   So different, this
man and this woman: a stream
  flowing in a field.
    —William Carlos Williams

The senryu itself first showed up unmistakably in Williams' poetry as a 1917 poem:

Chinese Nightingale

Long before dawn your light
Shone in the window, Sam Wu;
You were at your trade.
    —William Carlos Williams

The FOURTEENER LINE is discussed under *poulter's measure*.

FREE VERSE. If "verse" is defined as "metered language" and "prose" as "unmetered language," then the term "free verse" is a contradiction in terms because "verse" cannot be "free," for it is "metered." The only other possibility, then, is that "free verse" is "prose" broken into lines by some means or other—see Prose Poetry in The Sonic Level (chapter 1) and see *polyphonic prose*.

However, many poems written in such prosodies as are described in this book, such as podics, syllabics, and so forth, might be called "free verse" by people who do not recognize those prosodies as verse systems.

The GENETHLIACUM is an occasional poem written in honor of a birth:

Nursery Rime

"It's a wise child knows his father."

What shall I say of my son,
That he is firm, fair of skin?
That he rides his backside and can't know
He has not yet let the outside in?
There squalls a storm just begun.
I stand fast; he lies low.

What may I say of this bone
Wound in flesh partly mine—
Warp of my woof, thread of my skein—
He has come so supple to sup and dine,
To tangle the nets we have thrown
To veil the waters that won't drain.

He would swim where I recline.
Toss him a hook. Fish his schools:
He will lure us down, take us in.
He will build us a weir for fools—
He is no man's yet he is mine.
He is a death sign and a bulletin.

See *occasional poetry*.

GEORGICS are rhymed instructions or directions in the arts, sciences, or trades—versified handbooks. An excellent modern georgic is David Wagoner's "Staying Alive," widely anthologized.

The GESTE is discussed later under Narrative Poetry.

The GHAZAL is an Arabic form that has recently come into some popularity in the English-speaking world. It turns on a single rhyme, *aa ba ca da*, and so forth; it is shorter than the *qasida*, another Arabic couplet form.

A description of the GLEE is found under *balada*.

The GLOSA, GLOSE, or GLOSS is a poem that comments upon a *texte*, as in the *carol*, or as in this poem, which is written in *staves*.

Western Wind

Western wind, when wilt thou blow,
That the small rain down shall rain?
Christ! that my love were in my arms,
And I in my bed again.—Anonymous

Western wind, when wilt thou blow?
When shall the rivers begin to flow
Over this ice toward the sea?
When will the branches of the tree
Drop their mantles of rime and snow?
Western wind, when wilt thou blow,

That the small rain down shall rain?
Then may the willows in their train
Loosen their limbs upon the stream;
Then may birdsong burst this dream
Of winter to seek the sprouting grain,
That the small rain down shall rain.

Christ! that my love were in my arms
Where the grass greens and the bee swarms!
She is fair as the mountain heather,
Comely and kind as Maytime's weather
Over the land after April storms—
Christ! that my love were in my arms,

And I in my bed again
Where gladly have I slept and lain
Upon the pillow of her hair.
When shall I once more come there,
Her breast beneath the counterpane,
And I in my bed again?

—Wesli Court

GRANDE BALLADE—see *chant royal*.

The official Welsh meter, GWAWDODYN (gwow-dód-in) stanza,
is a quatrain with lines of of 9-9-10-9 syllables, respectively. Lines
one, two and four end-rhyme with each other. Line three may

rhyme internally, or a syllable before the end of the line may rhyme into the fourth line: *aa(bb)*[10]*a* **or** *aa(bx)*[10]*(ba)*—note that the superscript here indicates the ten-syllable line. GWAWDONYN HIR (gwow-dód-in heer) substitutes a nonasyllabic rhyming quatrain for the opening couplet, making this form a sestet: *aaaa(bb)*[10]*a* **or** *aaaa(bx)*[10]*(ba)*.

HABBIE is found under *Burns stanza* and *standard habbie*; see also *rime couée*.

The HAIBUN, a Japanese composite mode form, combines prose and verse.

The HAIKAI NO RENGA, the HAIKU, and the HANKA are discussed below under *katauta* and *renga*. For a poem that traces some of the development of Japanese poetry to the haiku, see "Paradigm" under *katauta*.

HENDECASYLLABICS is a quantitative accentual-syllabic Greek *line* eleven syllables long made up of a trochee **or** spondee, a dactyl, and three trochees, or two trochees and a spondee, in that order:

line   meters

```
        ´ ˘ | ´ ˘ ˘ | ´ ˘ | ´ ˘ | ´ ˘
  I.    xx  xxx  xx  xx  xx
  or
        ´ ´ | ´ ˘ ˘ | ´ ˘ | ´ ˘ | ´ ´
  2.    xx  xxx  xx  xx  xx
```

Here is a gibe, a verbal sneer at critics, written in hendecasyllabics (it is really the second half of the poem titled "Milton," shown earlier):

> *[Catullus]*
>
> O you chorus of indolent reviewers,
> Irresponsible, indolent reviewers,
> Look, I come to the test, a tiny poem
> All composed in a metre of Catullus,
> All in quantity, careful of my motion,

Like the skater on ice that hardly bears him,
Lest I fall unawares before the people,
Waking laughter in indolent reviewers.
Should I flounder awhile without a tumble
Through this metrification of Catullus,
They should speak to me not without a welcome,
All that chorus of indolent reviewers.
Hard, hard, hard is it, only not to tumble,
So fantastical is the dainty metre.
Wherefore slight me not wholly, nor believe me
Too presumptuous, indolent reviewers.
O blatant Magazines, regard me rather—
Since I blush to belaud myself a moment—
As some rare little rose, a piece of inmost
Horticultural art, or half coquette-like
Maiden, not to be greeted unbenignly.
                        —Alfred Tennyson

HEPTASTICH—see *septet.*

The HEROIC COUPLET is two iambic pentameter lines rhyming *aa.* See *heroic stanzas.*

The English-language HEROIC LINE, iambic pentameter blank verse, is discussed under *epic* in Narrative Poetry.

HEROIC OCTAVE—See *heroic stanzas* and the *sonnet.*

HEROICS are any verse forms that are written in iambic pentameter verse. See the *epic* in Narrative Poetry.

The HEROIC SONNET, so called, is eighteen lines long. It appends a *heroic couplet* to two stanzas of any kind of *heroic octave* or to four *heroic quatrains.*

There are several HEROIC STANZAS, all of which **must** be written in iambic pentameter lines: The *heroic couplet* rhymes *aa;* the *Sicilian triplet* rhymes *aba;* the *Italian quatrain* rhymes *abba;* doubled, it is the *Italian octave,* which constitutes the first part of the *Italian sonnet, abbaabba.* The *Sicilian quatrain* rhymes *abab;* doubled, it is the *Sicilian octave, abababab.* The *Sicilian quintet* rhymes *ababa.* The *Sicilian sestet* rhymes *ababab,* and the *Italian sestet* rhymes *abcabc*—either can end the *Italian sonnet.* The *Sicilian septet* rhymes *abababa.*

The HEXAMETER is discussed as the *classical hexameter* under *occasional poetry.*

HEXASTICH—see *sestet.*

The Welsh official meter HIR A THODDAID (heer ah thódd-eyed) is a quantitative syllabic sestet stanza; lines one through five have syllable counts of ten (they are decasyllabic lines); line six contains nine syllables (it is a nonasyllabic line). Lines one, two, three, four, and six rhyme. One syllable toward the end of line five cross-rhymes into the middle of line six:

lines   syllables and rhymes

1.   x x x x x x x x x a
2.   x x x x x x x x x a
3.   x x x x x x x x x a
4.   x x x x x x x x x a
5.   x x x x x x *x b x x*
6.   x x x *b x x x x* a

The Sons of David

> *"Lie still, ye thief, and hear the lady sing in Welsh."*
> *—the first part of King Henry IV, Act III, Scene I*

Lie still, ye thief, and hear the lady sing
In her own language, the confederates' tongue
Old Llywarch used, and Heledd, for their longing—
Blossom on branch, and osprey on the wind,
And Olwen's footprint in the morning mist.
Lie still, ye thief; listen to the song.

Lie still, lie still; and hear harp-music, far
Beyond Time's arras, feud, betrayal, war,
Bereavement and self-pity—all they are,
And all they were, they faced. They said, *Yea, sure!*
Look you, they said; they looked both near and high.
Lie still, ye rogue, lie still; hear the air.

Lie still, and listen, for the Cymri know
Measures of mirth and melodies of sorrow,
The dragon's track, drawn red across the snow,
White hawthorn, golden pear, the darker shadow
A girl's hair makes above the pillow's mound.
Hearken to the sound, and its echo.

Lie still, ye silly flouter of Glendower.
A fair young queen sings in her summer bower,
An old man in the winter of his power
fingers the harp-strings, and the golden shower,
the golden rain, descends to light our dark.
Lie still, Hotspur; hearken for an hour.
                                    —Rolfe Humphries

The HOKKU is described with the other Japanese forms in the sections on the *katauta* and *renga*.

HOMOSTROPHIC ODE—see *ode*.

The HORATIAN ODE will be found under *occasional poetry*.

A HORNPIPE is a sailor's dance—see "Hornpipe Epithalamium," under *epithalamion*.

HUDIBRASTICS is discussed in the section on *satirical poetry*.

The HUITAIN is discussed with the *ballade*.

HUMOROUS RENGA CHAIN—see *haikai no renga* under *renga*.

The HYMN is a sacred song. Various hymn forms are located with *liturgical poetry*.

Both HYMNAL OCTAVE and HYMNAL STANZA are discussed under *common measure* in the sections on Podics (in The Sonic Level) and Narrative Poetry.

The IDYLL is discussed under Narrative Poetry.

The IMPRECATION is a *curse*—see *liturgical poetry*.

For the INCANTATION see *liturgical poetry*.

"IN MEMORIAM" STANZA—see the *envelope*.

INTERLOCKING RUBAIYAT—see *rubaiyat*.

The INTERLUDE will be found in "Minor Dramatic Genres" in the companion volume of this book, *The Book of Literary Terms*.

INVOCATION—see *liturgical poetry*.

The IRREGULAR ODE is under *occasional poetry*.

The ITALIAN OCTAVE and the ITALIAN SESTET are found under Italian (*Petrarchan*) *sonnet* in the entry on the *sonnet* and under *octave*, *octet*, and *sestet*.

A description of the JEREMIAD is found in the companion volume of this book, *The Book of Literary Terms*. A poetic form is the Scottish *flyting*, which is listed under *forensic poetry*.

For the JINGLE see *nursery rhyme*.

KADDISH—see *liturgical poetry* and *occasional poetry*.

There are actually two Japanese forms that are called "KATAUTA"; both are formal, but only one is a stanza form per se, and both are based upon spontaneous "*utterances*," which, in the Japanese tradition, are sudden, *emotive words* or *epithets*. The first form of the katauta is an emotive question or its answer:

Am I in love? Birds are flying.
Do birds fly? I am in love.

A pair of such katautas is a *mondo*. Each line of the preceding couplet is a mondo. The katauta answer is not derived logically; it is intuited, as in the Zen *koan* or "unanswerable question," for Zen Buddhism is at the root of the haiku. The second kind of katauta is a stanza or poem form. It is made up of three parts arranged in lines of 5-7-7 syllables, these lengths being approximately breath-length, or the appropriate lengths in which to ask a sudden, emotive question and respond to it, also emotively. Seventeen syllables, as in the haiku, or nineteen, as in the katauta, are as many as can normally be uttered in one short breath; five to seven syllables are approximately equal to the utterance of an emotive question or its answer:

Why do these birds fly?
Where there is wind, there are wings.
Where there are wings, there is wind.

This following poem illustrates a number of the Japanese forms:

Paradigm

Why does the brook run?
The banks of the stream are green.   —MONDO

Why does the stream run?
The banks of the brook bloom
with roe and cup-moss, with rue.   —KATAUTA

The trees are filled with
cups. Grain in the fields, straw men
    talking with the wind.
Have you come far, water-
    borne, wind-born? Here are
hounds-tongue and mistletoe oak.   —CHOKA

 When the spears bend as
you walk through vervain or broom,
    call out to the brook—
it will swell in your veins as
you move through broom or vervain.   —WAKA (5-7, 5-7, 7)

Have you spoken aloud? Here,
where the swallows' crewel-work
    sews the sky with mist?
You must cut the filament.
You must be the lone spider.   —TANKA (5-7-5, 7-7)

The bole is simple:
Twig and root like twin webs in
    air and earth like fire.   —HAIKU (5-7-5)

For more information about Japanese forms, see the *renga*.

The KEATSIAN (ENGLISH) ode is with the other odes in the section on *occasional poetry*.

The KYRIELLE is a French normative syllabic poem form written in quatrains. All lines are octosyllabic (in English meters, tetrameter), and the fourth line is a refrain: *abaB cbcB*, etc.:

The Y2K Ball

Who is this that fingers the sax,
Blowing it down the dancers' backs,
Wielding it like Erato's axe?
    Why, it's Santa Claus's helper.

And who is this that whirls and spins
His arms on stage, who beats his skins,
Punishing them for their sins?
    Another one of Santa's helpers.

Who then is this that whacks the vibes?
What's the arc his mallet describes,
And where's the chart that he transcribes,
    This third of Santa's helpers?

Whose fingers hoof it along the keys
Jazzing among these melodies,
These carols with their alchemies?
    Another of Santa's helpers.

And who's the fellow in the race
To keep the rhythm and the pace
Bouncing upon his ringing bass?
    Why, it's Santa's plucky helper.

Who too are these that move along,
Weaving among the writhing throng
As though they were the slaves of song?
    All, all are old Santa's helpers.

Santa's chores have all been done,
The new millennium has begun—
So play and swing it, everyone!
    Each one of you Santa's helpers.
                        —Wesli Court

The French LAI family comprises both stanza and poem forms, and it is generally used to tell stories; see Narrative Poetry.

LAI NOUVEAU—see Narrative Poetry.

The LAMENT is a *complaint*; see also *blues*. This poem may or may not be by an Old English poet named "Deor," and it may or may not be autobiographical. The form is Anglo-Saxon prosody, as in the original. Alexander (see Bibliography), in his prefatory note to the poem, says, "The penultimate [next-to-last] stanza of Deor is longer than the others, is not followed by the usual refrain, and has a Christian tone which may seem out of place; but we have an insufficiently precise idea of what may have seemed consistent or inconsistent to an Anglo-Saxon audience to call this an interpolation."

However, one may be convinced on purely structural grounds that not only is this stanza an interpolation but so is the first line of the last stanza, which is merely a bridge from the interpolation. The reason the refrain does not appear between the stanzas is simply that the stanza would not have made sense if it were there, so the interpolator left it out and supplied a one-line bridge in order to justify the pagan poem to Christians. Without the penultimate stanza of the "original," the poem is perfectly tight structurally, so it has been left out here, together with the bridge:

Lament

Wayland knew the wanderer's weird.   [fate]
That willful earl bore his hurt,
Grief and yearning the only roadmates
Of bleak exile. Burdens bit
When Nithblad put blade to tendon,
Laid deft hands on the better man:

That passed. This will not last.

Beadohild mourned her murdered brothers,
Yet her plight pained her more,
For her womb bloomed with child.

As she grew great she could not keep
Clear in inwit what would be her fate: [mind]

That passed. This will not last.

All have heard of Hild's rape—
The Geat's lust could not be quelled;
Their love-gall ruined rest:

That passed. This will not last.

For thirty snows, thirty thaws
Theodoric ruled, which many know:

That passed. This will not last.

And many know Eormanric
Had wolf-wit. Wide Gothland
Gasped in the grasp of that grim king—
Through his reign theigns were grief-gripped,
Foresaw but sorrow, sighed for the fall
And grinding-down of that thrallman:

That passed. This will not last.

In the hall of the Heodenings I long held bardship,
Lived dear to my liege, Deor my name.
Many winters I dwelt in gladness;
My lord was kind—then came Heorrenda.
His lays were skilled. The lord of warriors
Laid on him my laurel crown:

That passed. This will not last.
                            —Anonymous Anglo-Saxon

LAPIDARY VERSE—see *satirical poetry*.
The LAY is discussed under Narrative Poetry.

LIGHT VERSE (*vers de société*) is humorous poetry; here is an example of vers de société in the form of a *ballade* with *envoy*:

Ballade for the Yale Younger Poets of Yesteryear

Tell me where, oh, where are they,
Those Younger Poets of Old Yale
Whose laurels flourished for a day
But wither now beyond the pale?
Where are Chubb, Farrar, and Vinal
With fame as fragile as a bubble?
Where is the late Paul Tanaquil,
And where is Lindley Williams Hubbell?

Where's Banks? Where's Boyle? Where's Frances Clai-
Borne Mason? Where is T. H. Ferril?
Dorothy E. Reid or Margaret Ha-
Ley? Simmering in Bad Poets Hell?
J. Ingalls' "Metaphysical
Sword" (hacking critics' weeds to stubble!)?
Young Ashbery (that is, "John L.")?
And where is Lindley Williams Hubbell?

Where's Alfred Raymond Bellinger
(If you'll allow me to exhale
Him *avec un accent français*)?
Where's Faust (Henri) or Dorothy Belle
Flanagan? Where is Paul Engle
(To rhyme whose surname gave me trouble)?
Hath tolled for all the passing bell?
And where is Lindley Williams Hubbell?

Prince of all poets, hear, I pray,
And raise them from their beds of rubble.
Where's Younger Carolyn Forché?
And where is Lindley Williams Hubbell?
                                    —R. S. Gwynn

Also see the *amphigory, clerihew, limerick, madsong*, and *nonsense verse*.

The LIMERICK is discussed with the *madsong*; see also Podics in *The Sonic Level*.

The LITANY is found in the *liturgical poetry* section. For an example, see William Dunbar's "Lament for the Poets" (under *complaint*).

The LITERARY BALLAD is discussed in the Narrative Poetry section.

The LITERARY EPITAPH is found among the *satirical poetry* forms.

LITURGICAL POETRY is the ritual and religious poetry of the church, and it includes such poem forms as the *benison* (blessing), *malison* (curse), *hymn* or *psalm* (song of praise), *invocation* (request for aid or succour), *prayer*, *antiphon*, and *litany*. This Old English "Hymn to the Creator" is attributed to Caedmon (d. 690?), the first Anglo-Saxon poet whose name is known. The form, as in the original, is *Anglo-Saxon prosody*. The *stichs* are broken here into *hemistichs* at the caesurae.

Hymn to the Creator
Now must we glorify
                    The guardian of Heaven,
The mood of our Maker,
                    The might of His marvels,
Warder of all;
                    How He, of all wonders
Ever Eldlord,
                    Formed the origin.
First he made
                    For the children of men
Heaven's hall—
                    Our holy Author!
Then Midgard,
                    This guardian of mortals—
Eldlord ever,
                    Framed afterward:
This Earth for man,
                    our almighty Maker!
                              —Caedmon

The *anthem*, a hymn of praise, like the *litany* (see Dunbar's "Lament for the Poets," under *complaint*), is derived from the Bible and is an *antiphon*, that is, it is responsive in nature. The antiphon is usually a responsive text chanted by the congregation following the reading of a *psalm* (*hymn*), and the *litany* is a prayer of entreaty recited by a leader and responded to by the congregation. Manoah Bodman, author of the following poem, may not have intended this to be a poem at all. It is an antiphon derived from the Bible, Job XLI:1–7. Bodman quotes the Biblical passage, and between questions he inserts his own responses. It is a prose-mode poem, and its prosodic structure is that of the Hebraic *grammatic parallel prosody*.

Canst Thou Draw?

Job XLI:1–7

Canst thou draw out Leviathan with an hook, or his tongue with a cord
*   which thou lettest down? Canst thou put an hook into his nose? or*
*   bore his jaw through with a thorn?*
Vain attempt!
Will he make many supplications unto thee?
Directly the reverse!
Will he speak soft words unto thee?
Terrible words!
Will he make a covenant with thee?
Distressing covenant!
Or, wilt thou take him for a servant forever?
Dreadful servant!
Wilt thou play with him, as with a bird?
Dismal play!
Or wilt thou bind him for thy maidens?
Strong cord!
Shall thy companions make a banquet of him?
Mournful banquet!
Shall they part him among the merchants?
Deadly shares!
Canst thou fill his skin with barbed irons?
Hopeless attempt!
Or his head with fish spears?
Despairing thought!
                              —Manoah Bodman

The *canticle* is a scriptural hymn for public worship. The *carol*, a joyous hymn, is found under its own heading.

   Charms are *incantations*. Here are some charms from the sixteenth and seventeenth centuries. They are rendered in their original forms. In one or two cases they have been augmented from fragments.

A SHEAF OF CHARMS

Two Charms for the Toothache

I.

Nail, I make my plaint to thee,
My aching tooth, it bothers me.
I take thy point to prick my gum,
Then hold thy neck between my thumb
And knuckle—with my peen tunk
You into this tree trunk.
My toothache now in thy wood stay,
From my jaw let it drop away
And bother me not evermore,
For if it do I shall be sore.

II.

Christ passed by his brother's door,
Saw Peter his brother lying on the floor,
"What aileth thee, brother?—
Pain in thy teeth?
Thy teeth shall pain thee no more:
In the name of the Father, Son, and Holy Ghost.
Amen."

Charm to Stanch Bleeding

Jesus was born in Bethlehem,
Baptized in River Jordan, when
The water was wild in the wood,
The person was just and good;

God spake, and the water stood:
And so shall now thy blood—
In the name of the Father, Son, and Holy Ghost.
Amen.

Charm Against a Magpie

Clean birds by sevens,
Unclean by twos;
The Dove, in the Heavens,
Is the one I choose.

Charm for a Burn or a Scald

There were three angels came from the East and West;
One brought fire, and another brought frost,
And the third, it was the Holy Ghost.
Out, fire, in frost, in the Name of the Father,
Son, and Holy Ghost.
Amen.

Charm for an Adder Bite

Or, to make an adder destroy himself.

Underneath this hazelen mot
There's a braggaty worm with a speckled throat,
Now! nine double hath he.
Now, from nine double to eight double,
From eight double to seven double,
From seven double to six double,
From six double to five double,
From five double to four double,
From four double to three double,
From three double to two double,
From two double to one double,
Now! no double hath he.

—Various Anonymous Poets

Curses are ritual *imprecations*. "The Blacksmiths," a curse from the anonymous Middle English, is, like *Piers Plowman* and *Sir Gawain and the Green Knight*, a late example of Anglo-Saxon alliterative verse. X. J. Kennedy, in his *Tygers of Wrath* (see Bibliography), says of this version that the translator "has preserved much of the rhythm and alliterative music of his original, from the fifteenth-century Arundel manuscript (3227 in the *Index of Middle English Verse*)." The caesurae here are indicated by line breaks rather than by spatial stepping.

The Blacksmiths

Sooty, swart smiths,   Smattered with smoke,
Drive me to death   With the din of their dents.
Such noise at night   No men heard, never!
What knavish cries   And clattering of knocks!
The crooked cretins   Call out, "Coal, coal!"
And blow their bellows   Till their brains burst:
"Huff, puff!" says that one;   "Haff, paff!" that other.
They spit and sprawl   And spill many spells;
They gnaw and gnash,   They groan together
And hold their heat   With their hard hammers.
Of bullhide are made   Their broad aprons;
Their shanks be shackled   For the fiery flinders;
They've heavy hammers   That are hard-hafted,
Stark strokes   On a steely stump:
LUS, BUS! LAS, DAS!   Rants the row—
So doleful a dream,   The devil destroy it!
The master lengthens little   And labors less,
Twines a two   And touches a trey:
Tick, tack! hick, hack!   Ticket, tacket! tyke, take!
LUS, BUS! LAS, DAS!   Such lives they lead,
These cobblemares: Christ give them grief!
May none of these waterburners   By night have his rest!
                    —Anonymous Middle English

Evensong is a formal lyric prayer sung in the evening; a synonym is *vespers*. *Morningsong* or *matins* is a prayer sung at dawn, and a *nightsong* is sung at midnight—see the entry on the *aubade*. The *requiem* is a poem for or hymn to the dead, like the Jewish *kaddish*; see *occasional poetry*.

LONG HYMNAL OCTAVE, LONG HYMNAL STANZA, LONG MEASURE, and LONG OCTAVE are all discussed with the *common measure* forms.

The LULLABY is a gentle song used to induce a baby to sleep. Here is a modern version of an old lullaby:

Rocket By, Baby

Rocket by, baby, in your space ship,
When you count down the rocket will zip.
When you blast off, go into free fall,
And off will go baby, cockpit and all.
—Wesli Court

The MADRIGAL is a song, often about love, written originally in two or three heptasyllabic or hendecasyllabic triplets followed by a *ritornello* (*return* or *refrain*) of one or two couplets in the same meter. Chaucer invented a strict form for English poetry. Written in iambic pentameter lines, it consists of three stanzas, the first of which is a triplet utilized as a *texte*, for all its lines become refrains in the following stanzas. The second stanza is a *quatrain*, lines three and four of which are lines one and two of the initial triplet. Stanza three is a *sestet* that repeats the triplet as the last three lines of the poem. This is the rhyme scheme: AB^1B^2 $abAB^1$ $abbAB^1B^2$.

Merciless Beauty

I. Captivity

Your two eyes will slay me suddenly—
The beauty of them I may not sustain,
They pierce and wound my heart with blade so keen.

Only your word will bind up instantly
My heart's hurt while still the wound is green;
    Your two eyes will slay me suddenly—
    The beauty of them I may not sustain.

Upon my troth, I tell you faithfully
That of my life and death you are the queen,

For with my death the truth shall soon be seen—
    Your two eyes will slay me suddenly—
    The beauty of them I may not sustain,
    They pierce and wound my heart with blade so keen.

II. Rejection

Your beauty has from your heart so chased
Pity, it is useless to complain,
For Danger winds your mercy in his chain.

Though I am guiltless, my death you have purchased—
I tell you true, I do not need to feign;
    Your beauty has from your heart so chased
    Pity, it is useless to complain.

Alas! that nature has in you compassed
Such great beauty, no man may attain
To mercy, though he starve because of pain.
    Your beauty has from your heart so chased
    Pity, it is useless to complain,
    For Danger winds your mercy in his chain.

III. Escape

Since I from Love have thus escaped so fat,
I never plan to be back in prison lean;
Since I am free, Love isn't worth a bean.

He may reply, answer this or that—
I snap my fingers, speak just what I mean.
    Since I from Love have thus escaped so fat,
    I never plan to be back in prison lean;

Love has struck my name clear off his slate,
And from my ledger he is stricken clean
Forevermore—there is no in-between.
    Since I from Love have thus escaped so fat,
    I never plan to be back in prison lean;
    Since I am free, Love isn't worth a bean.
                    —Geoffrey Chaucer

The MADSONG is any lyric sung by a madman or a fool, but there is a particular MADSONG STANZA in which many such lyrics traditionally appear. The *madsong stanza* is said to be a descendant of the main stanza of "The Cuckoo Song":

The Cuckoo Song
Sing cuckoo now! Sing cuckoo!
Sing cuckoo! Sing cuckoo now!

Summer is a-coming in,
Loudly sing cuckoo!
   It grows the seed
   And blows the mead,
And springs the wood anew—   } main stanza

   Sing cuckoo!

The ewe bleats after the lamb,
And after the calf, the cow;
   The bullock starts,
   The buck farts—   } main stanza
Merry sing cuckoo!

   Cuckoo, cuckoo!
Well sing ye, cuckoo,
Nor cease ye never, now!
          —Anonymous

Written in strong-stress prosody (podics), the first, second, and fifth lines of the main stanza (beginning with line three) are tripodic, and the third and fourth are dipodic. The lines rhyme or consonate a^3 b^3 c^2 c^2 b^3, d^3 e^3 f^2 f^2 e^3, and so on. The long lines often end on an unstressed syllable (a *falling ending*), and there are internal sonic effects, including alliteration and assonance.

Here is a modern take-off of "The Cuckoo Song":

Ancient Music

Winter is icummen in,
Lhude sing Goddamm,
Raineth drop and staineth slop,
And how the wind doth ramm!
         Sing: Goddammm.
Skiddeth bus and sloppeth us,
An ague hath my ham.
Freezeth river, turneth liver,
         Damn you, sing: Goddamm.
Goddamm, Goddamm, 'tis why I am, Goddamm,
         So 'gainst the winter's balm.
Sing goddamm, damm, sing Goddamm,
Sing goddamm, sing goddamm, DAMN.

                                    —Ezra Pound

The anonymous madsong following derives from the sixteenth
century, and there are many versions of it; this is a shorter one:

Tom O'Bedlam's Song

From the hag and hungry goblin
That into rags would rend ye,
         All the spirits that stand
         By the naked man
In the book of moons defend ye!

I slept not since the Conquest;
Till then I never waked
         Till the roguish boy
         Of love, where I lay,
Found me and stripped me naked.

The moon's my constant mistress
And the lonely owl my marrow;
         The flaming drake
         And the nighthawk make
Me music, to my sorrow.

I know more than Apollo,
For, oft when he lies sleeping,
    I behold the stars
    At mortal wars,
And the rounded welkin weeping.

The moon embraces her shepherd,
And the queen of love her warrior;
    While the first doth horn
    The stars of morn,
And the next the heavenly farrier.

With a host of furious fancies
Whereof I am commander,
    With a burning spear
    And a horse of air
To the wilderness I wander.

With a knight of ghosts and shadows
I'm summoned to a tourney
    Ten leagues beyond
    The wide world's end—
I think it is no journey.

                —Anonymous

Here is a contemporary madsong:

Odds Bodkin's Springsong

"Sweet heart and Honey-bird keeps no house."

In the sweet spring the cuckoo
Beaks his tune in the greenwood,
    Warbles of nestlings.
    His fellow nestlings
Starve as the old birds brood,

And I recall my borning,
My breeding and my calling.

I, Odds Bodkin,
Oddest of odd kin,
Remember the fledglings falling

Out of the nest that bred me,
Waning as I went waxing
Timber and tackle,
Great as a grackle,
Sleek as any waxwing.

Ah, my youth was sterling!
My foster folk went starveling
To stanch my hunger;
They grew no younger
Over their little starling

Until I grew so monstrous
The nest could not contain me.
I packed my kerchief
Full of mischief—
No sorrows could constrain me.

There's many a nest I've lain in
And many a housewren singing
Over many a fledgling
I've had a hand in
Hatching till I've gone winging.

Those nests are all blown over,
I'm old and draggle-feathered.
Now what I ponder
Wherever I wander
Is what it is I've fathered:

I've sired a choir of echoes
That comes alive in Maytime.
I've made a rimesong
That goes on timelong
To company my graytime.

Therefore I toast the homebird,
My lifelong enemy—
    His nesting wildwood,
    His nestling's childhood,
And wish him all my envy.
         —Wesli Court

The *limerick* is a form of *light verse* (*vers de société*). The alleged French ancestry of the limerick has been disputed. Some authorities feel it is a native English form, descended, as we have noted, from the madsong stanza, which in turn is traced from the main stanza pattern of the medieval "The Cuckoo Song" (shown earlier). However, the Anglo-Norman background of this form is probably not truly disputable, because it is clearly a podic form, and podic prosody developed after Chaucer, John Gower, and the Scottish Chaucerians adapted French syllabic verse to English accentual verse and adopted Norman rhyming.

The limerick is a quantitative accentual-syllabic *quintet* turning on two rhymes: *aabba*. Lines one, two, and five have an iamb and two anapests, in that order; lines three and four have either an iamb and an anapest, in that order, or two anapests. Line five can be merely a modified repetition of line 1 (*AabbA*), as the nineteenth-century poet Edward Lear practiced it, but one of the oldest identifiable limericks also used this device: "Tobacco" is from Michael East's *Second Set of Madrigals*, published in 1606. Whether East himself wrote it is moot.

Tobacco
O metaphysical tobacco,
Fetched as far as from Morocco,
    Thy searching fume
    Exhales the rheum,
O metaphysical tobacco!
         —Michael East (?)

Despite the popularity of the limerick in the twentieth century, the older folk tradition of the madsong can still be found in use. Here is a children's game song that was current in New England at least as late as the 1940s:

Street Song
Help! Murder! Police!
My mother fell in the grease!
    I laughed so hard
    I fell in the lard.
Help! Murder! Police!
            —Anonymous

Many experiments have been enacted with the limerick form. Among other things, it has been used with some success as a stanza pattern rather than as a poem form. Changing its hard and wrenched rhymes to consonances, however, produces some strange results:

A Robbery
Some thieves sacked the home of Miss Hughes
Who owned a remarkable nose.
    She cried, "Sirs! I shall sneeze
    And alert the police
If you don't get out of my house!"
            —Anonymous

But the form has settled down into, at its mildest, salacious suggestiveness—

Hornblower
A boozing musician named Rock
Just loved to blow jazz on his sock.
    In the midst of a riff
    One day he got stiff
When he grabbed, not his foot, but his crock!
            —Anonymous

—and, at its worst, its worst:

A Butcher

There once was a butcher named Simms
Who married a woman of whims.
        She said "No!" once too often,
        So he purchased a coffin
And made farewell love to her limbs.

                            —Anonymous

The MASK (MASQUE) is found under The Genres of Drama in the companion volume, *The Book of Literary Terms*. See also Dramatic Poetry in this volume.

MATINS—see descriptions of *morningsong* under *alba* and *liturgical poetry*.

For a discussion of the MESOSTICH, see the *acrostic*.

The MIRACLE PLAY is described in The Genres of Drama in *The Book of Literary Terms*; see also Dramatic Poetry in this volume.

MOCK FORMS—see *satirical poetry*.

The MONDO is described with the *katauta*.

MONK'S TALE STANZA is the *huitain* utilized as a stanza; see the *ballade*.

The MONODY is among the elegiac forms in the section on *occasional poetry*.

The MONOLOG (MONOLOGUE) is a form of Dramatic Poetry, described in that section.

A MONOSTICH is a poem of just one line; see *mote (motto)* and *posie*.

The MONOSTROPHE is a poem of but one stanza.

The MORALITY PLAY is discussed in "The Genres of Drama" in *The Book of Literary Terms*. See also Dramatic Poetry in this volume.

The MORNINGSONG is discussed in two places—under *alba* and *liturgical poetry*.

MORTUARY VERSE is found under *satirical poetry,* where it is discussed as the *literary epitaph*.

The Spanish MOTE (*motto*) is a monostich or a *distich* (*couplet*) that expresses a complete statement or thought. It can serve as a *texte* to be glossed in verse, as in the *glosa* (*glose, gloss*).

MOTTO—see *mote*.

The MYSTERY PLAY is discussed in "The Genres of Drama" in the companion volume, *The Book of Literary Terms*. See also Dramatic Poetry.

The NASHER is a form of *satirical poetry*. See *prose poem*, *rhymed prose*, and Ogden Nash's "Kindly Unhitch That Star, Buddy" (in the Glossary under *wrenched rhyme*).

The NIGHTSONG is included among liturgical poetry.

The NOËL is described with the *carol*.

An explanation of NONCE VERSE is found in the *occasionals*, under the *homostrophic ode*; it is also mentioned in the forenote to the Form Finder Index.

NONSENSE VERSE is often *children's poetry*.

The NURSERY RHYME, derived from the seventeenth century and often written in podic prosody, is a *jingle* for children, an *amphigory* or nonsense song.

The OBSEQUY is a form of *occasional poetry*, discussed under that listing; these are poems written for specific occasions, generally lyrical in nature. Two major forms are the *ode* and the *elegy*.

OCCASIONAL POETRY is written to celebrate a particular occasion, such as a birth (*genethliacum*), marriage (*epithalamion, epithalamium, prothalamion*), death (*elegy, obsequy, threnody, ode*), public event (*triumphal ode, coronation ode*) or person (*pæan, panegyric*), apology (*palinode*), and so forth.

An *ode* is any poem that celebrates an event or a person (an *encomium*); an *elegy* is a *eulogy* in verse, commemorating the death of someone, or it is a meditation upon that subject. The elegy was written in classical times in *elegiacs* (*elegiac meters,* the *elegiac distich, elegiac couplet*), a Greek quantitative accentual-syllabic couplet stanza whose first line is a *classical hexameter* composed **either** of spondees or dactyls in the first four feet, a dactyl in the fifth foot, and a spondee in the sixth: ´∪∪ | ´∪∪ | ´∪∪ | ´∪∪ | ´∪∪ | ´´ . The second line, a *classical pentameter*, is made up of two dactyls, a spondee, and two anapests, in that order: ´∪∪ | ´∪∪ | ´´ | ∪∪´ | ∪∪´ . Such a poem, comprised of any number of couplets, may or may not rhyme.

Elegies may, however, be written in any manner. Other forms of the elegy are the *epicedium*, an elegy for the dead delivered by a chorus; the *threnody,* a song of lamentation; the *monody,* an elegy for the dead delivered by a single person; the *pastoral elegy;* and the *coronach* or *dirge,* funeral hymns.

The ode has three more or less strict forms, the first of which is the *Pindaric ode*, derived from the *choral ode* of the *classical tragedy*, discussed in the companion volume of this book, *The Book of Literary Terms.* Here is a Pindaric ode that explains the form:

Ode on the Imitations of Immorality

Strophe

I warn you well beforehand, this will be
    An ode. Pindaric, none the less. Written
In strict decasyllabics and rimed. See,
    I believe in forms. My mom was bitten
By a dressmaker when she was gravid,
    And I've been patterning actually
All my life. I have my quirks. I've been avid
    For mannequins—I mean sexually—
Since puberty. When I pass department
    Store windows, I feel like heaving bricks and
Grabbing those luscious dummies. Deportment
    Is important, though (get set for the *stand*

Antistrophe

    Or *epode* which is coming up in just
A minute) in my line of work. You see,
    I teach college. That's right. Bread is a must,
Jack, and a man can sink pretty low. Me?
    I'm really a sales type, according to
The tests. But with my handicap, sales work
    Was out. Too many dolls around. Can you
Imagine me downtown? Don't be a jerk.
    So I'm one of these academic, gray
Flannel poets you hear about. You don't

Think much of my kind of punk? So okay.
Here's that *epode* I warned you about. Won't

Epode

You wait a minute while I think up a
New rime scheme? Sit down and have a cup of
Coffee. Okay. Come on back; I've got it
Figured out. It solved itself: we'll let it
    Go in heroic couplets. See, the *stand*
    Has to be in a different pattern, and
The *strophe* and *antistrophe* were in quatrains.
To be a poet you might not need brains,
    But you've got to have an ear, it seems to
    Me. Well, I've solved my problem. Not a few
Of the coeds are hot for me, but no
Sweat. They don't shake me. Long as I don't go
    Near the fashion classes, I'll never run
    Into a mannequin. I guess I'm done.
It was nice talking to you. Please try not
To judge me too harshly. You're all I've got.

The English or *Keatsian ode*, written in iambic pentameter measures, is thirty lines in length and is divided into three *decastichs* (ten-line stanzas), each of which combines the *Sicilian quatrain* (*abab*) with the *Italian sestet* (*cdecde*): *ababcdecde*:

The Man Hunter

"But we were born of risen apes, not fallen angels, and the apes were armed killers besides. And so what shall we wonder at? . . . The miracle of man is not how far he has sunk but how magnificently he has risen. We are known among the stars by our poems, not our corpses."   —ROBERT ARDREY

When I saw, spinning webs of sense and dust,
the heart-shaped spider of the womb's demands,
I raised myself upright upon the crust
of earth and issued it my first commands:
"Give me what I may take before the glass
of time is empty as a brain's white bowl

where slugs drink, where the mosses gorge and green."
I walked out of the forest, across the grass—
it withered underneath my callous sole,
for I could not forget what I had seen.

I saw the scarab in the turning earth
spinning murders from its golden shell;
I saw the rooting beast probing death,
but death must root if it would hope to dwell.
Therefore, I walked the trench of lambs and ewes
with winter's humour snowing in my bones,
and in my web of veins the scratching, dumb
dry tongue of the beast feeding on my dews.
Then, when at last I lay down in these stones,
I knew that more of us would one day come.

And you have come to find yourself in me
here where I lie, a skull transformed to stone.
My sightless eyes look out at you and see
that under the eons we are still alone—
but we are billions now who were a few
to forsake the forest and face time with a rock,
a naked rock held in a naked hand.
We face the ages still, and we bestrew
this cairn of stars with the remnants of our stock:
a jawbone here and there wearing to sand.

The Sicilian quatrain has sometimes been called the *elegiac stanza* because Thomas Gray's "Elegy in a Country Churchyard" was written in it. The *Horatian* or *homostrophic ode* may contain any number of stanzas, but all stanzas, though they are *nonce* (designed by the poet for the particular poem), must be alike (*homoeomeral*). A fourth type is the *Cowleyan* or *irregular ode*, an example of which would be William Wordsworth's "Ode: Intimations of Immortality."

The French *Ronsardian ode*, written in *quantitative syllabic prosody*, consists of any number of *heptastich* (seven-line) stanzas that rhyme and measure a^{10} b^4 a^{10} b^4 c^{10} c^{10} d^4 d^4 c^8. The Greek and

Italian *palinode* is a *recantation*, a song of retraction (*retractatio*). A set form consists of two strophes and two antistrophes. These are *nonce forms*, as in the ode, and like the ode the nonce patterns must be followed throughout the poem. The form of the first strophe is duplicated in the last antistrophe; the form of the second strophe is mirrored in the first antistrophe: *strophe A, strophe B, antistrophe B, antistrophe A*. The strophes, which may be the statement, are in fact the *ode*, and the antistrophes, the retraction, are the *palinode* proper. A *Horatian ode* is monostrophic.

A *triumphal ode* celebrates a victory; a *genethliacum* is a birthday ode; and an *epithalamion* or *epithalamium* is a marriage ode. Originally this latter poem was written in three *movements* or strophes: The first part was to be sung at the chamber door of the bridegroom and bride, and it was congratulatory in nature. It urged the newlyweds to lusty combat and was designed to muffle the sounds of that combat. The second strophe was intended to refresh the combatants and urge them to new efforts during the night. The third movement, sung in the morning, congratulated the couple on their performances, urged a truce until the next evening, and instructed them in their domestic and marital duties.

OCTASTICH—see *octave*.

The OCTAVE (*octastich, octet, ottavo,* sing., *ottavi,* pl.) is a stanza of eight lines in any meter or rhyme scheme. The *Italian octave*, which must be written in iambic pentameter lines, rhymes *abbaabba*—see the *Italian sonnet*. The *Sicilian octave*, also iambic pentameter, rhymes *abababab*. The *strambotto* is a Sicilian octave written in hendecasyllabic lines. For related forms see *ottava rima*, the *Sicilian sestet*, and the second ending for the *Italian sonnet*.

OCTET—see *octave*.

The ODE is described under *occasional poetry*.

OTTAVA RIMA, an Italian poem or stanza form, is an octave written in iambic pentameter lines and rhyming *ababahcc*. It is, in effect, a *Sicilian sestet* expanded by adding a *heroic couplet*. For related forms see the Italian and Sicilian *octaves*.

For examples of the OTTAVO (*octave, octet;* pl., *ottavi*), see the *canzone*.

The PAEAN, the PALINODE, and the PANEGYRIC may be found in *occasional poetry*. The pæan, like the panegyric, is a song of praise:

The Grand Chorus of Birds

Come on, then, ye dwellers by nature in darkness, and like to the
    leaves' generations,
That are little of might, that are moulded of mire, unenduring
    and shadowlike nations,
Poor plumeless ephemerals, comfortless mortals, as visions of
    creatures fast fleeing,
Lift up your mind unto us that are deathless, and dateless the date
    of our being:
Us, children of heaven, us, ageless for aye, us, all of whose
    thoughts are eternal;
That ye may from henceforth, having heard of us all things aright
    as to matters supernal,
Of the being of birds and beginning of gods, and of streams, and
    the dark beyond reaching,
Truthfully knowing aright, in my name bid Prodicus pack with
    his preaching.

It was Chaos and Night at the first, and the blackness of darkness,
    and hell's broad border,
Earth was not, nor air, either heaven; when in depths of the
    womb of the dark without order
First thing first-born of the black-plumed Night was a wind-egg
    hatched in her bosom,
Whence timely with seasons revolving again sweet Love burst out
    as a blossom,
Gold wings glittering forth of his back, like whirlwinds gustily
    turning.
He, after his wedlock with Chaos, whose wings are of darkness,
    in hell broad-burning,
For his nestlings begat him the race of us first, and upraised us to
    light new-lighted.
And before this was not the race of the gods, until all things by
    Love were united;
And of kind united with kind in communion of nature the sky
    and the sea are

Brought forth, and the earth, and the race of the gods everlasting
and blest. So that we are

Far away the most ancient of all things blest. And that we are of
Love's generation

There are manifest manifold signs. We have wings, and with us
have the Loves habitation;

And manifold fair young folk that forswore love once, ere the
bloom of them ended,

Have the men that pursued and desired them subdued, by the
help of us only befriended,

With such baits as a quail, a flamingo, a goose, or a cock's comb
staring and splendid.

All best good things that befall men come from us birds, as is
plain to all reason:

For first we proclaim and make known to them spring, and the
winter and autumn in season;

Bid sow, when the crane starts clanging for Afric, in shrill-voiced
emigrant number,

And calls to the pilot to hang up his rudder again for the season,
and slumber;

And then weave cloak for Orestes the thief, lest he strip men of
theirs if it freezes.

And again thereafter the kite reappearing announces a change in
the breezes,

And that here is the season for shearing your sheep of their spring
wool. Then does the swallow

Give you notice to sell your greatcoat, and provide something
light for the heat that's to follow.

Thus are we as Ammon or Delphi unto you, Dodona, nay,
Phœbus Apollo.

For, as first ye come all to get auguries of birds, even such is in all
things your carriage,

Be the matter a matter of trade, or of earning your bread, or of
any one's marriage.

And all things ye lay to the charge of a bird that belong to
discerning prediction:

Winged fame is a bird, as you reckon: you sneeze, and the sign's
as a bird for conviction:

All tokens are "birds" with you—sounds too, and lackeys, and
    donkeys. Then must it not follow
That we ARE to you all as the manifest godhead that speaks in
    prophetic Apollo?

                      —Algernon Charles Swinburne

The PANTOUM, a Malayan form, is an interlocking poem composed of quatrain stanzas, and all the lines are refrains. The meter
is generally iambic tetrameter or pentameter. The second and
fourth lines of each stanza become the first and third lines of the
following stanza: $A^1B^1A^2B^2$, $B^1C^1B^2C^2$ and so forth. It can be
ended with a *circle-back* to the two unrepeated lines of the first
stanza, or in a couplet made of those lines in reversed order: A^2A^1.

The Eunuch Cat

She went to work until she grew too old,
    Came home at night to feed the eunuch cat
That kept the mat warm and its eyeballs cold.
    She walked, but ran to wrinkles, then to fat,

    Came home at night to feed the eunuch cat,
Then went to bed, slept dreamlessly till eight,
    And waked. She ran to wrinkles, then to fat.
She fixed her supper, snacked till it was late,

Then went to bed, slept noisily till eight—
    Must I go on? She'll feed the cat no more.
She fixed her supper, snacked till it was late,
    Then died at dawn, just halfway through a snore.

    Must I go on?—she'll feed the cat no more
To keep the mat warm and its eyeballs cold.
    She died at dawn, just halfway through a snore;
She went to work until she grew too old.

                          —Wesli Court

The PASSION PLAY is described in The Genres of Drama in the
companion volume, *The Book of Literary Terms*.

The PASTORAL (PASTORALE), PASTORAL ELEGY, and PASTORAL ODE
are listed among the *bucolics* and *occasionals*, and the PASTOURELLE
under Narrative Poetry. Here is a *mock pastoral*:

A Pastorale of Sorts

    When green buds burst and birds began
    The summer's song, the cycle's plan;
        When grasses leapt for rain and sun,
        When snows had lost and warmth had won;
When cattle had been weaned from hay
    And grazed again where rivers ran,
        I came to you, you came to me,
            Under the lemon tree.

    No oranges for us, no pears,
    No subtleties nor coy despairs.
        The yellow fruit, sweet to admire
        Yet tart to taste, was our desire.
We'd wait together for the day
    When ripeness took us unawares.
        I read to you, you read to me,
            Under the lemon tree.

    We lingered there beneath those limbs;
    We counted lambs and chanted hymns.
        Your pinafore soon came unstarched.
        Our mouths went dry, our throats grew parched;
My knickers went from blue to gray.
    The days were brights, the nights were dims.
        I tired of you, you tired of me,
            Under the lemon tree.

    At last those golden fruits grew great
    With pursing juices—bitter freight!
        We plucked our pleasure, slit the skins
        And flavored nectar with our sins!
For several moments we were gay—
    We puckered, giggled, sighed, and ate.

> I toasted you, you toasted me,
> > Under the lemon tree.

> When finally we looked around
> The leaves were lying on the ground.
> > The sun had gone, the frosts returned—
> > We froze where lately we had burned.
> The flocks had fled, bleated away.
> > Though we'd recall the joys we'd found,
> > > I soured on you, you soured on me . . . ,
> > > > Under the lemon tree.

For another mock form, see R. S. Gwynn's "Ellenalliv for Lew: On His Retirement" under *villanelle*.

PENTASTICH—see *quintet*.

PATTERN VERSE—see *picture poem*.

The PETRARCHAN SONNET is the *Italian sonnet*, found under *sonnet*.

PHALACEAN VERSE—see *hendecasyllabics*.

For the PICTURE POEM, see *calligramme, concrete poem* (in chapter 1), and Spatial Prosody.

PIEDE—see the *canzone*.

The PINDARIC ODE is described under *occasional poetry*.

The PLAMPEDE is an *interlude*—see The Genres of Drama in the companion volume of this book, *The Book of Literary Terms*.

POLYPHONIC PROSE is a term invented by the American poet Amy Lowell to describe the medium that has been called "free verse," a misnomer and a contradiction in terms (see *free verse*). "Polyphonic" means "many-sounded," and other terms, such as Euphuism and Gongorism, have historically preceded Amy Lowell's term. For a full discussion of them, see the companion volume of this book, *The Book of Literary Terms*. Here is a poem written in one type of polyphonic prose—notice all the parallel structures in this piece. The most obvious one is the use of a refrain at the end of each paragraph. Another is the repetition of phrases—"tell me if"; the *catalogue* of actions is also in parallel—

"buying," "cheering," "throwing." See *grammatical parallelism* elsewhere in these pages. Particularly "polyphonic" is the sentence having to do with Pocahontas:

Cool Tombs

When Abraham Lincoln was shoveled into the tombs, he forgot
   the copperheads and the assassin . . . in the dust, in the cool
   tombs.
And Ulysses Grant lost all thought of con men and Wall Street,
   cash and collateral turned ashes . . . in the dust, in the cool
   tombs.
Pocahontas' body, lovely as a poplar, sweet as a red haw in
   November or a pawpaw in May, did she wonder? does she
   remember? . . . in the dust, in the cool tombs?

Take any streetful of people buying clothes and groceries,
   cheering a hero or throwing confetti and blowing tin horns
   . . . tell me if the lovers are losers . . . tell me if any get more
   than the lovers . . . in the dust . . . in the cool tombs.

—Carl Sandburg

For rhyming prose poems, see the *Nasher*.

A POSIE is a *verset*; see *distich*, *epigram*, *monostich*, and *mote* (*motto*).

POULTER'S MEASURE is an English accentual-syllabic *couplet* that alternates an *Alexandrine* line (see also *Spenserian stanza*) with the *septenary* or *fourteener*. There can be any number of couplets in a stanza or poem.

In English prosody the Alexandrine is a *line* of iambic hexameter verse:

ᵕ⁄ ᵕ⁄ ᵕ⁄ ᵕ⁄ ᵕ⁄ ᵕ⁄

xx xx xx xx xx xx

The fourteener was, in Latin verse, a *line* consisting of seven metrical feet. In English verse, the line contains fourteen syllables arranged in iambics, with a caesura appearing somewhere in the center of the line (after the third foot):

˘ ⁄ ˘ ⁄ ˘ ⁄ ˘ ⁄ • ˘ ⁄ ˘ ⁄ ˘ ⁄

xx xx xx xx • xx xx xx

A schematic of one couplet of poulter's measure looks like this:

lines   meters, caesurae, and rhymes

˘ ⁄ ˘ ⁄ ˘ ⁄ ˘ ⁄ ˘ ⁄ ˘ ⁄

1.   xx xx xx xx xx xa

˘ ⁄ ˘ ⁄ ˘ ⁄ ˘ ⁄ • ˘ ⁄ ˘ ⁄ ˘ ⁄

2.   xx xx xx xx • xx xx xa

PRAYER—see *liturgical poetry*.

PREGUNTA—see *forensic poetry*.

The PRIMER COUPLET is a dipodic (two-beat) distich rhyming *aa*:

˘   ⁄   ˘   ⁄

In Adam's fall

˘   ⁄   ˘   ⁄

We   sinned all.

The PROSE POEM will be found under the heading Prose Poetry in the section The Sonic Level. See also *parallel structure*, the *catalog poem*, *Nashers*, and *polyphonic prose*. For examples, see Whitman's "I Hear America Singing," Sandberg's "Cool Tombs," and "The Death of the Astronaut" in the section on the lai in Narrative Poetry.

The PROTHALAMIUM (PROTHALAMION) is a form of *occasional poetry*.

The PSALM is a sacred hymn—see *liturgical poetry*.

The Arabic QASIDA is a poem that may be as long as a hundred couplets long, all *couplets* rhyming *aa*:

Anacrontick Verse

Brisk methinks I am and fine,
When I drink my capering wine:
Then to love I do incline,
When I drink my wanton wine;

And I wish all maidens mine,
When I drink my sprightly wine:
Well I sup, and well I dine,
When I drink my frolic wine—
But I languish, lour and pine,
When I want my fragrant wine.
                    —Robert Herrick

Also see the *couplet, ghazal,* and *anacreontics.* Notice that this poem has a *running incremental refrain* that reappears as each even line.

The QUATERNION is a poem or other literary work written in four parts, each part treating of one of four subjects, as in Edgar Allan Poe's "The Bells," similar to the *triad.*

The QUATORZAIN is any fourteen-line form other than the *sonnet;* see the *bref double* and section X of "Reflections in an Attic Room" under *sonnet redoubled.*

The QUATRAIN is any stanza or poem form of four lines. It may be written in any prosody and line length, rhymed or unrhymed. The *envelope quatrain* rhymes *abba, cddc,* etc. The *"In Memoriam" stanza* is an iambic tetrameter envelope quatrain. The *Italian quatrain* is a *heroic envelope* and when doubled becomes the *Italian octave;* see the *sonnet.* Likewise, the *Sicilian quatrain, abab,* is also a heroic form that forms the quatrain stanzas of the *English sonnet,* and when doubled it becomes the *Sicilian octave.* The Spanish *redondilla* is an octosyllabic quatrain that rhymes *abba, abab,* or *aabb.* There are many examples of various types of quatrains throughout this volume. Other set forms of the quatrain are *ae freislighe, alcaics, awdl gywydd, ballad stanza, byr a thoddaid, casbairdne, common measure, deibhidhe,* the *englyns, gwawdodyn, kyrielle, pantoum,* the *rannaigheacts, rionnaird tri-Nard, rispetto, roundel, rubai, sapphics, seadna, sneadhbhairdne,* and *toddaid.*

The QUINTET (*pentastich*) is any poem or stanza of five lines. The *English quintet* rhymes *ababb.* The *envelope quintet* has a rhyme scheme of *abcba* or *abbba.* The *Sicilian quintet* is an iambic pentameter heroic form rhyming *ababa.* The octosyllabic Spanish *quintilla* is any quintet rhyming *ababa, abbab, ababb, abaab, aabab,* or *aabba.*

QUINTILLA—see *quintet*.

For RANDAIGECHT CHETHARCHUBAID and RANNAIGHEACHTS
BHEAG, GHAIRID, and MHOR, see the next entry.

All the RANNAIGHEACHT forms are Irish and syllabic. RANNAI-
GHEACHT GHAIRID (ron-áyach chárrid) is a *quatrain* stanza the first
line of which is three syllables in length, and the the remaining
three lines, seven syllables. Line three cross-rhymes with line four,
and all lines are supposed to end in monosyllables:

lines *syllables and rhymes*

  1. x x a
  2. x x x x x x a
  3. x x x x x x b
  4. x *x* b *x x* x a

In all the Irish forms the poem's ending circles back to the same
first syllable, word, or line with which it begins. When the lines in
this form end in disyllables the poem is called *randaigecht chetharchubaid garit recomarcach* (ron-di-guech chey-er-hu-did gár-red ray-
cúm-ar-cach).

RANNAIGHEACHT MHOR (ron-áyach voor) is a heptasyllabic
quatrain *consonating* (**not** rhyming) [*b(ac)*] [*a(bc)*] [*b(ac)*] [*a(bc)*]; in
each couplet there are at least two *cross-rhymes* (**not** consonances),
and the final word of the third line rhymes with a word in the center of the fourth line. The internal rhyme of the first couplet can
consonate rather than rhyme, but in the second couplet the
rhymes must be true. In each line two words must alliterate, and
the last word of line four must alliterate with the preceding
stressed word.

  1. x x *b x x x* (ac)
  2. x x *x x a x* (bc)
  3. x x *b x x x* (ac)
  4. x x (ac) *x a x* (bc)

Except that all the line endings of RANNAIGHEACHT BHEAG
(ron-áyah viog) are disyllabic, it is the same, as is DEACHNADH MOR

(da-gnáw moor) except that lines one and three are octosyllabic, lines two and four are hexasyllabic, and all line endings are disyllabic words.

The REDONDILLA is a *quatrain*.

The Japanese RENGA, according to Brower (see Bibliography), is "Linked verses. Historically two different forms, both involving more than one author. The earlier form, called *tanrenga*, or '*short renga*,' is a [*tanka*] whose first three lines were composed by one poet, and last two lines by another" (509). This final *couplet response* is the *hanka*. A *renga chain* or "*long renga*" is a poem made of a *sequence* of rengas and composed by two or more authors. The first triplet sets the subject; the succeeding couplet and all ensuing triplets and couplets amplify, gloss, or comment upon the first triplet The term *haikai no renga* applies to the humorous renga chain, and it means, specifically, "renga of humor" (Hoffman, 16).

By various stages the term "haiku"—a corruption and blending of the dissimilar words "hokku" and "haikai"—came to denote an independent *tercet* of 5-7-5 syllables. The *haiku* dropped all hankas, glosses, comments, and elaborations. It became a poem that had as its basis *emotive utterance*, an *image*, and certain other characteristics as well, including *spareness*, *condensation*, *spontaneity*, *ellipsis*, and a *seasonal element*. A distinction has sometimes been made between the haiku and the *senryu*, though both have exactly the same external form. The senryu is an inquiry into the nature of humankind, whereas the haiku is an inquiry into the nature of the universe.

The haiku is philosophically an outgrowth of Zen Buddhism. Haiku translated into English tend to appear, to Western eyes, overly sentimental and to fall victim to the *pathetic fallacy*—overstated *personification*. We do not understand that the Zen poet is trying to put himself or herself into the place of the thing perceived, empathizing with the inanimate object. Moreover, the Zen poet is trying to "become one" with the object and thus with all things.

The haiku has perhaps been best described as "a moment of intense perception." William Carlos Williams enunciated the American-British Imagist doctrine as "No ideas but in things." Both conceptions are, if not identical, at least quite similar, for both are based upon the *sensory level*. Williams' dictum and T. S. Eliot's "objective correlative" sever the observer from the perceived object, while at the same time preserving much of the **effect** of Zen empathy. An objective correlative is simply the vehicle of a metaphor. The theory is that if the correct object that correlates with the idea to be expressed (symbolizes that idea) is chosen, then the idea will arise through connotation and overtone without being stated denotatively. It is through this objectivity, finally, that the poet in English achieves empathy—which is only a way of saying there is no such thing as pure objectivity.

Here is a haiku by the classical Japanese writer Bashō:

Haiku
Will it soon be spring?
They lay the ground-work for it,
the plum tree and moon.
                                        —Bashō

And here is a *found haiku* (see *found poem*)—actually, it is a *senryu*:

An Amherst Haiku
    Will you bring me a
jacinth for every finger,
    and an onyx shoe?
—Emily Dickinson/Lewis Turco

For two other senryus, see *found poetry*; see also the *katauta*.
    RENGA CHAIN—see *renga*.
    The REQUIEM is described with *liturgical poetry*.
    A REVEILLE is an awakening song (see also the *alba* and *aubade*):

An Hymn to the Morning
Attend my lays, ye ever honored nine,	[the Muses]
Assist my labours, and my strains refine;	
In smoothest numbers pour the notes along	[meters]
For bright Aurora now demands my song.	[dawn goddess]

      Aurora, hail, and all the thousand dyes,
Which deck thy progress through the vaulted skies;
the morn awakes, and wide extends her rays,
On every leaf the gentle zephyr plays;   [breeze]
Harmonious lays the feathered race resume   [birds]
Dart the bright eye, and shake the painted plume.
      Ye shady groves, your verdant gloom display
to shield your poet from the burning day:
Calliope, awake the sacred lyre,   [Muse of Epic Poetry]
While thy fair sisters fan the pleasing fire:
The bowers, the gales, the variegated skies
In all their pleasures in my bosom rise.
      See in the east the illustrious king of day!
His rising radiance drives the shades away—
But oh! I feel his fervid leaves too strong,
And scarce begun, concludes the abortive song.
                    —Phillis Wheatley

RHOPALIC VERSE is a line (or several lines) beginning with a *monosyllabic* word followed by words each a syllable longer than the one before:

  1   2   3   4
Come, lover, hastily, violently,
And gather everything gatherable.

The next poem is an anonymous Irish bardic poem cast into a Welsh official meter, RHUPUNT (rhée-pint), for the purpose of this modern version. Rhupunt is a line of three, four, or five sections, each section containing four syllables. All but the last section rhyme with each other. The last section carries the main rhyme from line to line, or from stanza to stanza, depending on how the lines are set up; that is, each section can be written on the page as a single line of verse: *aaaB / cccB / dddB*, and so forth:

A Winter Song
I have one song:
Stags are groaning,

Clouds are snowing—
Summer is gone.

Swiftly the sun
Settles beyond
The horizon,
Louring and wan.

The wild geese mourn
Down the grey storm;
Fallen is fern,
Tattered and brown.

The bird's feather
Is clogged with hoar;
This is my lore—
Summer is gone.
      —Anonymous

The RIDDLE is a form of didactic poetry; it is a short lyric that poses a question, the answer to which lies hidden in hints. These verses are from the anonymous Welsh. The official meter rhupunt (just described) has been used. This version is one line longer than the original in order to fit the form: The answer to the riddle has been added as the last line.

A Riddle

Riddle me this—
Knew the Flood's kiss,
Has a snake's hiss,
This great creature,

Fleshless, boneless,
Senseless, bloodless,
Headless, footless,
Older nor younger

Than he started,
Never daunted,
Not live nor dead,
Ever useful—

God in Heaven,
What origin?
Great wonders Thine
Who made this bull.

In woods, in leas,
Ageless, griefless,
Ever hurtless,
Of equal age

With the Eras,
Older than hours
From Time's ewers;
Broad as the gauge

Of all the Earth.
He had no birth,
Nor has he girth
On land or sea.

Trust him to hum—
He will lie dumb
And will not come
If it need be.

Bull of the air
Beyond compare,
None may ensnare
Him in his den

On the sea-cliff.
He'll roar, he'll cough,
Mannerless oaf—
Savage again

Crossing the land
Roaring and grand,
Then hushed and bland,
Fey as a boy,

Then with a shout
Lashing about
Earth in a rout.
Wickedness, joy,

Hidden, yet seen
In his careen,
Heard in his whine
First here, then there,

Hurling, twirling,
Ever breaking,
Never paying
Bull of the air.

Blameless as sky,
He is wet, dry,
Often comes by.
Old Man-fashioned,

Like everything
From beginning
Unto ending—
He is the wind.
　　　　　—Anonymous

RIMAS DISSOLUTAS, a French form originally, and therefore originally a poem written in syllabic prosody, is basically a nonce form
for a stanza that may contain any number of lines; however, all lines
must be of equal length. The lines within a stanza do not rhyme,
but in subsequent stanzas corresponding lines **do** rhyme. If written
in sestets the rhyme scheme would be *abcdef abcdef ghijkl ghijkl*, etc.

RIME COUÉE, also a French form, is a sestet stanza comprised of two rhyming couplets of any one length plus two shorter lines, also of the same length. Each couplet is followed by one of the short lines, which rhyme with one another. If the couplets were four feet (or four syllables, or four stresses) long, and the short lines were two, a shorthand rhyme scheme for one stanza would look like this: $a^4a^4b^2a^4a^4b^2$; in the next stanza the rhymes would change. If the poem were written in iambics, a schematic diagram of one stanza would look like this:

lines   meters and rhymes

	´ ´ ´ ´		
1.	xx xx xx xa		
	´ ´ ´ ´		
2.	xx xx xx xa		
	´ ´ ´		
3.	xx xx xb		
	´ ´ ´ ´		´
4.	xx xx xx xc	*or*	xa
	´ ´ ´ ´		´
5.	xx xx xx xc	*or*	xa
	´ ´ ´		
6.	xx xx xb		

The Scottish *Burns stanza* or *standard habbie* is a variation: $a^4a^4a^4b^2a^4b^2$, with the rhymes changing in subsequent stanzas. Here are two stanzas of a longer poem written in Scots, a dialect of English that is closer to Middle than to modern English:

To a Mouse, on Turning Her up in Her Nest
With the Plough, November, 1785

Wee, sleekit, cow'rin, tim'rous beastie,
O, what a panic's in thy breastie!
Thou need na start awa sae hasty,
      Wi' bickering brattle!

I wad be laith to rin an' chase thee,
  Wi' murd'ring pattle!

I'm truly sorry man's dominion
Has broken Nature's social union,
An' justifies that ill opinion,
  Which makes thee startle
At me, thy poor, earth-born companion,
  An' fellow-mortal!
      —Robert Burns

RIME ROYAL. The septet stanza form in which Geoffrey Chaucer wrote *Troilus and Cressida* and others of his poems including "Complaint to His Purse" is sometimes called *Chaucerian stanza*, but more often *rime royal* because James I of Scotland used it. Written in iambic pentameter measures, it is a Sicilian triplet and a quatrain consisting of two heroic couplets, the first of which interlocks with the triplet (*ababbcc*):

Thoughts From the Boston Post Road
Today ten thousand vehicles have passed
  In cursing columns down the nearby Post
Road, left that sparrow on the billboard gassed
  Whose muddled instincts panic to the west
  Beyond the screws and monkey-wrenches tossed
 From mobile windows. But the west is east,
 And east is south, and south is north at least.

The land is shot for sparrows, shot for men.
  But for machines it's Paradise on Wheels!
The lubricated sky remembers when
  Its clouds were H2O, not high grade oils;
  And everywhere the graded turf recalls
 When it grew grasses rather than these goddam
 Vines of white concrete and black macadam.

If that poor sparrow ever manages
  To climb above our gamma-powered smogs,
Let him look down upon these acreages

> And see if apple trees are bearing cogs,
> Of if some tractor isn't laying eggs,
> Its mate a diesel truck that proudly roars
> To herald a new age of dinosaurs.

> We've done a grand job building road and rail.
> There's nowhere some good engine cannot roll
> (With some good man behind the driver's wheel),
> And I would not be worrying at all
> Except, this afternoon, out in the hall,
> I overheard my vacuum cleaner say,
> "They built Der Furor just the other day."

RIONNAIRD TRI-NARD (rún-ard tree-nard) is an Irish *quatrain* stanza of hexasyllabic lines ending in disyllables. Line two rhymes with line four, and line three consonates with both. In the second couplet there are two cross-rhymes but none in the first. In each line there is alliteration, and the ultimate syllable of line one alliterates with the first accented word of the second line. The poem ends with the same first syllable, word, or line with which it begins. The rhyme scheme showing the disyllabic line endings is: *(xa)(x[bc])(b[xc])(x[bc])*. Note that the letters in brackets indicate consonances rather than rhymes.

The RISPETTO, an Italian form, is any complete poem made up of two quatrains, usually written in iambic tetrameter measures, often rhyming *abab ccdd*. Following are two anonymous Gaelic poems rendered here in the form of a rispetto, but written in heptasyllabic quatrains. In the first, lines one and three consonate, and lines two and four rhyme; in the second, lines one and two consonate, and lines three and four rhyme: approximations of bardic meters and devices.

Two Epigrams

> When I stand with the young bloods,
> Then my fierce red blood is up;
> When I sit with the greybeards,
> I nod sagely in my cup.

Sad to see the sons of lore
Damned to the eternal fire
While these pigs, illiterate,
In God's glory coruscate.

—Anonymous Gaelic

The ROMANCE is discussed among the forms of Narrative Poetry.

The French RONDEAU is fifteen lines long and consists of three stanzas—a quintet, a quatrain, and a sestet, in that order, rhyming *aabba aabR aabbaR*. Lines nine and fifteen are short, a refrain consisting of the first *phrase* of the first line; thus, they are shorter than all the rest of the lines of the poem, which are all of the same length:

lines	rhymes and refrains	
1.	. . . R a	*1st line contains refrain*
2.	a	
3.	b	
4.	b	
5.	a	
6.	a	
7.	a	
8.	b	
9.	. . . R	*refrain*
10.	a	
11.	a	
12.	b	
13.	b	
14.	a	
15.	. . . R	*refrain*

This example was written by an Afro-American poet early in the twentieth century:

We Wear the Mask

We wear the mask that grins and lies,
It hides our cheeks and shades our eyes—
This debt we pay to human guile;
With torn and bleeding hearts we smile,
And mouth with myriad subtleties.

Why should the world be otherwise,
In counting all our tears and sighs?
Nay, let them only see us while
We wear the mask.

We smile, but, O great Christ, our cries
To thee from tortured souls arise.
We sing, but oh the clay is vile
Beneath our feet, and long the mile;
But let the world dream otherwise,
We wear the mask.

Paul Lawrence Dunbar

The RONDEAU REDOUBLED has five quatrain stanzas plus one quintet stanza to end it, and lines are supposed to be of equal length, except for the last, which is a repeton consisting of the first few words of line one of the poem. There are four other refrains as well: **all** of lines one through four, which makes stanza one a *texte*, for line one ends stanza two; line two ends stanza three; line three ends stanza four; and line four ends stanza five. In this rhyme scheme capital R stands for the repeton, and the other capitals are numbered with superscripts to differentiate the refrains: $(RA^1)B^1A^2B^2, babA^1, abaB^1, babA^2, abaB^2, babaR$.

Jason Potter

from Bordello

Suddenly, nothing was left of all those
years we'd spent together in the same house,
under that old mansard that bent and rose
above us, gracefully guarding. The spruce

in the dooryard spired out of the grass
like a steeple, pulling us taut as bows—
both generations. But age is a noose:
suddenly, nothing was left of all those

mornings and nights. I, Jason Potter, chose
to lay away my helpmeet and my spouse
in a lone bed. So ended my repose.
Years we'd spent together in the same house

became beads to tell, the string broken—loose
time come unstrung. Still, outside, the spruce grows,
and it is nature to try to mend loss.
Under that old mansard that bent and rose

over the life we'd built, my blood still flows
in fever now and then. I make my truce
with flesh through these paid women whom I use.
Above us, guarding and graceful, the spruce

used to seem a symbol of common use
and fulfillment of self and heart—those blues
tipping sheer limbs sharply; strong and close
and clean, the bole and needles of pure hues....
Suddenly, nothing was left.

Another French poem form is the RONDEL, which is thirteen
lines divided into two quatrains and a quintet rhyming *Abba abAB
abbaA*. These love songs following are by the Anglo-Norman poet
Charles d'Orleans (1391–1465).

The Seige

To his Mistress, to succour his heart that is beleaguered by jealousy.

My Love, strengthen this castle of my heart,
    And with some store of pleasure give me aid,
For Jealousy, with all who take his part,
    About the failing tower strong siege has laid.

Nay, if to break his grip thou art afraid,
Too weak to make his cruel force depart,
    At least strengthen this castle of my heart,
And with some store of pleasure give me aid.

Nay, let not Jealousy, for all his art,
    Be master, and the tower in ruins laid
    That still, ah Love! thy gracious rule obeyed.
Advance and give me succour on thy part;
My Love, strengthen this castle of my heart,
    And with some store of pleasure give me aid.
                        —Charles d'Orleans

The French RONDEL SUPREME is a poem consisting of two *quatrains* and a *sestet* rhyming *ABba abAB abbaAB*, the capital letters
representing refrains. All lines must be of the same length. Like his
older contemporary Chaucer, d'Orleans wrote in Middle English,
but in his work accentual-syllabic prosody is not developed into a
cohesive system, as Chaucer's was.

Confessional

My ghostly father, let me confess,
First to God and then to you,
That at a window—do you know how?—
I stole a kiss of great sweetness.

It was done without advisedness,
But it is done, not undone now.
My ghostly father, let me confess,
First to God and then to you.

But it shall be restored, doubtless,
For kisses one should rebestow,
And that to God I make this vow,
Otherwise, I ask forgiveness.
My ghostly father, let me confess,
First to God and then to you.
                        —Charles d'Orleans

The RONDELET, which is French, is a poem of a single *septet* with two rhymes and one refrain: *AbAabbA*. The refrain is tetra-syllabic or dimeter, depending on what prosody is being used, and the rest of the lines are twice as long, octasyllabic or tetrameter.

The Swift Replies

> The swift replies
> Fall from air to the ear in Spring.
> The swift replies
> To the phoebe who sounds her sighs,
> To dovecall, the catbird crying—
> And when the owl goes questioning,
> The swift replies.
>
> —Wesli Court

The French RONDINE is a poem twelve lines in length divided into a septet and a quintet rhyming *abbaabR aabbaR*. As in the ron-deau, the refrain consists of the first *phrase* of the first line.

Rondine of the Rare Device

"If you can kiss the mistress, never kiss the maid."

> The maid will do if you are not ambitious—
> Why split the stalk if twigs will make the besom?
> Why kill the roots if one may steal the blossom?
> The garden is a plot of sundry pleasures
> Filled with winding paths and rare devices,
> Here a fountain, there a Grecian column—
> The maid will do.
>
> Rose O'Morning winds upon the trellis,
> All hips and nettles, snags and lures at random.
> Is desire the better part of wisdom?
> Brown-eyed Susan smiles from her bed of grasses—
> The maid will do.
>
> Wesli Court

The RONSARDIAN ODE is in the section on *occasional poetry*.

For the ROUND see *caccia*, *catch*, and *glee* (all three under *balada*), and *roundelay*.

The English ROUNDEL is a poem similar to the rondine: eleven lines and three stanzas, a quatrain, a triplet, and a quatrain rhyming *abaRb Rbbab abbaRb*—the refrain, which is made up of the first phrase of the first line, in this case also rhymes with the *b* lines:

The Way of the Wind
The wind's way in the deep sky's hollow
None may measure, as none can say
How the heart in her shows the swallow
    The wind's way.

Hope nor fear can avail to stay
Waves that whiten on wrecks that wallow,
Times and seasons that wane and slay.

Live and love, till the strong night swallow
Thought and hope and the red last ray,
Swim the waters of years that follow
    The wind's way.
            —Algernon Charles Swinburne

The English ROUNDELAY is any simple poem with a refrain, but John Dryden invented a complicated set form that is twenty-four lines long—four sestets—and turns on only two rhymes. Except for the first and second lines of stanza one and lines three and four of stanza four, all the rest are repetons or refrains, each being used at least once elsewhere in the poem in a particular order: $abA^1B^1A^2B^2$ $A^1B^1A^3B^3A^2B^2$ $A^3B^3A^4B^4A^2B^2$ $A^4B^4abA^2B^2$.

Roundelay
Chloe found Amyntas lying,
        All in tears, upon the plain,
Sighing to himself, and crying,

"Wretched I, to love in vain!
Kiss me, dear, before my dying;
　　Kiss me once and ease my pain."

Sighing to himself, and crying,
　　"Wretched I, to love in vain!
Ever scorning, and denying
　　To reward your faithful swain:
Kiss me, dear, before my dying;
　　Kiss me once, and ease my pain!

"Ever scorning, and denying
　　To reward your faithful swain."
Chloe, laughing at his crying,
　　Told him that he loved in vain.
"Kiss me, dear, before my dying;
　　Kiss me once, and ease my pain!"

Chloe, laughing at his crying,
　　Told him that he loved in vain;
But repenting, and complying,
　　When he kissed, she kissed again—
Kissed him up before his dying;
　　Kissed him up and eased his pain.
　　　　　　　　—John Dryden

The Arabic RUBAI is a *quatrain* poem rhyming *aaba*; used as a
stanza form, the poem becomes a RUBAIYAT. The *interlocking rubaiyat* is a form of *chain verse* which picks up the third line of the
preceding stanza as the main rhyme of the second stanza, and so
on: *aaba bbcb ccdc*. Normally, the last stanza would use as its third
line the main rhyme of stanza one: *zzaz*.

Rubaiyat of Beauty and Truth

"A man of gladness seldom falls into madness."

A man of gladness seldom falls into madness,
A man of goodness descends not to badness,

A chap of parts seldom falls apart
To become thereby a sorry and sad mess.

A fellow with guts has a lot of heart,
A woman who's sour is likely a tart.
That person who broods will soon lose his goods,
A glutton who gorges develops a wart.

Silverbrowed people never wear hoods,
Dragglehaired women always wear snoods
When they walk in the wind, except for a few
Who like to wear waterwings when it floods.

All of these sayings are truer than true,
Though less true for me than they are for you.
So take it from me, for a word to the wise
Is better than oneandahalf, maybe two.

Borrow a truism, try it for size,
See it if won't help you humorize,
For a man of gladness seldom falls into madness
Below his chin or over his eyes.

—Wesli Court

The RUNE is a letter of the Anglo-Saxon alphabet, believed to have magical powers, as indeed it did, for those who could read. By extension, any magical English language poem may be called a "rune"—see Amergin's "The Mystery," under *chant*.

The SAPPHIC LINE is composed of two trochees, a dactyl, and two trochees, in that order, although certain substitutions are allowed at prescribed places. This is a Sapphic line: ⁄◡ ⁄◡ ⁄◡◡ ⁄◡ ⁄◡. A spondee may be substituted for a trochee in lines one and two, feet two and five; and in line three, foot five—see the italicized sections of the diagram below.

A fuller discussion of the Greek quantitative accentual-syllabic *quatrain* stanza, SAPPHICS, is given in the section on Phrasing (in chapter 1). It is made up of three Sapphic lines plus an *adonic line*.

Here is a diagram:

lines   meters

```
        ´   ´   ´   ´   ´
 1.    xx  xx xxx xx  xx
        ´   ´   ´   ´   ´
 2.    xx  xx xxx xx  xx
        ´   ´   ´   ´   ´
 3.    xx  xx xxx xx  xx
        ´   ´
 4.    xxx xx
```

An example, "Sapphic Stanzas in Falling Measures," is found in the section on Phrasing.

SATIRICAL POETRY (SATIRICS) is poetry of mockery, including *mock forms*. The *epitaph* is *lapidary verse*—that is, a gravestone *inscription* (**not** to be confused with the *epigraph*). It is one of the two major short forms of *satirics*, the other being the *epigram*, which has been defined as terse verse with a cutting edge. The *clerihew*, a particular type of epigram, was invented by E. Clerihew Bentley (1875–1956). It is a quatrain in dipodic meters rhyming *aabb*, the first line of which is both the title and the name of a person:

SIGMUND FREUD
Became annoyed
When his ego
Sailed to Montego.

SIGMUND FREUD
Became more annoyed
When his id
Fled to Madrid.

SIGMUND FREUD
Grew most annoyed
When his superego
Tried Montenegro.

SIGMUND FREUD
Was nearly destroyed
When his alter-ego
Showed up in Oswego.

KARL JUNG
Found himself among
Archetypes
Of various stripes.
                —Wesli Court

All epigrams are satirical or at least witty mockery, and all forms may be utilized in this minor genre, in which case they are *mock forms*—see "A Pastorale of Sorts" (under *pastoral*) and R. S. Gwynn's "Retirement into Gentle Go Not Do" (under *villanelle*). *Capitolo* is satirical *terza rima*—see *canzone*. The *literary epitaph* (*mortuary verse*) is also satirical; it has been described as terse verse for the long gone:

> *This Morning Tom Child, the Painter, Died*
> Tom Child had often painted Death,
> But never to the Life, before:
> Doing it now, he's out of breath;
> He paints it once, and paints no more.
>   —Samuel Sewall

Skeltonics, which is a short-lined, bumptiously rhymed satiric form, is listed separately later. An opposite prosody is the *Nasher*, also used as a vehicle for mockery—see Ogden Nash's "Kindly Unhitch That Star, Buddy," in the Glossary under *wrenched rhyme*. *Hudibrastics* are irregular tetrameter lines rhymed humorously in couplets. The *fabliau*, mentioned earlier, is a satiric form, as is the *sirvente*, a lyric satire on religion or public matters.

SÉADNA, an Irish *quatrain* stanza, alternates octosyllabic lines having disyllabic endings with heptasyllabic lines having monosyllabic endings. Lines two and four rhyme; line three rhymes with the stressed word preceding the final word of the fourth line. In the second couplet there are two cross-rhymes, and there is alliteration in each line, the ultimate word of the fourth line alliterating with the preceding stressed word. The ultimate syllable of the first line alliterates with the first stressed word of the second line. As in Irish tradition, the poem ends with the same first syllable, word, or line with which it begins. A simplified rhyme scheme is: *[(xa)] [b] [c(xc)] [bcb]*; note that lines are enclosed in brackets, and disyllabic endings in parentheses. Here is a diagram:

lines   syllables and rhymes

1.   x x x x x x xa
2.   x x x x x x b
3.   x x x x x x xc
4.   x b x c x x b

SÉADNA MÓR (sháy-na moor) is identical excepting that lines two and four end in trisyllables.

The SEDOKA is a Japanese form made of two *katautas* (5-7-7, 5-7-7 syllable count). A *volta* takes place between the two triplet stanzas and, though the poem may be a *dialogue*, it is written by a single author:

Dialogue

   I am wearing blue
in honor of the sky. Shall
you wear green to honor earth?

   I will don rainbows:
I will wear snow on my back—
white, allcolor forever.

The Japanese SENRYU is found under *haiku* and under *renga*.
For the SEPTENARY, see *poulter's measure*.

The SEPTET (*heptastich*) is a seven-line poem or stanza form. The iambic pentameter *Sicilian septet* rhymes *ababab a*. *Rime royal* and the *rondelet* are septet forms.

The SEQUENCE or *cycle* is a series of related poems—see *companion poem*.

SERIES—see *sequence*.

The SERENADE is a secular *evensong*, a love song sung at eventide:

A Serenade of Youth, an Envoy in Middle Age

> *"'Tis Midsummer moon with you; you are mad."*

Diana, Lady of the Sky,
What do you dream as Earth turns by
    Beneath your silver stare?
Do you, like us who lie below,
Go slumbering within your glow
And dream that lightning eons flow
    Into those vacuums where
The echoes of eternity
Reverberate infinitely
And shadows whisper quietly,
    Dissolving in a sigh?

My Lady, maiden Moon, do you
In your unending voyage through
    The amethystine skies,
With everlasting hope dream of
Some strange, celestial form of love
Known only in those worlds above?
    And do your cratered cries
Resound through space and time and soul
To form at last a perfect whole
While luminary bodies roll
    Through the galaxial blue?

Fair Moon, you are a lucky thing.
Although you have no song to sing,
    Your beams touch your desire,
And Earth, encircled by your power,
Blossoms like some nocturnal flower
Out of a darkling sylvan bower—

Blooms with the coldest fire.
I would that I might be a moon,
A grain within some starry dune
Whose love might not end quite so soon
        In death's chill moldering.

Envoy:
        Now you are not alone.
The astronauts have scuffed your crust;
Science has satisfied its lust.
Romance is settled into dust—
        Diana, you are stone.

An *evensong* (*vespers*) is a prayer, or simply an *air* or *nocturne*, sung in the evening, and a *nightsong* is a formal lyric prayer sung at midnight. See the section on *liturgical poetry*. See also the *alba* (*aubade*).

The SERMON, a liturgical form, is found in The Genres of Nonfiction in *The Book of Literary Terms*.

The SESTET (*hexastich*) is any stanza or poem of six lines. The iambic pentameter *Italian sestet* rhymes *abcabc*, and it forms the second stanza of an *Italian sonnet*. The *heroic sestet*, equally iambic pentameter, rhymes *abbacc* or *ababcc*. The *stave* is also a sestet stanza. The Spanish *sextilla* rhymes either *aabccb* or *ababcc*, and it is octasyllabic.

The SESTINA is of Medieval French origin, attributed to Arnaut Daniel in the late twelfth century and used by other Gallic poets and by Italians including Petrarch and Dante (from whom it received its Italian name). The popularity of the poem in English is primarily a twentieth century phenomenon, however, particularly in the United States. The six *end words* or *teleutons* of the lines of the first stanza are repeated in a specific order as end words in the five succeeding sestet stanzas. The order of the repetition of the end words is ABCDE FAEBDC CFDABE ECBFAD DEACFB BDFECA and, in the envoy, BE (line 37) DC (line 38) FA (line 39). In English the sestina is generally written in iambic pentameter or, sometimes, in decasyllabic meters. Its thirty-nine lines are divided into six sestet stanzas and a final triplet envoy (or *envoi*). In the envoy the six teleutons are also picked up, one of them being buried in and one finishing each line.

The order in which the end words are repeated appears to have its roots in numerology, but what the significance of the pattern was originally is now unknown. The sequence of numbers is 6-1-5-2-4-3. Obviously, the series is just 1-2-3-4-5-6 with the last three numbers reversed and inserted ahead of the first three: 6-1-5-2-4-3. If the end words of stanza one are designated ABCDEF (the capital letters signifying repetitions) and the sequence 615243 is applied to it, the order of repetitions in the second stanza will be FAEBDC. Apply the sequence to the second stanza, and the third stanza will be CFDABE. Continuing the process will give us ECBFAD in the fourth stanza, DEACFB in the fifth, and BDFECA in the sixth sestet. The order of repetition in the three lines of the envoy is BE / DC / FA.

The oldest British example—a double sestina, actually—is by Philip Sidney, "You Goat-Herd Gods," from his sixteenth century *Arcadia*; the version given later in this section has had its spelling modernized. It is not merely a double sestina (twelve sestet stanzas rather than six), but a pastoral dialogue or *eclogue* as well.

In the nineteenth century, Algernon Charles Swinburne wrote another double sestina titled "The Complaint of Lisa"; his "Sestina," which Swinburne made to rhyme *ababab* as well, turned its stanzas into Sicilian sestets and increased the difficulty of the form, but some of the earliest French and Italian sestinas also rhymed, so this was not really an experiment. Edmund Gosse, a contemporary, also wrote a "Sestina," and, as sometimes was the fashion, he italicized the teleutons. Not long after the turn of the twentieth century, Ezra Pound returned to the dramatic mode of Sidney and wrote the monologue "Sestina: Altaforte"; this, together with his "Sestina for Isolt," set off a steady trickle, if not a flood, of traditional and experimental sestinas.

The problem with the sestina is, generally, that the repeated end words can be obtrusive. To draw the reader's attention *away* from the repetitions, poets often enjamb their lines so that sentences and phrases are not end-stopped on the teleutons, or they may use, on occasion, homographs of the end words, like wind (as in "south wind") and wind (as in "wind your own clock"), or even such ploys as can and toucan. However, in his "Age and Indifferent Clouds," Harry Mathews deliberately used such words as "hippopotamus" and "bronchitis," thus drawing the reader's attention *to* the teleutons rather than away from them, and the beginnings of the lines doubled the difficulty by making puns and ringing variations on six herbs and plants, which might go unnoticed because the end words take so much of the reader's attention. Donald Justice's "Sestina: Here in Katmandu" has no envoy and its line lengths vary, generally between four stresses and one, and Alan Ansen's "A Fit of Something Against Something" is a "diminishing sestina," which starts out normally but then begins to lose words until in the envoy all that's left are the teleutons of each line—see *diminishing verse.*

In 1979 Wesli Court took advantage of the obsessive quality of the sestina's repetitions in "The Obsession," one of the poems in a sequence titled *Letters to the Dead* that rings the changes on the rhymed iambic pentameter sestet. The first line of "The Obsession" contains all six of the end words, and the same basic line is repeated incrementally as the first line of succeeding stanzas. Each time the line is repeated the syntax is transposed by hypallage; nonetheless, the line always makes sense. Because all six endwords do appear in this line, a particular problem arises at the envoy, for it cannot be of three lines. Instead, the refrain line reappears a seventh time as a one-line envoy rather than as the normal triplet, but with the sense of the original first line reversed.

Sestina in Indian Summer

"Everything is good in its season."

After the frost summer returns and settles
Into the orchard. The sluggish yellowjacket
Describes its ovals over the bright windfall,
And the leaves begin to color our landscapes
The russet of oak and the maples' ocher.
This is no time for us to think of winter

And its white song, no time to sing of winter,
Of fires on our hearths, before our settles,
Running along the backlog turning ocher
And crimson. The chestnut falls from its jacket
Into roots; sunlight lies long on our landscapes.
We listen in the night to hear the wind fall

And wonder when it will rise again to fall,
To take the leaves and pile them into winter
Among the stooks that walk across our landscapes.
It is enough for now that the wind settles
Into breeze and the grass removes its jacket
Of frost while the landscapes of maple, oak, or

Chestnut put on their robes of russet, ocher,
Saffron, and settle in to wait for the fall.
Asters and cedars have the yellowjacket
Along the brook, and we will not now inter
Our languid hours where the dragonfly settles
Among the rushes. The warmth of the land escapes

Slowly eastward toward the stony coasts, capes
And bays where the vacant beach wears a choker
Of brown kelp, a necklace of shells that settles
Into the sand. We wait and ignore the fall
Of leaves, the failing summer, and the winter
Impending. We hear the late yellowjacket

Circle, the horsechestnut fall from its jacket
Of thorns; we watch color transform our landscapes,
Knowing that the allcolor of our winter
Is nascent beneath this flowering of ocher.
This renaissance of summer is but windfall.
Soon we will hunker down upon our settles

In sweater and jacket. Backlogs of oak or
Maple will burn; their smoke will stitch our landscapes
To the winter weather that falls and settles.

You Goat-Herd Gods

A Dialogue between Strephon and Klaius

Strephon. You goat-herd Gods who love the grassy mountains,
You nymphs that haunt the springs in pleasant valleys,
You satyrs joyed with free and quiet forests,
Vouchsafe your silent ears to plaining music
Which to my woes gives still an early morning
And draws the dolor on till weary evening.

Klaius. O Mercury, foregoer to the evening,
O heavenly huntress of the savage mountains.
O lovely star, entitled of the morning,
Which that my voice does fill these woeful valleys,
Vouchsafe your silent ears to plaining music
Which oft hath Echo tired in secret forests.

Strephon. I that was once free-burgess of the forests,
Where shade from sun and sports I sought at evening;
I that was once esteemed for pleasant music
Am banished now among the monstrous mountains
Of huge despair, and foul affliction's valleys,
Am grown a screech-owl to my self each morning.

Klaius. I that was once delighted every morning,
Hunting the wild inhabitants of forests,
I that was once the music of these valleys,
So darkened am, that all my day is evening,
Heart-broken so, that mole-hills seem high mountains
And fill the vales with cries instead of music.

Strephon. Long since, alas, my deadly, swinish music
Hath made itself a crier of the morning
And has with wailing strength climbed highest mountains:
Long since my thoughts more desert be than forests;
Long since I see my joys come to their evening
And state thrown down to over-trodden valleys.

Klaius. Long since the happy dwellers of these valleys
Have prayed me leave my strange, exclaiming music
Which troubles their day's work, and joys of evening.
Long since I hate the night, more hate the morning;
Long since my thoughts chase me like beasts in forests,
And make me wish myself laid under mountains.

Strephon. Me seems I see the high and stately mountains
Transform themselves to low, dejected valleys;
Me seems I hear in these ill-changed forests,
The nightingales do learn of owls their music;
Me seems I feel the comfort of the morning
Turned to the mortal serene of an evening.

Klaius. Me seems I see a filthy, cloudy evening
As soon as sun begins to climb the mountains;
Me seems I feel a noisome scent, the morning
When I do smell the flowers of these valleys;
Me seems I hear, when I do hear sweet music,
The dreadful cries of murdered men in forests.

Strephon. I wish to fire the trees of all these forests;
I give the sun a last farewell each evening;
I curse the fiddling finders-out of music:
With envy I do hate the lofty mountains
And with despite despise the humble valleys;
I do detest night, evening, day, and morning.

Klaius. Curse to myself my prayer is, the morning:
My fire is more than can be made with forests;
My state more base than are the basest valleys;
I wish no evenings more to see, each evening;
Shamed I have my self in sight of mountains
And stopped my ears, lest I grow mad with music.

Strephon. For she whose parts maintained a perfect music,
Whose beauty shone more than the blushing morning,
Who much surpassed in state the stately mountains,

In straightness passed the cedars of the forests,
Has cast me, wretched, into eternal evening
By taking her two suns from these dark valleys.

Klaius. For she, to whom compared, the Alps are valleys,
She, whose least word brings from the spheres their music,
At whose approach the sun rose in the evening,
Who, where she went, bore in her forehead morning,
Is gone, is gone from these our spoiled forests,
Turning to deserts our best pastured mountains.

Strephon, **Klaius.** These mountains witness all, so shall these valleys,
These forests too, made wretched by our music:
Our morning hymn is this, and song at evening.

—Philip Sidney

Sestina

I saw my soul at rest upon a day
       As a bird sleeping in the nest of night,
Among soft leaves that give the starlight way
       To touch its wings but not its eyes with light;
So that it knew as one in visions may,
       And knew not as men waking, of delight.

This was the measure of my soul's delight;
       It had no power of joy to fly by day,
Nor part in the large lordship of the light;
       But in a secret moon-beholden way
Had all its will of dreams and pleasant night
       And all the love and life that sleepers may.

But such life's triumph as men waking may
       It might not have to feed its faint delight
Between the stars by night and sun by day,
       Shut up with green leaves and a little light;
Because its way was as a lost star's way,
       A world's not wholly known of day or night.

All loves and dreams and sounds and gleams of night
        Made it all music that such minstrels may,
And all they had they gave it of delight;
        But in the full face of the fire of day
What place shall be for any starry light,
        What part of heaven in all the wide sun's way?

Yet the soul woke not, sleeping by the way,
        Watched as a nursling of the large eyed night,
And sought no strength nor knowledge of the day,
        Nor closer touch conclusive of delight,
Nor mightier joy nor truer than dreamers may,
        Nor more of song than they, nor more of light.

For who sleeps once and sees the secret light
        Whereby sleep shows the soul a fairer way
Between the rise and rest of day and night,
        Shall care no more to fare as all men may,
But be his place of pain or of delight,
        There shall he dwell, beholding night as day.

Song, have thy day and take thy fill of light
        Before the night be fallen across thy way;
Sing while he may, man hath no long delight.
                        —Algernon Charles Swinburne

The Obsession

Last night I dreamed my father died again,
A decade and a year after he dreamed
Of death himself, pitched forward into night.
His world of waking flickered out and died—
An image on a screen. He is the father
Now of fitful dreams that last and last.

I dreamed again my father died at last.
He stood before me in his flesh again.
I greeted him. I said, "How are you, father?"
But he looked frailer than last time I'd dreamed

We were together, older than when he'd died—
I saw upon his face the look of night.

I dreamed my father died again last night.
He stood before a mirror. He looked his last
Into the glass and kissed it. He saw he'd died.
I put my arms about him once again
To help support him as he fell. I dreamed
I held the final heartburst of my father.

I died again last night: I dreamed my father
Kissed himself in glass, kissed me goodnight
In doing so. But what was it I dreamed
In fact? An injury that seems to last
Without abatement, opening again
And yet again in dream? Who was it died

Again last night? I dreamed my father died,
But it was not he—it was not my father,
Only an image flickering again
Upon the screen of dream out of the night.
How long can this cold image of him last?
Whose is it, his or mine? Who dreams he dreamed?

My father died. Again last night I dreamed
I felt his struggling heart still as he died
Beneath my failing hands. And when at last
He weighed me down, then I laid down my father,
Covered him with silence and with night.
I could not bear it should he come again—

I died again last night, my father dreamed.

—Wesli Court

For the SEXAIN and SEXTILLA, see *sestet*.
The SHAKESPEARIAN SONNET is described in the *sonnet* section.
SHANTY—see *chantey*.
SHAPED STANZA—see the The Typographical Level in chapter 1.
The SHORT COUPLET is in the section on the *couplet*.

SHORT HYMNAL OCTAVE, SHORT HYMNAL STANZA, SHORT MEAS-URE, and SHORT OCTAVE, all of them English forms, are all found under *common measure.*

SHORT PARTICULAR MEASURE is a *sestet stanza* that has three iambic feet in lines 1, 2, 4 and 5, and four feet in lines 3 and 6; the usual rhyme is *aabaab.* For an example, see the anonymous "The Maid's Complaint" under *objective syntax* in the Glossary; also see *common measure.*

SHORT RENGA (*tanrenga*)—see *renga.*

SICILIAN OCTAVE—see *octave.*

SICILIAN SEPTET—see *septet.*

SICILIAN SONNET—see *sonnet.*

For the Italian forms called SICILIAN OCTAVE, see *octave*; SICILIAN QUATRAIN, see *quatrain*; SICILIAN QUINTET, see *quintet*; SICILIAN SEPTET, see *septet;* and for the SICILIAN SESTET, see *sestet.* The SICILIAN SONNET is found under *sonnet.* For the SICILIAN TERCET, see *tercet*; for the SICILIAN TRIPLET, see *triplet.*

For the Italian SIRIMA, see *canzone.*

The SIRVENTE is described under *satirics.*

SKELTONICS, or *tumbling verse*, which is insistently rhymed dipodic couplets, was the creation of the sixteenth-century poet John Skelton, who, among other things, evidently proclaimed himself the first official court poet of England or *Poet Laureate*— that is, wearer of the classical *crown of laurel* indicating victory in athletics or war, or preeminence in poetic composition. There is no set point at which the rhymes may change in Skeltonics, and every now and again a tripod may be thrown in to thicken the brew.

Skelton has been called the last of the English Medieval poets by some, and by others the first of the English Renaissance poets. No doubt he was both, for he wrote not only in podic prosody, like the anonymous English poets since Chaucer, but in accentual-syllabic prosody as well, like the Scottish Chaucerians, Chaucer himself, and almost all other English poets up through the nineteenth century.

The "head" of the title of the following poem is a skull, like that in "Memento Mori" (under *cautionary verse*), for Skelton was a priest, though a highly unusual one. In the original the title continues into an *epigraph*, "that was sent to him from an honorable gentlewoman for a token, Skelton, Laureate, devised this ghostly meditation in English, covenable, in sentence, commendable, lamentable, lacrimable, profitable for the soul." The last line of this poem was originally in French: "mirez vous y," which is rendered here in English.

Though Skelton was the last English poet of any note before the nineteenth century priest Gerard Manley Hopkins to use alliterative stress verse, his podics were idiosyncratic: He made lines of the hemistichs and rhymed them insistently. We have come to call this system "Skeltonics," in his honor, or "tumbling verse." (Interestingly enough, Hopkins also invented a system of strong-stress verse, which he called "sprung rhythm.")

Upon a Dead Man's Head

Your ugly token
My mind hath broken
From worldly lust,
For I have discussed
We are but dust,
And die we must.
It is general
To be mortal.
I have well espied
No man may him hide
From Death hollow-eyed,
With sinews withered,
With bones shivered,
With his worm-eaten maw
And his ghastly jaw
Gaping aside—
Neither flesh nor fell.
Then, by my counsel,
Look that ye spell
Well this gospel:
For whereso we dwell
Death will us quell
And with us mell.

For all our pampered paunches
There may be no franchise
Nor worldly bliss
Redeem us from this.
Our days be dated
To be checkmated
With draughts of death
Stopping our breath—
Our eyes sinking,
Our bodies stinking,
Our gums grinning,
Our souls burning.
To whom, then, shall we sue
For to have rescue,
But to sweet Jesu
On us then for to rue?
O goodly Child
Of Mary mild,
Then be our shield
That we be not exiled
To the dread dale
Of bootless bale,
Nor to the lake
Of fiends black.
But grant us grace
To see thy Face,
And to purchase
Thine heavenly place,
And thy palace
Full of solace
Above the sky
That is so high,
Eternally
To behold and see
The Trinity!
Amen.

Mirror you thus.
                              —John Skelton

Sneadhbhairdne (sna-vúy-erd-ne), a syllabic Irish *quatrain* stanza form, alternates octasyllabic and tetrasyllabic lines, both ending in disyllabic words. Lines two and four rhyme; line three consonates with both. Every stressed word in the fourth line must rhyme, and there is alliteration as in *rionnaird tri-nard*. The poem circles back to the first syllable, word, or line with which it began, as in all the Irish forms: *(xa)(xb)(bc) [bb(xb)]*:

lines   syllables and rhymes

1.   x x x x x x (x a)
2.   x x (x b)
3.   x x x x x x (b c)
4.   b b (x b)

The soliloquy is a form of Dramatic Poetry, which has its own earlier section.

The Japanese somonka is an epistolary love poem made up of two *tankas* written by different authors. The first is a declaration of love, the second a response.

Find the Italian sonetto rispetto under *sonnet*. For an example, see stanza XI in "Reflections in an Attic Room" under *sonnet redoubled*.

The word song is a synonym for *lyric*.

Find song measure with the other *edda measures*.

The word sonnet originally meant simply "little song," but it has come to denote a fourteen-line poem written in iambic pentameter measures and rhymed in various ways. The *Petrarchan* or *Italian sonnet* has an *Italian octave,* which is made up of two *Italian quatrains* (*abbaabba*), after which a *volta* or *turn* takes place, a shift in direction or thought, which is pursued in the succeeding sestet, which is either an *Italian sestet* (*cdecde*) or a *Sicilian sestet* (*cdcdcd*).

The *envelope sonnet* rhymes *abbacddc efgefg* or *efefef*. The *Sicilian sonnet* combines a *Sicilian octave* and a *Sicilian* or *Italian sestet*; the rhymes change at the volta: *abababab cdecde* or *cdcdce*.

The Italian and Sicilian octaves and *ottava rima* (*abababcc*) are *heroic octaves*. The *sonetto rispetto* combines one stanza of ottava rima or one iambic pentameter rispetto (*ababccdd*) with either an Italian or a Sicilian sestet (*abababcc defdef* or *dedede,* or *ababccdd efgefg* or *efe-fef*). *The English* or *Shakespearean sonnet* has three *Sicilian quatrains* (*abab cdcd efef*) followed by a volta and a *heroic couplet* (*gg*).

The *Spenserian sonnet* has three *interlocking Sicilian quatrains* (*abab bcbc cdcd*) plus a volta and a heroic couplet (*ee*); the *terza rima sonnet* has interlocking *Sicilian triplet* (*aba*) stanzas *aba bcb cdc ded*, a turn, and a heroic couplet. All these couplet, triplet, quatrain, sestet, and octave forms are *heroic stanza forms* because they are written in iambic pentameter measures, as are quintet and septet forms written in the same measures, such as the *Sicilian quintet* (*ababa*) and the *Sicilian septet* (*abababa*).

Other *quatorzain* forms are the *blues sonnet* (see *blues* stanza) and the *sonetto rispetto,* discussed earlier.

The SONNET REDOUBLED (SONNET REDOUBLÉE) is a *sequence* of fifteen sonnets. Each of the fourteen lines in the first sonnet (the *texte*) becomes, in order, the final line in the following fourteen sonnets. A variation of this pattern makes each of the lines in the texte the first line in the following fourteen sonnets:

Reflections in an Attic Room

Texte. (Shakespearian sonnet)

As if one needed to begin to write;
As though one had to have a pen at hand,
Paper smoothening to the touch of night,
Light sifting across the page like wind and sand.

This is the scrivener's fallacy, the hour
Abraded by sand and wind, by willful words:
They scrape at vision, they scarify and scour—
The urn becomes a scattering of shards;

The wind, a voice freed of its hollow shell
Noting nothings echoing in the bone

Bleaching among the dunes of time that swell:
They shift, remembering they once were stone.

Sit stony-eyed; watch the words curl and come
Stillborn to life between the joint and thumb.

I. (Petrarchan sonnet with Italian sestet)

Dear Father: You are dead. What's there to say?
Yet I'll go on to say it, as you know,
Or may not, as the case may be. Just so,
Our monologues continue on their way,
Two streams of silence rising out of clay,
Passing each other in the essential flow
Of stars and atoms. Watch them rise and go,
Falling in vortices of night and day:

The grass grows green, the suns and planets turn
Upon a field of sable. Brine turns to blood,
I turn to you as day turns into night,
As flesh turns in to earth. I cannot spurn
The flame you gave to me upon the flood
As if one needed to begin. To write

II. (Petrarchan sonnet with Italian sestet)

Is useless. "Poetry makes Nothing happen,"
As Auden said. It happens anyhow,
Rising upon the eternal tide of Now,
Engulfing everything—the field, the aspen,
Herb, rock and furrow. So we sigh, grasp pen,
Ink and paper, then we sit down to plow
Another row of letters. We endow
The meadow with another seed to open.

And when it does, what will the blossom be?
Another flower in a sea of flowers?
A blooming and a withering of the land
That once was ocean, that once more shall be sea

Rising to blood again to invest these hours
As though one had to have a pen in hand?

III. (Petrarchan sonnet with Italian sestet)

Here in an attic study rising to
A peak in the winter dark, one thinks at times
Of love; one thinks of synonyms and rhymes
That come as close as words are wont to do
To what it once was like when the flesh was new
And closed with flesh in torrid zones and climes.
What was it like? Whose were those pantomimes
Between the sheets that got the rave reviews?

Those sheets—those wrinkled sheets: they press in close
Upon recall. The books that line these shelves
Are filled with love songs yellowing and trite:
Verbena pressed between the leaves verbose.
Our sheets untwine, leaving to our selves
Paper smoothening to the touch of night.

IV. (Petrarchan sonnet with Italian sestet)

The attic listens to the scratching pen.
Outdoors, the wind has sunk. The snow is deep,
The neighbors in their steads are fast asleep,
Dreaming of when they will awake again.
Nothing is happening, nor will it when
They lift their lids to look into the deep
Trance of wakening. The ink will keep
The stillness that inhabits books and men,

Will keep it and disgorge it as the leaf
Turns, veined and sere, and then begins to brown
Under the rooftree, beneath the moving hand.
The words accumulate, become a sheaf
Of seasons as the silence filters down,
Light sifting across the page like wind and sand.

V. (Petrarchan sonnet with Italian sestet)

Imagine this: a battering at the door;
The voice of anguish pleading, "Give us curds,
Crusts, crumbs of meaning—pray you, give us words!
We need the Secret Name, and so much more—
A sense of purpose from your ample store
Of synonyms and antonyms! Rewards
Undreamt await if you extend towards
Your fellow man a portion of your lore!"

But the knocker lies against the stolid wood,
The panel does not echo. The empty hall
Contains but peeling paper and a sour
Smell of waiting. It must be understood
There is no understanding, only gall:
This is the scrivener's fallacy. The hour

VI. (Petrarchan sonnet with Italian sestet)

Is late. The atmosphere is thick. The earth
Is running down. The fishes in the sea
Are drowned in silt. Each blade of grass, each tree
Is blighted. There has been a monstrous birth,
And plenitude has been transformed to dearth—
The Magi slouch away from Galilee.
"The pen is mightier than the sword," but see
It beaten into shares of slender worth:

It settles in its rut and plows its row.
The poisonous sun and parching raindrops slough
From brow and temple. Emaciated birds,
Before the wrinkled seed can sprout and grow,
Seize it for ivied towers wearing down,
Abraded by sand and wind, by willful words.

VII. (variant Petrarchan sonnet with Sicilian sestet)

Go, little book, and bear thy wordy freight
Away from me as fast as e'er thou may—

I'm sick to death of everything you say.
I wrote you out in sundry hours late
When I long since ought to have hit the hay—
But did I seek sweet dreaming? Did I sate
The wingéd Pegasus on an early date,
In a timely moment? Nay, I say you, neigh!

I entertained the nightmare in my room.
I watched that grim old nag bend to devour
The grain of bitterness, the oats of doom,
The silage of depression. Little, sour
Book, I loathe thy messages of gloom—
They scrape at vision, they scarify and scour.

VIII. (Petrarchan sonnet with Sicilian sestet)

Build me more stately vessels, O my Soul!
I have a pot to piss in, sure enough,
But I've a fancy for more fancy stuff:
Amphorae full of oils, a wassail bowl,
Kraters of flowers. Ceramics is my goal:
A funerary urn, built good and tough,
Of alabaster so that, when I slough
This clay, my ash won't end up in a hole.

But what is this? I look into my heart
And find a crock chock-full of feeble words;
A thunder-jug beladen with a fart;
Stained paper, and a nest of nestling turds—
And as I watch, the paper falls apart;
The urn becomes a scattering of shards.

IX. (nonce sonnet with envelope refrain in the octave)

I wrote a book called *Curses and Laments*.
There was, it seems, a modicum of scents
In such an exercise, but only that:
A modicum, for it relieves frustration,
But changes nothing else in God's creation.

You pucker up and whistle in your hat;
You break a little wind when you're intense—
I wrote a book called *Curses and Laments*.

You take a certain pleasure in the smell
Of fire and brimstone. They can go to Hell,
Those bastards that have muscled you around.
Leave them a curse and then go underground
To breathe the air where you have loosed to dwell
A wind, a voice freed of its hollow shell.

X. (Bref double/quatorzain)

What will we talk about beneath the stone?
"I have a little dust stuck in my eye."
"Today the worms are restless. I can feel
Them turning." "Pardon me, I have a cold—
I cannot stop my coughin'." "Thought I'd die
Of laughter when my nasty neighbor went
Out in the rain and caught her death." "I saw
Pale Ryder the other day—he's looking old
And out of sorts." "I wait for the telephone
To ring, but my children never seem to call.
Perhaps it's out of order—the reaper-man
Doesn't service the equipment he has sold."
Perhaps it's much like life—we'll merely lie
Noting nothings echoing. In bone-

XI. (sonetto rispetto)

Yards poets slowly accumulate.
I sometimes wonder if, on Judgment Day,
We'll all rise up in glory to afflate,
Converse, and each recite his latest lai.
Can rime be so perverse? In Plato's State
We'd all be banished—even the great Good Gray
Poet. But where in God's name could we go—
To that grand Writers' Conference Below?

But even there we would, it seems to me,
Be welcomed none too warmly to pause or dwell.
There'd be the Devil to pay, inevitably,
For there are limits to tolerance in Hell.
If we are left alone with our poetry
Bleaching among the dunes of time, that's well.

XII. (terza rima sonnet)

So Limbo's won and Paradise is lost.
My attic room is filling up with smoke:
I sit and talk with Geoffrey, Will—a host

Of my confreres. We pass the time with joke
And bawdry. There is little else to do—
The centuries lie heavy as a yoke

Upon the roof; the crackling of the glue
In all our bindings shatters this still air.
Our words and verse go whistling up the flue.

We pilgrims to Perdition sit and stare
Into the silence of sere marrow-bone.
I proffer the hemlock cup—they do not dare

Accept, for if they drank I'd be alone.
They shift, remembering they once were stone.

XIII. (variant Spenserian sonnet)

And in my pipe smoke I can just discern
The outlines of a sonnet redoublée,
A skeleton of what is my concern:
The meaning of it all. My smoke is gray.

I ponder carefully these artful rounds
And think about the things I have to say—
I try some lines aloud. The noise redounds
To my House of Fame, and meters ricochet

From the sloping walls to die upon my ears.
Where are the hare of soul, the baying hounds
Of the Apocalypse? Where are the tears
Condensed from feelings language seldom sounds?

My room is silent; my pen is chill and dumb.
Sit stony-eyed with words that curl and come.

XIV. (nonce sonnet)

Now it is almost done, this foolish thing
That I have penned. The lines have nearly jelled,
And I must ask if I have felt compelled
To write, or merely willed myself to sing

This song that few will ever care to read.
And was I born, or was I merely made,
Concocted of myself—the man of trade,
Not the Bard God conjured out of need

To cure the universe? I do not care.
To be a poet of whatever sort
Will help to pass this journey to the Court
Of Ultimate Decisions. This is fare

I pay and eat—these lines that fall and come
Stillborn to life between the joint and thumb.
                                        —Wesli Court

SPATIAL POETRY (SPATIALS) is explained in The Typographical
Level. See also *concrete poem*, *picture poem*, and *shaped stanza*.

SPENSERIAN STANZA can be found in two places, in the section
on Narrative Poetry, and in the listing of *ballade*.

For the SPLIT COUPLET, see the *couplet*.

The Scottish STANDARD HABBIE is described with *rime couée*.

The STAVE is the stanza of a drinking song or of a hymn, both of
which have refrains. Lines generally are tetrameter or shorter.
More specifically, the term may be applied to a *sestet* comprised of

three couplets and ending with a refrain: *aabbcC*, *ddeecC*, and so forth. An even stricter version has a refrain as both lines one and six; therefore, only the center couplet rhyme would change: *AabbaA*, *AaccaA*, etc. For an example of this type of stave, see "Western Wind," under *glosa*. The strict stave is a variation of the *couplet envelope,* that is, two couplets rhyming *aa* enclosing another rhyming couplet: *aabbaa*, *ccddcc*, and so forth. Other couplet forms are found among the *couplet*, *didactics*, *cywydd llosgyrnog*, *gwawdodyn*, *hir a thoddaid*, *rime couée*, *sestet*, and *short particular measure*. For a relative, see *envelope stanza*.

Here is a simple stave that uses incremental repetition in a couplet refrain:

Corinna Singing

When to her lute Corinna sings,
Her voice revives the leaden strings
And doth in highest notes appear
As any challenged echo clear;
But when she doth of mourning speak,
Even with her sighs the strings do break.

And as her lute doth live or die,
Led by her passion, so must I,
For when of pleasure she doth sing,
My thoughts enjoy a sudden spring,
But if she doth of sorrow speak,
Even from my heart the strings do break.
                         —Thomas Campion

The Italian STRAMBOTTO will be discovered with the *octave*.

Both the SYNONYMOUS PARALLEL and the SYNTHETIC PARALLEL are found in the section Syntax, and under *parallel structure*. Also see *free verse*, *prose poem*, and the companion volume, *The Book of Literary Terms*.

TAIL—see *cauda*.

For the TAILED SONNET, see *caudate sonnet*.

TAIL-RHYME STANZA is another term for *Burns stanza* or *standard habbie*; see also *rime couée*.

The Japanese *tanka,* like the katauta, takes two forms, both of which are externally alike in that they are quintet poems with lines, in this order, of 5-7-5-7-7 syllables. In the first tanka form, called the *waka,* one subject is treated in the first two lines, another in the next two, and the last line is a *refrain* or *paraphrase* or *restatement*: 5-7, 5-7, 7. The first two lines are a *dependent clause* or a *phrase*, and the last three an *independent clause*.

The second type of tanka consists of two parts. The first three lines are an independent unit ending in a noun or verb after which a turn takes place: 5-7-5, 7-7. The *triplet* is an observation, and the *couplet* is a comment on the observation.

The TANRENGA is discussed under *renga*.

The Welsh TAWDDGYRCH CADWYNOG (tówdd-girch ca-dóy-nog) is, like rhupunt, a single line of three, four, or five sections, but each section may, optionally, appear on the page as a single line. Each section is four syllables in length, and the sections rhyme *abbc*. Each of these sections rhymes, in **at least** one other line of verse, with its corresponding section. After two lines (a couplet or eight sections), the rhymes may change. Here are the rhymes for four possible lines (sixteen sections): (*abba*) (*abba*) (*cddc*) (*cddc*).

TELESTICH is described at the beginning of this section on lyric forms, under *acrostic*.

The TERCET is any complete poem of three lines, a *tristich*—see the *triad*. The *enclosed tercet* rhymes *aba* (see *enclosed triplet*), and the *Sicilian tercet* is an enclosed tercet written in iambic pentameter meters (see the *Sicilian triplet*).

The American TERZANELLE is a *villanelle* written in *terza rima*. Like the latter, it is nineteen lines in length: five *interlocking triplets* plus a concluding quatrain in which the first and third lines of triplet one reappear as refrains. The center line of each triplet is a repeton reappearing as the last line of the succeeding triplet with the exception of the center line of the penultimate stanza, which reappears in the quatrain. This is the rhyme and refrain scheme for the triplets: A^1BA^2 *bCB* *cDC* *dED* *eFE*. The poem may end in one of two ways: fA^1FA^2 or ffA^1A^2. Every line is the same metrical length.

lines	rhymes, repetons, refrains	lines	rhymes, repetons, refrains
1.	A^1	10.	d
2.	B	11.	E
3.	A^2	12.	D
4.	b	13.	e
5.	C	14.	F
6.	B	15.	E
7.	c	16.	f
8.	D	17.	A^1 or F
9.	C	18.	F or A^1
		19.	A^2

This is a disguised terzanelle—all the triplet stanzas have been run together to look like a solid block of printing:

Terzanelle in Thunderweather

"A winter's thunder's a summer's wonder."

This is the moment when the shadows gather
Under the elms, the cornices and eaves.
This is the silent heart of thunderweather.
The birds are quiet now among the leaves
Where wind stutters, then moves steadily
Under the elms, the cornices and eaves—
These are our voices speaking guardedly
About the sky, about the sheets of lightning
Where wind stutters, then moves steadily
Into our lungs, across our lips, tightening
Our throats. Our eyes speak in the dark
About the sky, about the sheets of lightning
Illuminating moments. In the stark
Shades that we inhabit there are no words
For our throats. Our eyes speak in the dark

Of things we cannot say, cannot ignore.
This is the moment when the shadows gather,
Shades that we inhabit. There are no words—
This is the silent heart of thunderweather.

TERZA RIMA is an accentual-syllabic Italian stanza form consisting of any number of interlocking, enclosed *triplet stanzas.* The first and third lines of a stanza rhyme; the second line rhymes with the first and third lines of the following stanza. In other words, the ending of the second line of any stanza becomes the rhyme for the following stanza: *aba bcb cdc ded;* a *circle-back ending* would be *eae* in this case, but the poem usually ends in a *couplet* rhymed from the second line of the last triplet: *yzy zz.* The TERZA RIMA SONNET is a fourteen-line *quatorzain* in iambic pentameter, rhyming *aba bcb cdc ded ee. Capitolo* is satirical terza rima, as in the first two stanzas of "Canto Due" of "Canzone" under *canzone,* shown earlier (note that each of the first two sestet stanzas is made up of two *terza rima triplets*). Several sections of "Reflections in an Attic Room" in the *sonnet redoubled* entry are terza rima sonnets.

A synonym for TETRASTICH is *quatrain.*

The TEXTE is a set of lines to be glossed by the remainder of the poem. For verse forms that utilize a texte, see the *carol,* the *glosa* or *glose,* the *rondeau redoubled,* and the *sonnet redoubled.*

The THRENODE (THRENODY) is found among *occasional poetry.*

THRIME is a synonym for *triplet.*

TODDAID (todd-eyed) stanzas are Welsh quatrains that alternate between ten-syllable and nine-syllable lines. A syllable toward the end of the first line cross-rhymes somewhere in the middle of the second, and the same effect is reproduced in lines three and four. Lines two and four rhyme with each other.

1. x x x x x x *x a* x x
2. x x x *a* x x x x b
3. x x x x x x x *c* x x
4. x x x x *x c* x x b

Following is a modern version of an anonymous medieval Welsh poem. In order to render it into modern English, two of the twenty-four official Welsh meters have been used: *toddaid* (todd-eyed) in the longer stanzas, and *cyhydedd fer* (cuh-hée-dedd ver) in the final couplet. This medieval poem is written from a woman's viewpoint, that of the child's mother, and it is an exception to the sadness and despair that seem to suffuse those early medieval British poems that have been spared to posterity.

Huntsong for a Small Son

Dinogad's coat is specked with spots—
I made it out of pelts of stoats.
Flingabout, fling! Flingabout, flingabout!
Eight times the song we'll sing.

When your daddy went to the hunt,
Shouldered his spear, his staff in hand,
He called to the hounds that were hale and fleet,
"Fido, fetch! Bowser, trail!"

He caught fish in his little boat
Like a dragon after a shoat.
When your daddy climbed up the craggy rock
He brought back boar, buck, stag,

A stippled game-hen from the hills
And a trout from Oak Fountain Falls.
At whatever your Daddy cocks his spear,
There he strikes bear, lynx, fox.

This is no boast, this is no lie—
If it escapes, then it can fly.

> —Anonymous

TODDAID BYR is a couplet made of one decasyllabic line paired with a hexasyllabic line. In the former the main rhyme appears before the end of the line, and the succeeding syllables are linked by assonance, alliteration, or rhyme with the early syllables of the latter line:

lines	rhymes and syllables
1.	x x x x x x x A x b
2.	b x x x x A

For examples, see lines three and four of the quatrains of "Hunt-song for a Small Son," just given.

The Irish TRIAD is a loose poem form (not a bardic meter) that lists three things and considers their effect. Although this epigram is from the Middle English, it illustrates the form. Here are two versions of the same poem. The first follows the original form; the second is cast into the Welsh sestet form *cywydd llosgyrnog* (ców-idd llos-gír-nog).

The Rule of Three

I.

When I consider these things three,
I may never then blithe be:
The first is that I shall away;
The second, I know not which day;
The third fills me with my most care—
I know not whither I shall fare!

II.

When I consider these things three
I may never then go blithely:
I shall, firstly, wend away;
Secondly, I know not the hour.
The third fills me with my most fear—
I know not where I shall fare.

—Anonymous

The French TRIOLET is an octave poem turning on only two rhymes and including two refrains: *ABaAabAB*. Every line is the same metrical length.

Jasper Olson

from Bordello

I take my women any way they come—
I'm Jasper Olson, brother. Hard and fast
I play this game. Though some folks think I'm dumb,
I take my women any way they come,
and come they do. There's no time to be numb
in this life—grab it now and ram the past.
I take my women any way they come.
I'm Jasper Olson, brother, hard and fast.

The TRIPLET is any stanza consisting of three lines. The *enclosed triplet* rhymes *aba*; the *Sicilian triplet* is an enclosed triplet written in iambic pentameter meters. There are two Welsh englyns that are triplet stanza forms, *englyn milwr* (én-glin mée-loor) and *englyn penfyr* (én-glin pén-vir), two of the twenty-four official bardic meters of Wales.

Englyn milwr turns on one rhyme or consonance, and each line has a count of seven syllables. The rhymes change for each stanza.

The putative author of this piece, the sixth-century poet "Llywarch Hen," was perhaps not a historical bard but a Welsh national persona who appears in various poems, like King Arthur, but even in translation a particular personality comes through. This is not the case with most groups of anonymous poems, so perhaps Hen did exist after all:

The Head of Urien

I carry a severed head.
Cynfarch's son, its owner, would
Charge two warbands without heed.

I bear a great warrior's skull.
Many did good Urien rule;
On his bright breast, a grey gull.

I bear a head at my heart,
Urien's head, who ruled a court;
On his bright breast the crows dart.

I bear a head in my hand.
A shepherd in Yrechwydd-land,
Spear-breaker, kingly and grand.

I bear a head at my thigh,
Shield of the land, battle-scythe,
Column of war, falcon-cry.

I bear a head sinister.
His life great, his grave bitter,
The old warrior's savior.

I bear a head from the hills.
His hosts are lost in the vales.
Lavish it with cries and hails.

I bear a head on my shield.
I stood my ground in the field,
Near at hand—he would not yield.

I bear a head on my greaves.
After battlecry he gives
Brennych's land its laden graves.

I bear a head in my hand,
Gripped hard. Well he ruled the land
In peace or in war's command.

I cut and carried this head
That kept me fearless of dread—
Sever my quick hand instead!

I bear a head from the wood,
Upon its mouth frothing blood
And, hereafter, on Rheged!

My breast quaked and my arm shook;
My heart was stone, and it broke.
I bear the head that I took.

—Llywarch Hen

The work following has also been attributed to Llywarch Hen. The form used here is englyn penfyr. Its lines consist, respectively, of 10-7-7 syllables. The lines rhyme *AAA* (the capitals signify the main rhyme); one, two, or three syllables occur at the end of the first line after the main rhyme. These syllables are echoed by assonance, alliteration, or secondary rhyme in the first few syllables of the second line; the main rhyme ends the second and third lines:

lines   syllables and rhymes

1.   x x x x x x x x A b
2.   *b x x x x x* A
3.   x x x x x x A

The Corpse of Urien

The handsome corpse is laid down today,
Laid under this earth and stone—
Curse my fist! Owain's sire slain!

The handsome corpse is now broken
In the earth, under the oak—
Curse my fist! My kinsman struck!

The handsome corpse is bereft at last,
Fast in the stone he is left—
Curse my fist! My fate is cleft!

The handsome corpse is rewarded thus,
In the dust, under greensward—
Curse my fist! Cynfarch's son gored!

The handsome corpse is abandoned here
Under this sod, this gravestone—
Curse my fist! My liegelord gone!

The handsome corpse is here locked away,
Made to rest beneath the rock—
Curse my fist! How the weirds knock!

The handsome corpse is settled in earth
Beneath vervain and nettle—
Curse my fist! Hear fate rattle!

The handsome corpse is laid down today,
Laid under this earth and stone—
Curse my fist! This fate was mine!
                    —Llywarch Hen

For other triplet forms see *tercet, terza rima, terzanelle, tristich, triversen,* and *villanelle.*

The TRISTICH is found under *tercet.*

The TRIUMPHAL ODE, a celebration of victory, is a form of *occasional poetry.* See "In Praise of Owain Gwynedd" under *cyhydedd naw ban.*

Discussions of the American TRIVERSEN and TRIVERSEN STANZA are found in the sections Podics and Overtone. Here is a poem written in triversen stanza:

Hot Moon
The maize is shin high
    behind the fences
        of the village by the lake,

and in the blue haze
    above the mouth of the river
        seagulls call in the sun,

climb and fall
    where waters meet waters
        and fish lie over ledge.

TROILUS STANZA is another term for *rime royal.*

TUMBLING VERSE is *Skeltonics*.

TWIME is a synonym for *distich* and *couplet*.

TYPEWRITER POEM—see Spatial Prosody.

The UTTERANCE is found under *katauta*.

A VALEDICTION is a farewell—see *commiato*, *envoi*. See also the last section of the *canzone*.

The VENUS AND ADONIS STANZA is a form of the *heroic sestet*; it combines a Sicilian quatrain with a heroic couplet and rhymes *ababcc*.

For VERS DE SOCIÉTÉ see *light verse*.

VERSE ESSAY—see *didactic poetry*.

VERSET—see *epigram*, *mote* (*motto*), *posie*.

The French VILLANELLE, like the terzanelle, is a poem of five triplet stanzas and a concluding quatrain, but it turns on only two rhymes. Lines one and three of triplet one are refrains, the first of which reappears as lines six, twelve, and eighteen; the second reappears as lines nine, fifteen, and nineteen: A^1bA^2 abA^1 abA^2 abA^1 abA^2 abA^1A^2 or, sometimes, in reverse order: abA^2 A^1. Every line is the same metrical length.

The House on the Hill

They are all gone away,
    The House is shut and still,
There is nothing more to say.

Through broken walls and gray
    The winds blow bleak and shrill:
They are all gone away.

Nor is there one to-day
    To speak them good or ill:
There is nothing more to say.

Why is it then we stray
    Around the sunken sill?
They are all gone away,

And our poor fancy-play
    For them is wasted skill:
There is nothing more to say.

There is ruin and decay
    In the House on the Hill:
They are all gone away,
There is nothing more to say.
        —Edwin Arlington Robinson

Do Not Go Gentle into That Good Night

Do not go gentle into that good night,
Old age should burn and rave at close of day;
Rage, rage against the dying of the light.

Though wise men at their end know dark is right,
Because their words had forked no lightning they
Do not go gentle into that good night.

Good men, the last wave by, crying how bright
Their frail deeds might have danced in a green bay,
Rage, rage against the dying of the light.

Wild men who caught and sang the sun in flight,
And learn, too late, they grieved it on its way,
Do not go gentle into that good night.

Grave men, near death, who see with blinding sight
Blind eyes could blaze like meteors and be gay,
Rage, rage against the dying of the light.

And you, my father, there on the sad height,
Curse, bless me now with your fierce tears, I pray.
Do not go gentle into that good night.
Rage, rage against the dying of the light.
        —Dylan Thomas

Here is a *mock villanelle* written in reverse syntax and sending up Dylan Thomas' "Do Not Go Gentle into That Good Night":

Ellenalliv for Lew: On His Retirement

An Assbackwards Dylanic

In graduate school Lew Turco was the champion of two parlor tricks for which alone we would never have forgotten him, even if he had written nothing: one was the trick of being able to recite anything backwards, and to do it instantly; the second and more impressive was the trick of improvising on the spot a Dylan Thomas poem, not ever one we would quite remember, though each new Turco-Thomas poem did sound at least faintly familiar and certainly authentic. —DONALD JUSTICE

Retirement into gentle go not do.
Dies he until stops never poet a.
Do to tasks undone many have still you.

Start they what of half finish ever few.
You with compared they're when away fade they.
Retirement into gentle go not do.

Renown first their on rested have some, true.
Promises early to up live few, hey!
Do to tasks undone many have still you.

Writes who man the to given be must due
Does he what for reward small too is pay
Retirement into gentle go not do.

Yield to not and, find to, seek to, strive to.
Truth its holds still saw ancient this that pray
Do to tasks undone many have still you.

Sleep you before go to miles have you, Lew
Forth travel you may so, anew breaks day.
Retirement into gentle go not do.
Do to tasks undone many have still you.
                                    —R. S. Gwynn

Other interlocking forms are the *rubaiyat, Spenserian sonnet, terza-nelle,* and *terza rima.*

The VIRELAI is to be found under the *lai,* in Narrative Poetry.

The WAKA is with the other Japanese forms in the section on Overtone and under *katauta* and *renga.*

For the WHEEL; see the *bob and wheel.*

Narrative Poetry

The French ALEXANDRINE LINE is a line of twelve syllables, but in English prosody it is iambic hexameter verse (˘ ´|˘ ´|˘ ´|˘ ´|˘ ´| ˘ ´), and in English poetics it is usually paired with a *septenary* or *fourteener*, a line of iambic heptameter verse with a central caesura taking place somewhere after the third foot, usually after the fourth foot (˘ ´|˘ ´|˘ ´|˘ ´|•|˘ ´|˘ ´|˘ ´) to form a *couplet* of *poulter's measure*:

˘ ´|˘ ´|˘ ´|˘ ´|˘ ´|˘ ´
(˘ ´|˘ ´|˘ ´|˘ ´|•|˘ ´|˘ ´|

The Alexandrine line appears in the *Spenserian stanza*, which consists of eight iambic pentameter lines plus the concluding Alexandrine. It is the stanza in which the most unreadable *epic* in the English language is written: Edmund Spenser's *The Faery Queen*, although it may in fact not be an epic at all but an interminable *romance*, (described later). Also see the *classical hexameter* in the *epic*.

ART BALLAD—see *ballad* (in this section).

ART EPIC—see *epic* (in this section).

The BALLAD is a relatively short lyric verse tale meant to be sung. There are distinctions to be made between literary ballads and folk ballads; the latter were passed down through oral traditions from *balladeer* to balladeer (a wandering *minstrel, gleeman, jongleur, minnesinger, bard*, or *scop*, an old English court or household poet-harpist-singer). On the other hand, the *troubadour* (who composed in the langue d'oc in Provence, northern Italy, and northern Spain) and *trouvère* (who composed in the langue d'oïl in northern France) were medieval French literary poets, composers of gestes and songs.

First, English-language literary ballads are usually written in accentual-syllabic prosody; folk ballads are often done in some podic meter. Further, the literary ballad's author is usually known, whereas the folk-ballad's author is usually anonymous. Third, because the literary ballad is still whole, it follows a more or less normal narrative pattern, but as the folk ballad was passed down from hand to hand, it has often—but not always—become eroded, and only the high points, or *crises* and *climaxes*, remain. This phenomenon is called *"leaping and lingering"*—the folk ballad leaps from high point to high point, skipping connecting passages, and lingers on each a while before it leaps again. Here is a Scottish folk ballad that uses a number of sonic techniques, particularly repetition and incremental repetition—notice that **every line** is some sort of *refrain*. Notice, too, that the poem is not end-rhymed; it consonates:

Lord Randal

"Oh where have you been, Lord Randal, my son?
And where have you been, my handsome young man?"
"I've been at the greenwood; mother, make my bed soon,
For I'm weary with hunting and wish to lie down."

"And who met you there, Lord Randal, my son?
And who met you there, my handsome young man?"
"Oh, I met with my true-love; mother, make my bed soon,
For I'm weary with hunting and wish to lie down."

"And what did she give you, Lord Randal, my son?
And what did she give you, my handsome young man?"
"Eels fried in a pan; mother, make my bed soon,
For I'm weary with hunting and wish to lie down."

"And who got your leavings, Lord Randal, my son?
And who got your leavings, my handsome young man?"
"My hawks and my hounds; mother, make my bed soon,
For I'm weary with hunting and wish to lie down."

"What happened to them, Lord Randal, my son?
What happened to them, my handsome young man?"
"They swelled up and died; mother, make my bed soon,
For I'm weary with hunting and wish to lie down."

"I fear you are poisoned, Lord Randal, my son.
I fear you are poisoned, my handsome young man."
"Oh yes, I am poisoned; mother, make my bed soon,
For I'm weary with hunting and wish to lie down."

"O what will you leave me, Lord Randal, my son?
O what will you leave me, my handsome young man?"
"Twenty-four milk cows; mother, make my bed soon,
For I'm weary with hunting and wish to lie down."

"And what for your sister, Lord Randal, my son?
And what for your sister, my handsome young man?"
"My gold and my silver; mother, make my bed soon,
For I'm weary with hunting and wish to lie down."

"What's left for your brother, Lord Randal, my son?
What's left for your brother, my handsome young man?"
"My houses and lands; mother, make my bed soon,
For I'm weary with hunting and wish to lie down."

"What of your true-love, Lord Randal, my son?
What of your true-love, my handsome young man?"
"I leave her hellfire; mother, make my bed soon,
For I'm weary with hunting and wish to lie down."
                                                    —Anonymous Scots

If one splits one *fourteener couplet* (see the *Alexandrine line* and
poulter's measure) in this manner:

(⌣ ⁄ | ⌣ ⁄ | ⌣ ⁄ | ⌣ ⁄ | • | ⌣ ⁄ | ⌣ ⁄ | ⌣ ⁄
(⌣ ⁄ | ⌣ ⁄ | ⌣ ⁄ | ⌣ ⁄ | • | ⌣ ⁄ | ⌣ ⁄ | ⌣ ⁄

at the caesura

(˘ ʹ | ˘ ʹ | ˘ ʹ | ˘ ʹ | •
| ˘ ʹ | ˘ ʹ | ˘ ʹ
(˘ ʹ | ˘ ʹ | ˘ ʹ | ˘ ʹ | •
| ˘ ʹ | ˘ ʹ | ˘ ʹ

and adds *abcb* rhyme, one will achieve a quatrain of *common measure* or *ballad stanza*. Here is a *literary ballad* written in ballad stanza:

The Unquiet Grave
"The wind doth blow today, my love,
    And a few small drops of rain;
I never had but one true love—
    In a cold grave she has lain.

"I'll do as much for my true-love
    As any young man may;
I'll sit and mourn all at her grave
    For a twelvemonth and a day."

The twelvemonth and a day being spent,
    The dead began to speak:
"Oh, who sits weeping on my grave
    And will not let me sleep?"

"It is I, my love, sits on your grave,
    And will not let you sleep;
For I crave one kiss of your clay-cold lips,
    And that is all I seek."

"You crave one kiss of my clay-cold lips?
    But my breath smells musty strong!
If you have one kiss of my clay-cold lips,
    Your time will not be long.

"'Tis down in yonder garden green,
    Love, where we used to walk—
The finest flower ever seen
    Is withered to a stalk.

"The stalk is withered sere, my love,
       So will our hearts decay;
So make yourself content, my love,
       Till you are called away."
                                    —Anonymous

Although this poem does not have a refrain, many ballads do, like "Lord Randal."

BALLAD STANZA—see the *ballad.*

The BEAST EPIC has animals as its personae. Otherwise, see the *epic.*

The CHANSON DE GESTE is a medieval epic or tale of *chivalry,* from the French chevalier or "horseman," the mounted knight in armor. It is written in prose *laisses* or *cantos.*

The CHANTE-FABLE is a medieval French compound mode *romance* (described later) written in alternating verse and prose passages.

Find the CINEMA EPIC described in the *epic.*

CLASSICAL HEXAMETER—see the *heroic line* in the *epic.*

Find the COMPOUND-MODE EPIC in the *epic.*

The DREAM ALLEGORY or DREAM VISION is a medieval verse narrative in which the narrator, who is usually also the protagonist, falls asleep and experiences adventures having symbolic import.

The EPIC is a long *heroic narrative* that tells of the fabulous exploits of a person who is often of superhuman stature and nature, as in the Chaldean *Epic of Gilgamesh* whose semidivine hero was the sovereign of the city of Erech in ancient Babylonia. The problematic Greek poet Homer may or may not actually have lived or written either of the epics attributed to him, *The Iliad* and *The Odyssey.* Such narratives as these and the anonymous Old English *Beowulf* are sometimes called *primary epics* or *folk epics.* A *secondary*, *art*, or *literary epic* is one whose author is definitely known, as for instance *The Aeneid* of Virgil, *Paradise Lost* and *Paradise Regained* by John Milton, and *John Brown's Body* by Stephen Vincent Benét.

Gilgamesh is a *prose epic*, written in *grammatical parallels*, but most epics of the Western world are written in verse. The *heroic line* is that *metrical line* in which the major epics of a particular culture are traditionally written. The Greek heroic line is the *classical hexameter*, a quantitative accentual-syllabic verse line that consists of six verse feet, the first four of which are **either** spondees (´´) or dactyls (´ ◡ ◡), followed by a dactyl in the fifth foot and a spondee in the sixth foot: (´ ◡ ◡ | ´´ | ´´ | ´ ◡ ◡ | ´ ◡ ◡ | ´´).

The English heroic line is *iambic pentameter*, often *blank verse* (the term "blank" means simply *unrhymed*—**any** unrhymed, metered verse is blank verse, to be distinguished from *free verse*.), in which a *caesura* generally appears after the third foot: (◡ ´ | ◡ ´ | ◡ ´• | ◡ ´ | ◡ ´).

John Brown's Body by the American Stephen Vincent Benét (1898–1943) is a *compound mode epic*, partly prose, partly verse, written in the twentieth century. It has sometimes been described as a *cinema epic* because the structure is *episodic*, flashing from one part of the American Civil War to another, alternating action, lyrics, narration, monologue, long-shots and close-ups, even passages taken from books written by characters depicted in the epic—a sort of literary *montage*, which is a cinematic technique. It is also a most readable and enjoyable epic, easily transferred to the stage, as has been done very successfully.

The epic traditionally begins *in medias res*—at a low point in the middle of the main action, with the *epic question*—the poet addressing the Muses, begging for their aid in the vast undertaking the poet proposes to undertake, and asking them to tell him why these tragic things occurred in the first place. As the epic progresses, these questions are answered through *exposition* and *flashback*—a jump back in time to some previous time and action; for a discussion of narrative techniques, see the companion volume, *The Book of Literary Terms*.

The *epic catalog* (see *distributio* in *The Book of Literary Terms*) is an itemizing, a list of things such as the list of ships that carried the Greek troops to Troy or the names of the fallen angels in *Paradise Lost*. Because the folk epic was a product of the *aural tradition*—that is, it was not only spoken (delivered *orally*) but extemporaneously composed aloud—its author(s) drew upon a stock of conventions including *stock situations*, combinations of circumstances; *refrains*, repeated lines; *burdens*, repeated stanzas; *epithets*, stock descriptions (see *topoi* in *The Book of Literary Terms*; singular, *topos*), stock themes or motifs; and *machinae*, interventions of the gods (see *deus ex machina*), all of which are *epic formulae* (formulas) for composition, and all of which are covered in *The Book of Literary Terms*.

An EPYLLION is a shorter epic, composed originally in dactylic hexameter verse, sometimes equated with the idyll.

The French FABLIAU is a ribald story in verse. Also see *fable*.

FOLK EPIC—see *epic*.

The Middle English GESTE is a story in verse or prose, a *romance*.

For the FOURTEENER and the fourteener couplet, see the *ballad* and *ballad stanza*.

HEROIC LINE—see the *Alexandrine line,* and the *iambic pentameter blank verse line* in the *epic*.

The IDYLL is an *episode* (see the companion volume *The Book of Literary Terms*) out of the legendary past, as in Tennyson's romantic Arthurian *cycle* or *sequence, The Idylls of the King*.

The LAY (LAI) is a short story in verse—actually, this story following is written in a form of *lyric prose*:

The Death of the Astronaut

I. Prologue

Flaming, he rose; flaming, he
came down—a circle bent and broken.
Through his dark sight the magnified
world burst upon his senses. In token
of flesh wedded to the wooden tree
with golden spikes, he died,

his carnival face stripped of its hoses,
bright air frothing like bloody
steam from the imaginings of his eyes
and the silences of his body.
Below, folk looked out of their houses—
the night was filled with fireflies.

II.

Before the omen of fire, before
the pillar of my reentry was a sword
splitting the thin sky, and a sound
tailed out behind like a whispered word
that should have been a roar,
I saw darkness standing off the ground.

I had been sent star-probing
one other time. It had been the same—
the instruments, the hard boost;
the man with a man's name
stunned within steel, flung
into too much freedom, kept just

busy enough not to notice
time gibbering in a labyrinth of dials.
The clock-watcher had become the clock
jabbing its hands at incredible numerals.
I was too slow to understand much of this.
I made my brain record, my hands work.

At last I could pause. When
first I looked outward, I saw a clear
green hemisphere, slow as a recollected sea,
beating against the weir
of space, clouds rising like a thin
spume above an inaudible plangency.

It was then, for a moment, I felt
like an idea lost in a bubble—
but just for a moment. Out of a cone
somewhere among the rubble
of data which my mind held,
there came a voice, its tone

urgent and made of earth. My lips
responded: I felt them writhe,

the breath rustle between.
My hands were lithe
and sure on the controls; my eyes were whips
skimming dials, quick and keen.

Time lay catatonic. Below, men went
stumbling and falling while I—
I! a man as well—might never fall,
but remain a strange light in a foreign sky
no longer sky but firmament.
The infinite swallows the infinitesimal.

III.

At this point—no. Strike that. Points dissolve.
A circle moving beneath the prickle of stars
has no mathematics. Nevertheless,
somewhen within that curse
I programmed, I felt the earth revolve.
A pentacle of solitude was drawn; the press

of distances was nearly tangible.
I listened. In my ear
a static crackle grated its beetle note.
All I could hear
was the mouth of silence approaching like the mandible
of a mantis. Slate

is the color of fear; its scent is dust.
The chill the Caesars know in their sepulchres
began to breech
the armor I wore in that Circus
Maximus. My phones were dead. Just
filament and wire stood within reach

of my stilled hands—nothing sentient.
I saw sunrises fade and burn
among fleets of sparks. The moon blossomed
like a lily carved of bone: the vast urn

which nourished it went
arching coldly about stars. Sterile, chasmed,

my catafalque of steel
reeled through tracks the ancient
gods are said to have harrowed
among the planets. But there was only trenchant
emptiness there, a wheel
of silence; wheels within wheels, darkness arrowed

with blue light.
I probed fiery axes with eyes
gone stark, grown calm as immobility:
I watched the sun rise
for the final time. My sight
flamed out; nevertheless, I could see:

IV.

The Earth receded. It became small,
and I saw that it was flat,
borne by an enormous turtle
waddling down a jet road. The plate,
our planet, was fastened to the beast's shell
with golden wire that looked like sunlight. A kettle

containing darkness and angels hung suspended,
upside-down, above the burden
and the burdened. There was commerce
between Earth and Heaven.
Men ascended
a great ladder shaped like a cross

whose base was rooted in the rim
of the world; its crossbar bore
the kettle's lip. The ladder was of wood
fastened with golden nails. One star
topped the emblem.
I watched the carnival recede

till a monstrous serpent formed of mist
rose by the wayside, looped its coils
about the universe and swallowed.
Vast emptiness. The blood boils.
I feel my cave of steel tossed
by furious winds. I am a wick tallowed

and ignited. Darkness is lurid
with voices hissing prayers, songs—
a litany of absence.
It is I who sing!
This is my torrid
hymn. Who listens?

V. Epilogue

Below, the folk in their houses quietly
heard the public announcement,
went out to their yards to search the skies.
They stood and waited there. Summer was silent,
save for the crickets. Suddenly,
the night air burned with plunging fireflies.

The strict French form of the *lai* is a *nonet* stanza written in
quantitative syllabics rhyming *aabaabaab*: the lines rhyming *a* are
five syllables long, but the *b* lines are only two syllables in length.
In a poem consisting of more than one stanza, the succeeding
stanzas have their own rhymes:

lines   syllables and rhymes

1.   x x x x a
2.   x x x x a
3.   x b
4.   x x x x a
5.   x x x x a
6.   x b
7.   x x x x a
8.   x x x x a
9.   x b

A later and more complicated development of the lai is the LAI NOUVEAU, an octave stanza. The opening *a* lines form a *texte,* which is used as alternating refrain lines in succeeding stanzas, as in the *villanelle.* Line one ends stanza two, line two ends stanza three, and so on to the final stanza where they are reunited in reverse order in a couplet. Though the *main rhyme* (*a*) is ordinarily continued from stanza to stanza, the short-line rhymes may vary: $A^1A^2baabaa \ldots aazaazA^2A^1$. Notice that the syllable counts are the same for the lai nouveau as for the lai:

lines   *syllables, rhymes and refrains*

1.	x x x x A^1
2.	x x x x A^2
3.	x b
4.	x x x x a
5.	x x x x a
6.	x b
7.	x x x x a
8.	x x x x a
9.	x x x x A^1
10.	x x x x A^2
11.	x c
12.	x x x x a
13.	x x x x a
14.	x c
15.	x x x x A^2
16.	x x x x A^1

LITERARY BALLAD—see *ballad.*
LITERARY EPIC—see *epic.*
METRICAL ROMANCE—see *romance.*
Find the MOCK EPIC in the *epic.*

The MOCK-HEROIC TALE is a travesty of some of these forms. Here is a mock tale written in faux Middle English—although one might think that some of these words are anachronisms, the only word that is not to be found in a Middle English vocabulary is the word "te" (tea); even the word crompid (crumpet) is authentic:

The Tale of Gergrundehyde the Gode

A Medieval Romance

Thorowe the mede, the mede, the mede,
  Rideth a knyght uppen his stede,
Straghte inne air he holdeth hise launce.
    Thorowe the medewe he dooth praunce,
      Dooth praunce.

Under the wode, the wode, the wode,
  Wandreth Gergrundehyde the Gode;
Ferles his eyen, noble hise staunce,
    Fressh from the batailfelds of Fraunce,
      Of Fraunce.

Serchyng the realme, the realme, the realme,
  A pecok ploume uppen hise healm,
Serchyng the realme for hise lady fayre,
    Floures al laced among hire heire,
      Hire heire.

Eanded atte last, atte last, atte last,
  Hise serche been overe, his serche been past.
Heir stondeth his luve inne dragounnes leir,
    Nefere was mayden boren so rere,
      So rere.

"Namore have fere, have fere, have fere,
  Eow I shal save thoh yt tak a yer."
"I fere ne longer, my galaunt knyght.
    My fate ys al uppen thy might,
      Thy myght."

The dragoun ys spered, ys spered, ys spered,
  Spitted uppen the knyghtes broodswerd.
The bataile lastes thorowe the nyght
    Untill the dragoun ys putte to flyght,
      To flyght.

"Curteis, gode knyght, gode knyght, gode knyght,
    My trowthe to thee I heer do plight."
"Pardonne me, lasce, preye pardonne me,
    Ne woldest eow rather tak some te,
        Some te?"

Thorowe the mede, the mede, the mede,
    Rideth the knyght uppen hise stede
Beryng hise mayden nobly borne,
    Crompids uppen the sadel horne,
        Dul horne.

Under the wode, the wode, the wode,
    Wandreth Gergrundehyde the Gode.
"Pardonne me, lasce, myght I troublen eow?"
    "Certes, gode sire. Oon lumpe or two,
        Or two?"

                                    —Wesli Court

Another French form, the PASTOURELLE (PASTORALE), is a humorous story narrated by a knight who takes advantage of a country wench, or who is outwitted by his intended victim. This poem
following is a late Middle English pastourelle that is simultaneously a narrative, a dramatic poem, and a complaint. It appears
here in a modern version that reproduces its original form except
that the final stanza—which the preceding three stanzas so obviously call for but which was missing from the source—has been
newly supplied:

Now Springs the Spray
As I rode out upon a day,
In my straying
I heard somewhere a little fey
Maiden sing,
"May the clod cling!
Woe is she who in love-longing

Must live, aye!
Now springs the spray—
All for love I cannot sleep,
Try ever as I may!"

Soon as I heard that merry tune
I rode there.
I found her in an arbor soon,
In a leafy lair.
With joy to spare
I asked of her, "Thou maiden fair,
Why sing you, 'Aye!
Now springs the spray—
All for love I cannot sleep,
Try ever as I may!'"

She answered to me maidenly
With these words few:
"My lover, he hath shorn and sheared me
Of his love true;
He changes anew.
If I may say so, he shall rue
This evil day!
Now springs the spray—
All for love I cannot sleep,
Try ever as I may!"

I cried, "The gods have sent me, dear,
To comfort thee
In this green, leafy bower here—
Prithee, come near me."
"Sir, I agree."
We clasped and kissed until, I fear,
She cried out, "Aye!
Now springs the spray—
All for love I cannot sleep,
Try ever as I may!"

                              —Anonymous

POULTER'S MEASURE—see the *Alexandrine line* and the *fourteener* (under *ballad*).

PRIMARY EPIC—see *epic*.

A ROMANCE (METRICAL ROMANCE) is a long chivalric poem about the adventures of the Knights of the Round Table or other courtly figures.

SECONDARY EPIC—see *epic*.

SEPTENARY—see the *Alexandrine line* and the *fourteener* (under *ballad*).

The VIRELAI keeps the syllable counts of the *lai*; the difference is that it is an interlocking form, for the long lines of a succeeding stanza pick up the rhyme of the short lines in the preceding stanza: *aabaabaab bbcbbcbbc*, and so forth.

Bibliography

Alden, Raymond MacDonald, ed. *English Verse: Specimens Illustrating Its Principles and History*. New York: Henry Holt, 1903.

Alexander, Michael, ed. *The Earliest English Poems*. Hammondsworth: Penguin, 1966.

Allingham, William, ed. *The Ballad Book*. New York: White, Stokes, and Allen, 1866.

Baker, David, ed. *Meter in English, A Critical Engagement*. Fayetteville: University of Arkansas Press, 1996.

Bell, H. Idris, and David Bell, eds. *Dafydd ap Gwilym: Fifty Poems*. London: The Honourable Society of Cymmrodorion, 1942.

Bone, Gavin David, ed. *Anglo-Saxon Poetry*. Freeport, Maine: Books for Libraries, 1970.

Boulton, Marjorie. *The Anatomy of Poetry*. London: Routledge & Kegan Paul, 1953.

Bridges, Robert. *Milton's Prosody*. Oxford: Oxford University Press, 1893.

Brogan, T. V. F. *The New Princeton Handbook of Poetic Terms*, Princeton, N.J.: Princeton University, 1994.

Brower, Robert H., and Earl Miner. *Japanese Court Poetry*. Stanford, Calif.: Stanford University Press, 1961.

Carney, James, ed. *Medieval Irish Lyrics*. Berkeley: University of California, 1967.

Carroll, Paul, ed. *The Young American Poets*. Chicago: Follett, 1968.

Chaucer, Geoffrey. *The Poetical Works*, with "Memoir" by Sir Harris Nicolas and "Essay on the Language and Versification of Chaucer" by T. Tyrwhitt, 6 vols. London: William Pickering, 1852.

———. *The Poetical Works*, ed. F. N. Robinson. Boston: Houghton Mifflin, 1933.

Clancy, Joseph P., ed. *The Earliest Welsh Poetry*. London: Macmillan, 1970.

Cohen, Helen Louise. *Lyric Forms From France*. New York: Harcourt, Brace, 1922.

Conybeare, John Josias, ed. *Illustrations of Anglo-Saxon Poetry.* New York: Haskell House, 1964.

Corbett, P. J., *Classical Rhetoric for the Modern Student.* New York: Oxford, 1965.

Court, Wesli. *The Airs of Wales.* Philadelphia: Temple University Poetry Newsletter, 1981.

———. *Courses in Lambents.* Oswego, N.Y.: Mathom, 1977.

———. *Curses and Laments.* Stevens Point, Wis.: Song, 1978.

Courthope, W. J. *The History of English Poetry,* 6 vols. London: Macmillan, 1895–1920.

Cummings, E. E. *95 Poems.* New York: Harcourt, Brace, 1958.

Cushman, Stephen. *William Carlos Williams and the Meanings of Measure.* New Haven, Conn.: Yale University, 1993.

Davie, Donald. *Articulate Energy.* New York: Harcourt, Brace, 1958.

Davison, Edward Lewis. *Some Modern Poets, and Other Essays.* New York: Harper & Bros., 1928.

Dunbar, William. *Poems,* ed. James Kinsley. Oxford: Clarendon, 1958.

Eliot, T. S. *The Three Voices of Poetry.* New York: Cambridge University, 1954.

Empson, William. *Seven Types of Ambiguity.* London: Chatto and Windus, 1930.

Felkin, F. W. *The Craft of the Poet, An Outline of English Verse Composition.* New York: Henry Holt, 1926.

Finch, Annie. *The Ghost of Meter.* Ann Arbor: University of Michigan, 1993.

Ford, Patrick K., ed. *The Poetry of Llywarch Hen.* Berkeley: University of California, 1974.

Frank, Roberta. *Old Norse Court Poetry.* Ithaca, N.Y.: Cornell University Press, 1978.

Gardner, John, tr. and ed. *The Complete Works of the Gawain-Poet.* Chicago: University of Chicago, 1965.

Gioia, Dana. *Can Poetry Matter?* Saint Paul: Graywolf, 1992.

Gordon, R. K. *Anglo-Saxon Poetry.* London: J. M. Dent, 1926.

Greene, David H., ed. *Anthology of Irish Literature.* New York: New York University, 1971.

Gross, Harvey. *Sound and Form in Modern Poetry.* Ann Arbor: University of Michigan Press, 1964,

Henryson, Robert. *Poems and Fables,* ed. H. Harvey Wood. Edinburgh: Oliver and Boyd, 1958.

Hoagland, Kathleen, ed. *1000 Years of Irish Poetry.* Old Greenwich, Conn.: Devin-Adair, 1947.

Hoffman, Yoel, ed. and tr. *Japanese Death Poems.* Rutland, Vt. and Tokyo: Charles E. Tuttle, 1986.

Holden, Jonathan. *Style and Authenticity in Postmodern Poetry.* Columbia: University of Missouri Press, 1986.

Humphries, Rolfe. *Green Armor on Green Ground.* New York: Charles Scribner's Sons, 1956.

Justice, Donald. *Of Prosody: Notes for a Course in Contemporary Poetry.* Iowa City: privately circulated, 1959.

Kaiser, Rolf. ed. *Medieval English.* Berlin: Rolf Kaiser, 1961.

Kapan, Bernard, ed. *Freedom and Form: American Poets Respond.* Hattiesburg: University of Southern Michigan, 1977 (special issue of *The Mississippi Review,* vi:1, 1977).

Kennedy, X. J., ed. *Tygers of Wrath.* Athens: University of Georgia, 1981.

Knott, Eleanor. *Irish Classical Poetry.* Dublin: Colm O Lochlainn, 1960.

———. *Irish Syllabic Poetry* 1200–1600, Dublin and Cork: Cork University, 1935.

Langland, William. *Piers the Plowman,* tr. and ed. Margaret Williams. New York: Random House, 1971.

———. *The Vision of William Concerning Piers the Plowman,* ed. Walter W. Skeat. Oxford: Clarendon, 1888.

Leach, MacEdward, ed. *The Ballad Book.* New York: A. S. Barnes, 1955.

Lowes, John Livingston. *Convention and Revolt in Poetry.* Boston: Houghton Mifflin, 1919.

MacKay, Charles. *The Lost Beauties of the English Language.* New York: J. W. Bouton, 1874.

Malof, Joseph. *A Manual of English Meters.* Bloomington: Indiana University, 1970.

Malone, Kemp, ed. *Ten Old English Poems.* Baltimore: Johns Hopkins University, 1941.

Matthews, Brander. *A Study of Versification.* Boston: Houghton Mifflin, 1911.

Maxim, Hudson. *The Science of Poetry and the Philosophy of Language.* New York: Funk & Wagnalls, 1910.

Myers, Jack, and Michael Simms. *Longman Dictionary and Handbook of Poetry.* New York: Longman, 1985.

O'Connell, Richard, ed. *Irish Monastic Poems*. Philadelphia: Atlantis Editions, 1975.

———. *More Irish Poems*. Philadelphia: Atlantis Editions, 1976.

Omond, T. S. *A Study of Metre*. London: Grant Richards, 1903.

———. *English Metrists*. London: Oxford, 1921.

Packard, William. *The Poet's Dictionary*. New York: HarperCollins, 1989.

Percy, Thomas. *Reliques of Ancient English Poesy*, ed. Henry B. Wheatley, 3 vols. New York: Dover, 1966.

Poe, Edgar Allan/Herbert Spencer. *The Philosophy of Style/The Philosophy of Composition*. New York: Pageant Press, 1959.

Preminger, Alex, ed. *Encyclopedia of Poetry and Poetics*. Princeton, N.J.: Princeton University, 1965; rev. ed., 1993.

[Puttenham, George]. *The Arte of English Poesie*, ed. Edward Arber. Kent, Ohio: Kent State University, 1970.

Raffel, Burton, tr. and ed. *Poems from the Old English*. Lincoln: University of Nebraska, 1964.

Reinfeld, Linda. *Language Poetry, Writing as Rescue*. Baton Rouge: Louisiana State University Press, 1992.

Reiser, Max. *Analysis of Poetic Thinking*. Detroit: Wayne State University, 1969.

Rhys, Ernest, ed. *The Prelude to Poetry: The English Poets in Defence and Praise of Their Own Art*. London: Dent, 1927.

Salamon, Russell. *Parent[hetical Pop]pies*. Cleveland: Renegade Press, 1964.

Savage, Henry Littleton. *The Gawain Poet*. Chapel Hill: University of North Carolina, 1956.

Sidgewick, Frank, ed. *Legendary Ballads*. Philadelphia: J. B. Lippincott, n. d.

———, and E. K. Chambers, eds. *Early English Lyrics*. London: Sidgwick and Jackson, 1966.

Skelton, John. *The Complete Poems*, ed. Philip Henderson. London: J. M. Dent, 1959.

Thorpe, Benjamin, ed. *Codex Oxoniensis: A Collection of Anglo-Saxon Poetry*. London: William Pickering, 1842.

Tolkien, J. R. R. *Finn and Hengest: The Fragment and the Episode*. Boston: Houghton Mifflin, 1983.

Turco, Lewis. *The Book of Forms*. New York: E. P. Dutton, 1968.

———. *The Book of Literary Terms*. Hanover, N.H.: University Press of New England, 1999.

————. *Creative Writing in Poetry*. Albany: State University of New York, 1970.

————. *Emily Dickinson, Woman of Letters*. Albany: State University of New York Press, 1993.

————. *The New Book of Forms*. Hanover, N.H.: University Press of New England, 1986.

————. *Poetry: An Introduction through Writing*. Reston, Va.: Reston, 1973.

————. *The Public Poet: Five Lectures on the Art and Craft of Poetry*. Ashland, Ohio: Ashland Poetry Press, 1991.

————. *Visions and Revisions of American Poetry*. Fayetteville: University of Arkansas Press, 1986.

Untermeyer, Louis. *The Forms of Poetry*. New York: Harcourt, Brace, 1926.

————. *The Pursuit of Poetry*. New York: Simon & Schuster, 1969.

Warhaft, Sidney, et alia, eds. *English Poems 1250–1800*. New York: St. Martin's, 1966.

Warren, Alba H., Jr. *English Poetic Theory 1825–1865*. New York: Octagon, 1976.

Welch, Robert. *A History of Verse Translation from the Irish 1789–1897*. New York: Barnes & Noble, 1988.

Whitelock, Dorothy, ed. *The Anglo-Saxon Chronicle*. New Brunswick, N.J.: Rutgers University, 1961.

Williams, Gwyn, ed. *An Introduction to Welsh Poetry*. London: Faber and Faber, 1953.

————, ed. *Presenting Welsh Poetry*. London: Faber and Faber, 1959.

————, tr. *Welsh Poems Sixth Century to 1600*. Berkeley: University of California, 1974.

Williams, Miller. *Patterns of Poetry*. Baton Rouge: Louisiana State University Press, 1986.

Wimsatt, W. K., ed. *Versification: Major Language Types*. New York: Modern Language Association, 1972.

Wood, Clement. *Poets' Handbook*. New York: Greenberg, 1940.

Woods, Susanne. *Natural Emphasis: English Versification From Chaucer to Dryden*. San Marino, Calif.: Huntington Library, 1984.

Wrinn, Mary J. J. *The Hollow Reed*. New York: Harper & Bros., 1935.

Yasuda, Kenneth. *The Japanese Haiku*. Rutland, Vt.: Charles E. Tuttle, 1957.

308   Acknowledgments

Continued from page iv

"The Tale of Gergrundehyde the Gode" is from *Courses in Lambents: Poems* by Wesli Court (Oswego: Mathom Publishing Company), © 1977. Reprinted by permission of the author.

"Love Curse," and "Robin and Makyn" by Robert Henryson, v. Wesli Court, are from *Courses in Lambents: Poems* by Wesli Court (Oswego: Mathom Publishing Company), © 1977, and from *The New Book of Forms* by Lewis Turco (Hanover: University Press of New England), © 1986. Reprinted by permission of the author.

"Rocket By, Baby" by Wesli Court is from *Light Year '84*, ed. Robert Wallace (Cleveland: Bits Press), © 1983. Reprinted by permission of the author.

"Jolly Rutterkin" by John Skelton/Wm. Cornish, Jr., "Lord Randal" from the anonymous Scots, "Upon a Dead Man's Head" by John Skelton, and "You Goat-Herd Gods" by Philip Sidney, all v. Wesli Court, are from *Poetry: An Introduction Through Writing* by Lewis Turco (Reston: Reston Publishing Co.), © 1973. Reprinted by permission of the author.

"Complaint to His Purse" by Geoffrey Chaucer, v. Wesli Court, "The Magi Carol," and "The Morbid Man Singing" are from *Poetry: An Introduction Through Writing* by Lewis Turco (Reston: Reston Publishing Co.), © 1973, and from *The New Book of Forms* by Lewis Turco (Hanover: University Press of New England), © 1986. Reprinted by permission of the author.

"In Summer" by Hywel ab Owain Gwynedd, "Huntsong for a Small Son" by Anonymous, "Lament for Owain ab Urien" by Taliesin, "Love in Exile" by Dafydd ap Gwilym, "My Choice" by Hywel ab Owain Gwynedd, "Spring Song" from the Anonymous Welsh, "Winter" from the anonymous Welsh, "The Corpse of Urien" by Llywarch Hen, "The Grave" by Dafydd Benfras, "The Head of Urien" by Llywarch Hen, "The Mystery" by Amergin, "To a Girl" by Cynddelw Brydedd Mawr, all v. Wesli Court, are from *The Airs of Wales* by Wesli Court (Philadelphia: *Poetry Newsletter* of Temple University), © 1981, and from *The New Book of Forms* by Lewis Turco (Hanover: University Press of New England), © 1986. Reprinted by permission of the translator and author.

"The Wanderer" by an anonymous Anglo-Saxon author, v. Wesli Court, is from *Song* 7 (Spring), © 1979. Reprinted by permission of the author.

"Virelai Avortée en Forme de Rondeau Acrostiche" and "Partsong for Gorgon-zola" are from *Curses and Laments* by Wesli Court (Stevens Point: Song Magazine), © 1978. Reprinted by permission of the author.

"Hornpipe Epithalamion," "Bref Double à l'Écho," and "The Swift Replies" are from *Curses and Laments* by Wesli Court (Stevens Point: Song Magazine), © 1978, and from *The New Book of Forms* (Hanover: University Press of New England), © 1986. Reprinted by permission of the author.

"Rubaiyat of Beauty and Truth" by Wesli Court is from *Edge City Review* 2:1, © 1966. Reprinted by permission of the author.

"Now Springs the Spray" by an anonymous Middle English author, v. Wesli Court, is from *Spoon River Quarterly* 6:4 (Fall), © 1981. Reprinted by permission of the author.

"Confessional" by Charles d'Orleans, "The Death of Conain" from the anony-mous Gaelic, "Evil It Is" by Anonymous, "Gnomic Verses" by Anonymous, "Merciless Beauty" by Geoffrey Chaucer, "The Monks' Massacre" from the Anonymous Old English, "The Ruin" by an anonymous Anglo-Saxon author, and "The Shepherd's Carol" by an anonymous Middle English author, all v. Wesli Court, "Haiku" by Basho, v. Lewis Turco, and "Terzanelle in Thunderweather" by Wesli Court, are from *The New Book of Forms* by Lewis Turco (Hanover: Uni-versity Press of New England), © 1986. Reprinted by permission of the publisher.

"The Curse of Death" from the anonymous Anglo-Saxon, v. Wesli Court, is from *Willow Springs Magazine* 4 (Spring), © 1979.

"l(a", copyright © 1958, 1986, 1991, by the Trustees for the E. E. Cummings Trust, from *Complete Poems 1904–1962* by E. E. Cummings, edited by George J. Firmage. Reprinted by permission of Liveright Publishing Corporation.

"An Amherst Haiku" and "The Harper of Stillness" by Emily Dickinson/Lewis Turco are from *The New Book of Forms* (Hanover: University Press of New En-gland), © 1986, and from *Emily Dickinson, Woman of Letters* (Albany: State Univer-sity of New York Press), © 1993. Reprinted by permission of the author.

"Dirge" is from *Selected Poems* by Kenneth Fearing (Bloomington: University Press), © 1956, copyright not renewed, and from *Poetry: An Introduction Through*

Writing, by Lewis Turco (Reston: Reston Publishing Co.), © 1973. Reprinted by permission of Lewis Turco.

R. S. Gwynn's "Ballade for the Yale Younger Poets of Yesteryear" was originally published in *The Sewanee Review,* and "Ellenalliv for Lew: On His Retirement" was originally published in *The Formalist*. They are reprinted here by permission of the author.

"God's Grandeur" by Gerard Manley Hopkins is from *Poems of Gerard Manley Hopkins* (London: Oxford University Press), © 1918. *Public domain*.

"Aberdovey Music" and "The Sons of David" are from *Green Armor on Green Ground* by Rolfe Humphries (Charles Scribner's Sons), © 1956, and from *The Collected Poems of Rolfe Humphries* (Bloomington: Indiana University Press), © 1965. Reprinted by permission of the latter publisher.

"Ancient Music" and "In a Station of the Metro" by Ezra Pound were first published in 1913 and are in the *public domain*.

"The House on the Hill" is from *The Children of the Night* by Edwin Arlington Robinson, © 1897. *Public domain*.

"She" is from *Parenthetical Poppies* by Russell Salamon (Cleveland: Renegade Press), uncopyrighted, and from *Poetry: An Introduction Through Writing* by Lewis Turco (Reston: Reston Publishing Co.), © 1973. Reprinted by permission of the author and the editor.

"Chicago" by Carl Sandburg is from *Poetry* (March 1914); "Cool Tombs" is from *Cornhuskers* by Carl Sandburg (New York: Holt, Rinehart and Winston), © 1918, and from *Poetry: An Introduction Through Writing* by Lewis Turco (Reston: Reston Publishing Co.), © 1973. *Public domain*.

"Do Not Go Gentle Into That Good Night" by Dylan Thomas, from *The Poems of Dylan Thomas.* Copyright © 1952 by Dylan Thomas. Reprinted by permission of New Directions Publishing Corp.

"Balada of Uncertain Age" by Lewis Turco is from *Amelia* 4:1, © 1990. Reprinted by permission of the author.

"Nasnas" is from *A Cage of Creatures* by Lewis Turco (Potsdam: Banjo Press), © 1978. Reprinted by permission of the author.

"Rondine of the Rare Device" by Lewis Turco is from *Light Year '87*, ed. Robert Wallace (Cleveland: Bits Press), © 1986. Reprinted by permission of the author.

"Ode on the Imitations of Immorality" by Lewis Turco is from *The Carleton Miscellany*, 3:2, © 1962. Reprinted by permission of the author.

"A Serenade of Youth, an Envoi in Middle Age" by Lewis Turco is from *Confrontation* 48–49 (Spring/Summer), © 1992. Reprinted by permission of the author.

"Pocoangelini 7" is from *Pocoangelini: A Fantography and Other Poems* by Lewis Turco (Northampton: Despá Press), © 1971. Reprinted by permission of the author.

"The Shadowman" by Lewis Turco is from *The Formalist*, 4:2, © 1993, and from *Contemporary Authors Autobiography Series*, vol. 22, ed. Joyce Nakamura (Detroit: Gale Research), © 1995. Reprinted by permission of the author.

"A Pastorale of Sorts" by Lewis Turco is from *First Poems* (Francestown: Golden Quill Press), © 1960, and from *Poetry: An Introduction Through Writing* by Lewis Turco (Reston: Reston Publishing Co.), © 1973. Reprinted by permission of the author.

"Sapphic Stanzas in Falling Measures" by Lewis Turco is from *The Kansas Quarterly* 23:1–2, © 1992. Reprinted by permission of the author.

"Jason Potter," "Jasper Olson," "Will Somers," and "Lafe Grat" by Lewis Turco are from *Pocoangelini: A Fantography and Other Poems* by Lewis Turco (Northampton: Despá Press), © 1971, and from *Bordello*, poems, with prints by George O'Connell (Oswego: Grey Heron/Mathom), © 1996. Reprinted by permission of the author.

"Requiem for an Old Professor" by Lewis Turco is from *Patterns of Poetry*, ed. Miller Williams (Baton Rouge: Louisiana State University Press), © 1986. Reprinted by permission of the author.

"The Death of the Astronaut" is from *Legends of the Mists* by Lewis Turco (Kew Gardens: New Spirit Press), © 1993. Reprinted by permission of the author.

"Dialogue" and "Paradigm" by Lewis Turco are from *Poetry: An Introduction Through Writing* by Lewis Turco (Reston: Reston Publishing Co.), © 1973, and from *Seasons of the Blood* (Rochester: Mammoth Press), © 1980. Reprinted by permission of the author.

"The Old Professor and the Sphinx" is from *Awaken, Bells Falling: Poems 1959–1967* by Lewis Turco (Columbia: University of Missouri Press), © 1968, copyright renewed by Lewis Turco in 1996, and from *Poetry: An Introduction Through Writing* by Lewis Turco (Reston: Reston Publishing Co.), © 1973. Reprinted by permission of the author.

"For Lewis Turco" by Richard Wilbur and "For Richard Wilbur" by Lewis Turco were published originally as "The Birth of a Verse Form" in *The Formalist*, 8:1, © 1997 William Baer, and subsequently, with "Rubliw for Dana Gioia," as part of *A Garland of Rubliws* (Dresden, Maine: Mathom Bookshop), © 1997. Reprinted by permission of the authors and William Baer.

"Marriage" and "Chinese Nightingale" by William Carlos Williams were originally published in 1916 and 1917 respectively and are in the *public domain*; "Marriage" in haiku version is reprinted from *Poetry: An Introduction Through Writing*, by Lewis Turco (Reston: Reston Publishing Co.), © 1973.

"On Gay Wallpaper" by William Carlos Williams, from *Collected Poems: 1909–1939, Volume 1.* Copyright © 1938 by New Directions Publishing Corp. Reprinted by permission of New Directions Publishing Corp.

General Index

Page numbers in **bold** indicate glossed entries in the text. Page numbers in *italics* indicate poems quoted in text.

Library of Congress Cataloging-in-Publication Data

Turco, Lewis.
    The book of forms : a handbook of poetics / by Lewis Turco.—3rd ed.
      p.   cm.
    Includes bibliographical references and index.
    ISBN 1–58465–041–9 (cl. : alk. paper)— ISBN 1–58465–022–2 (pbk. :
alk. paper)
    1. Poetics. 2. Versification.   I. Title.
PN1042.T78   2000
808. 1 — dc21   99–39099